# ROBERT

## A MAN FOR ALL SEASONS

*Gie me ae spark 'o Nature's fire*
*That's a' the learning I desire.*

# ROBERT BURNS

## A MAN FOR ALL SEASONS

*The natural world of*
*Robert Burns*

by

John Young

*with illustrations by*

Keith Brockie

*and*

Donald Watson

SCOTTISH CULTURAL PRESS

First published 1996
Scottish Cultural Press
PO Box 106, Aberdeen AB11 7ZE
Tel: 01224 583777 • Fax: 01224 575337

**British Library Cataloguing in Publication Data**
A catalogue record for this book is available from the British Library


ISBN: 1 898218 60 9



Illustration Acknowledgements:
Robert T Smith: pp. 7. 11, 20, 44, 53, 59, 65, 83, 135, 151, 172, 180
B S Turner: pp. 120, 173
Laurie Campbell: pp. 31, 56
Black & White line drawings: Donald Watson
All other illustrations: J Young


Printed and bound by BPC-AUP Aberdeen Ltd
Aberdeen, Scotland

# CONTENTS

*The social, friendly, honest man,*
*Whate'er he be,*
*Tis he fulfills great Nature's plan,*
*And none but he.*

# FOREWORD

How delightful it is to accept John Young's invitation to contribute a foreword for this highly acceptable work. How appropriate also that it should be published in time to commemorate Burns in 1996, the bicentenary year of the poet's death.

We, within the Burns' movement, along with many folk with a more passing interest in the National Bard, speak of Robert Burns as the real countryman, the man who lived close to nature and more importantly, a man singularly conscious of the flora and fauna around him. Now, however, we have been presented with conclusive proof of these concepts, thanks to this book's exhaustive lists of the innumerable references to nature in the poet's works. They encompass flower and tree, bird and mammal, fish and insect, even the very louse observed that day in kirk on a young lady's fine Lunardi bonnet!

I can assure you that John Young is the ideal person for this great task. He has dipped into his wide knowledge and love of the Bard's poetry. At the same time he has used as the tools of his compiling trade the essential concordance texts by J B Reid (1889) and James Mackay (1990).

The other major ingredient in the production of this book is the writer's wide ranging interest in and knowledge of wildlife in all its many facets. John is currently an Area Officer with Scottish Natural Heritage, based in Airlie, Angus, with special responsibility for Caenlochan and Den of Airlie National Nature Reserves in North Tayside. This gives him the joy of overseeing an area with rare alpine plants, deer, wild cat, nesting eagles and fascinating waterfowl; while his beat also boasts of woodland, rich farming country, and great beaches and cliffs still housing nesting auks and kittiwakes.

Yes, I commend the writer, and his major opus, to you and to all those with an interest in Robert Burns, and of the natural history of our land. It is an absolute 'must' for the bookshelf.

It is both a work of reference for the scholar, speaker or mere taster of Burns' verse, while proving an ideal book into which to dip on a winter's evening. Its message is that if our image of nature in the Bard's poetry covers chiefly a mouse, a mountain daisy or a certain mare Maggie which saved her master Tam, we are merely scratching the surface.

I imagine my Burnsian and naturalist friend John Young has compiled this book neither for fame nor fortune. Rather it has been compiled in fond memory of a family member to whom it is dedicated.

It is thus a labour of love, and this you will appreciate as you read and use it. Your knowledge and your vision will be expanded.

Wilson Ogilvie                                                    Dumfries, January 1996

Past President, Dumfries Burns Club;
Past President, The Burns Federation;
Convener Scottish Literature Committee, The Burns Federation.

**for Hazel**

*Here lies a rose, a budding rose,*
*Blasted before its bloom;*
*Whose innocence did sweets disclose*
*Beyond the flower's perfume.*
*To those who for her loss are grieved,*
*This consolation's given -*
*She's from a world of woe relieved,*
*And blooms a rose in heaven.*


*To relish nature is to walk with God*

# INTRODUCTION

The notion that Robert Burns was inspired by 'nature' has been espoused and perpetuated for well over a century by a long list of writers and speakers – with the notable exception of Hugh MacDiarmid who, in 1926, said that Burns was 'no realist or observer of nature'.

That nature – in the strict sense of natural history, or an appreciation of wild landscape, plants and animals – did literally influence his thinking and permeate his works, cannot now be doubted.

*While briers an woodbines budding green,*
*An paitricks scraichin loud at e'en,*
*An morning poussie whiddin seen,*
    *Inspire my Muse,*
*This freedom, in an unknown frien'*
    *I pray excuse.*

*I am nae poet, in a sense;*
*But just a rhymer like by chance.*
*An hae to learning nae pretence;*
    *Yet, what the matter?*
*Whene'er my Muse does on me glance,*
    *I jingle at her.*

*Your critic-folk may cock their nose,*
*And say, 'How can you e'er propose,*
*You wha ken hardly verse frae prose,*
    *To mak a sang?'*
*But, by your leaves, my learned foes,*
    *Ye're maybe wrang.*

*What's a' your jargon o your schools,*
*Your Latin names for horns an stools?*
*If honest Nature made you fools,*
    *What sairs your grammars?*
*Ye'd better taen up spades and shools,*
    *Or knappin-hammers.*

*A set o dull, conceited hashes*
*Confuse their brains in college-classes,*
*They gang in stirks, and come out asses,*
*Plain truth to speak;*
*An syne they think to climb Parnassus*
*By dint o Greek!*

*Gie me ae spark o Nature's fire,*
*That's a' the learning I desire;*
*Then, tho I drudge thro dub an mire*
*At pleugh or cart,*
*My Muse, tho hamely in attire,*
*May touch the heart.*

Extract from *Epistle to J Lapraik*

Within the full range of the natural scene, Burns referred to the various natural elements on many occasions – Landscape (835 times); Flowers (446); Trees (457); Mammals (91); Birds (366); Seasons (223); other miscellaneous wildlife (112) and the elements (350). A quite remarkable total of some 2,880 references, unsurpassed by any other poet, then or since.

Thankfully, he also viewed 'nature' in its totality, to include the essential, inescapable relationships and behavioural aspects of the main influence on the environment – fellow man!

The main objectives of this book are: firstly, to analyse and catalogue the natural history records contained in Burns' writings, primarily to provide justification in describing him as a *bona fide* naturalist – and especially conservationist – some 150 years before the latter term was either coined or the theme popular. Secondly, to present the proof, if that were required, that his undoubted love of nature was founded on factual knowledge and not just the gleanings of a romantic ploughman poet. Thirdly, my main reason for attempting complete listings, rather than snatching at examples which would have been sufficient to prove the various points, is that I do sincerely hope that future generations of young 'students of nature' will find these lists a historically interesting base from which to progress through Robert Burns, to value not only his philosophy, but also to appreciate that his undoubted genius was enhanced significantly by a love of landscape and living things – which remains to this day our most vital natural heritage and one we must all strive to conserve in Scotland. To this end I have also included some of his references taken from *The Merry Muses of Caledonia* (hereafter *MMC*), a collection of suppressed poems of a bawdy nature. I have not considered it prudent to quote these in full, but serious students may consult the edition to place such records in context. A great deal of confusion still exists regarding the authenticity of many of these works attributed to Burns.

While I have made an attempt to be comprehensive I cannot claim not to have overlooked other natural history records, and I would of course be pleased to have these brought to my attention. Where names are clearly repetitive in lines or chorus, I have not necessarily included each one. Similarly, at the risk of seeming inconsistent, I have erred on the side of caution by inclusion of names and terms when more accurately they may be referrable to the descriptive.

Where I have quoted excerpts from his writings to support the text, I have attempted to retain Burns' original punctuation and spelling. In addition, I have attempted to retain a style of being factually correct and informative, while avoiding jargon, gobbledygook and trying to extend and impress with the usual form of verbal hurly.

Over the years a great deal of scientific confusion has occurred with the use of local names. I have attempted to clarify these by listing those known to have been used in South-west Scotland during the mid-eighteenth century; and in addition have given the Scots and Gaelic in abbreviated check lists to aid rapid reference. The Gaelic was of course widely spoken in southern Scotland prior to Burns' lifetime, giving way to the Lallans. Obviously, many place names and local names for plants and animals have been derived from that ancient language which has unfortunately died out in Lowland Scotland. For a full historical introduction and chronology of Burns and his life, I can recommend reading the excellent official Bicentenary Edition (1986) authorised by the Burns Federation. Suffice it here to give the briefest details as may have been recorded by the man himself.

**1759**   *Born at Alloway, near Ayr, 25th January*
I was born a very poor man's son. My father was gardener to a worthy gentleman of small estate. Had he continued in that station I must have marched of to be one of the little underlings about a farm-house; but it was his dearest wish and prayer to have it in his power to keep his children under his own eye until they could discern between good and evil.

**1766**   *At Mount Oliphant*
Though it cost the schoolmaster some thrashings, I made an excellent English scholar; and by the time I was 10 or 11 years of age, I was a critic in substantives, verbs and particles. In my infant and boys days too, I owed much to an old woman who resided in the family. She had, I suppose, the largest collection in the country of tales and songs concerning devils, ghosts, fairies, brownies, witches, warlocks, and other trumpery. This cultivated the latent seeds of poetry. We lived very poorly; I was a dextrous ploughman for my age.

**1777**   *At Lochlea*
My father entered on a larger farm about 10 miles further in the country. For four years we lived comfortably here. My reputation for bookish knowledge, a certain wild logical talent, and a strength of thought (made me) generally a welcome guest. My reading was enlarged, my life flowed on much in the same course til my 23rd year. *Vive l'amour et vive la bagatelle* were my sole

principles of action. A difference commencing between my father and his landlord, after three years tossing in the vortex of litigation, my father was just saved from the horrors of jail by a consumption which, after two years promises, carried him away.

**1784**  *At Mossgiel, near Mauchline*
When my father died, my brother and I took a neighbouring farm. But the first year from unfortunately, buying bad seed, the second from a late harvest, we lost half our crops. [Then came] a most melancholy affair [Jean Armour], which I cannot yet bear to reflect on. I gave up my part of the farm to my brother and made what little preparation was in my power for Jamaica.

**1786**  *Scots poems chiefly in the Scottish dialect printed at Kilmarnock*
Before leaving my native country for ever, I resolved to publish my poems. My vanity was highly gratified by the reception I met with from the public, and besides, I pocketed all expenses deducted, nearly £20.

**1786–8**  *Visits to Edinburgh*
I had taken the last farewell of my few friends when a letter from Dr Blacklock to a friend of mine overthrew all my schemes. His opinion that I would meet with encouragement in Edinburgh for a second edition fired me so much that away I posted to that city. At Edinburgh I was in a new world. By all probability I shall soon be the tenth worthy, and the eighth wise man of the World.

I see the time not distant far when the popular tide shall recede with silent celerity and leave me a barren waste of sand.

**1787**  *Edinburgh edition of the poems, 'Printed for author and sold by William Creech'*
I guess I shall clear between two and three hundred pounds by my authorship; with that sum I intend to return to my old acquaintance, the plough, and to commence Farmer.

*Tours the Borders and the Highlands*
My journey thro' the Highlands was perfectly inspiring; and I hope I have laid in a new stock of poetical ideas.

**1787–96**  *Contributes songs to James Johnston's 'The Scots Musical Museum'*
An engraver, James Johnston, in Edinburgh, has, not from mercenary views, but from an honest Scotch enthusiasm, set about collecting all our native songs. I have been absolutely crazed about it.

**1788**  *Marries Jean Armour and farms Ellisland, near Dumfries*
I have married 'my Jean' and taken a farm. With the first step I have every day more and more reason to be satisfied, with the mast it is rather the reverse.

**1789**  *Appointed Exciseman*
£50 a year for life, and a provision for widows and orphans, you will allow, is no bad settlement for a poet.

**1791**  *Gives up Ellisland and settles as an Exciseman in Dumfries*
I have sold to my landlord the lease of my farm. I have not been so lucky in farming.

**1793**  *'The Second Edition' of the Poems, 'considerably enlarged', 2 vols., Edinburgh*
A few books which I very much want are all the recompense I crave, together with as many copies of this new edition of my own works as Friendship or Gratitude shall prompt me to present.

**1795**  *The Excise*
I am on the Supervisors' list, and in two or three years I shall be at the head of that list. The moment I am appointed supervisor I may be nominated on the collectors' list. A collectorship varies much from better than two hundred a year to near a thousand. They have, besides a handsome income, a life of complete leisure. A life of literary leisure, with a decent competence, is the summit of my wishes.

**1796**  *The last illness*
I fear the voice of the bard will soon be heard among you no more! For these eight or ten months I have been ailing, sometimes bedfast and sometimes not; but these last three months I have been tortured with an excrutiating rheumatism, which has reduced me to nearly the last stage.

**1796**  *Died at Dumfries, 21 July*

# Scotland's Landscape During Burns' Lifetime

It is now extremely difficult for us, after only two centuries – which in evolutionary terms is minute – to conjure an accurate image of how the landscape in Southern Scotland would have appeared to Burns and others in the mid-eighteenth century and thus to place his natural history records in context. The hills are of course a permanent feature of size, shape and position, but they too have not escaped being significantly modified as far as vegetational cover – and thus as a wildlife habitat and landscape feature – are concerned.

Previously covered in either oak, hazel or pine forest, that 'high' woodland was systematically destroyed. The Southern Uplands in general – and more specifically, the hills he knew well including Corsincon, Dalpeddar, Moffat and Criffel – would almost certainly have been totally clad in heather, interrupted only by isolated remnants of pine, birch and rowan.

As sheep numbers inevitably increased, burning was used as the main method of heather destruction, allowing coarse grass types to colonise the scorched areas before the heather could possibly recover. Early burning was not controlled and the temperatures produced in such fires are now known to be extremely high, and invariably completely damage the root systems of both heather and trees, making natural regeneration virtually impossible, other than from future wind-borne seeds.

To assist the grazing regime further, crude open drains began to appear, often destroying botanically-rich wet flush areas but perhaps more importantly, altering the whole, rather finely balanced, hydrological systems. This encouraged a rapid 'run off', potentially releasing prematurely a huge volume of either rain water or snow melt, temporarily flooding the feeder burns, tributaries and eventually the major river systems.

We can safely assume a dramatic succession on the hills from tree cover, giving way to dominant heather, which in turn was crudely improved by burning then draining to produce a coarse grazing sward suitable for hardy sheep. Upland drainage in the river catchment areas had in turn three major effects on the environment.

The subsequent 'flood' gouged or cleared out the valuable fish spawning beds which were usually composed of the finer granulated rock particles or gravel found mainly in the tributaries. By the time the proverbial flood was variously augmented, and had conjoined with the main river system it was usually sustaining a very powerful surge. This flooded low-lying farmland where it was not protected by bankings; 'backing up' field drains where they existed; damaging bridges; and sweeping off and drowning valuable farm stock. From a purely biological aspect, it then carried away accumulated silt soil and riverside vegetation, including trees, from the 'slow' bends, loops and islands that naturally formed a barrier or obstruction to the free flowing torrents. These pockets of riverside vegetation were not only invaluable to the conservation of aquatic vegetation and animals but were an integral part of the fascinating and beautiful riverside scene.

Eventually, and inevitably, a huge volume of silt was water-borne and subsequently deposited in the estuaries, no doubt enriching the sandy shores to the benefit of most invertebrates; but it did also cause immense problems in harbours and navigational channels in an era when dredging was not possible.

Following the demise of the larger areas of trees which originally covered the hills, lower based woodlands other than those of private estates became vulnerable and were rapidly being depleted to the extent of being classed as remnants. Timber remained the main fuel source, although peat was being cut, and coal mined, though not winned in quantities that would be viable and affordable to the bulk of the population – at least in volumes to suppress the destruction of trees, which were a 'free' source. In addition, the better quality timber, often the hardwoods, were also used for buildings, furniture, farm implements including carts, wheels and hand tools, with huge volumes being turned to charcoal to 'feed' the new iron smelters and the flourishing tan bark trade.

The crude, dirt roads mainly followed the old cattle drove routes, usually roughly parallel to the rivers. Townships eventually developed at the strategic stopping places; often they had a former military significance or were so sited to allow exploitation of a natural resource, such as shallow coal seams. From these settlements, fields were cleared to produce grain and some root crops like potato and turnip; but predominantly to provide grazing and hay for cattle and horses.

The first field clearings were small, badly drained (if at all), and usually demarcated and/or protected, either by stone walls built from the 'cleared' stones or surrounded by a dense thicket or hedge, of predominantly hawthorn. The cultivation was on the rig system and would have allowed large areas of rushes and bracken to persist, with the so-called 'field weeds' such as thistles, ragwort, docks and foxgloves being allowed to flourish too. Such swards that were developed and regularly grazed would have carried a large percentage of clovers and many other flowering plants associated with old mature meadows. Margins of most fields would typically be characterised by profuse growth of bramble, dog rose and hawthorn, while elsewhere on uncleared land one would expect a secondary or shrub layer with blackthorn, hazel, alder and willow.

Dominant trees that survived would have been mainly of Scots pine, oak, ash, birch and rowan, under which the humus-rich soils would have produced such typical colourful delights as primrose and harebell.

Prior to effective land drainage, the wet areas of lochan, flush, marsh and bog must have provided an extensive mosaic of still waters, supporting huge populations of insects, invertebrates, amphibians, mammals, and fish, but especially birds.

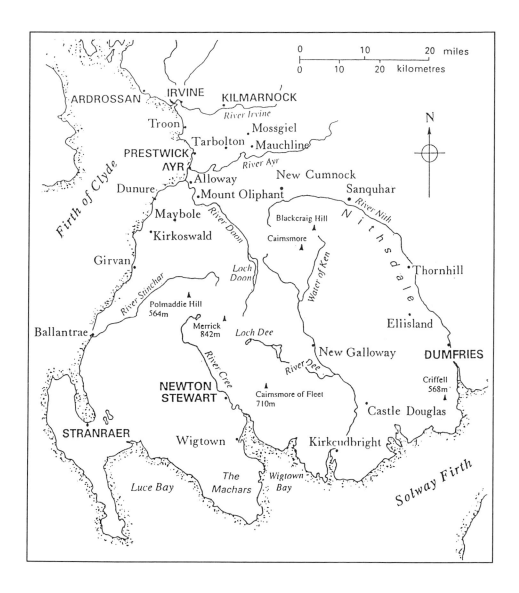

Map of Burns' Country

This scenario, even if necessarily somewhat hypothetical, clearly indicates an immense diversity of very rich wildlife habitat being present in south-west Scotland during Burns' lifetime.

Historians can only speculate at the range and density of some species and groups, with a myriad of weed-infested fields providing an abundant seed source for species such as partridge and linnet, overgrown margins with attendant songthrush and blackbirds; reed lined ponds with water lily, coots, teal and majestic swans. The lowland scene would give way to tree-clad glens, reaching upwards to the remaining grouse moors and grassy hillocks with the wild calls of lapwing, curlew and golden plover. All of course were then living free from the 'learned' ravages perpetuated on the land in the name of so called progress.

One can only now be wistful of high water quality, pure air and a land surface uncontaminated by sitka spruce and agricultural chemicals – a veritable natural paradise compared to the legacy that greedy insensitive 'silly' man has left his children to inherit in the new twenty-first century. Need one continue to debate or speculate that such natural quality so influenced and inspired such an intelligent, romantic observer of nature as our National Bard – Robert Burns – a man who observed, loved, cared, defended: and was thus our first Scottish campaigning conservationist.

# Acknowledgements

I am pleased to record thanks to Allan Allison, Jim Allan, David Balharry, John Cameron, John Craig, Stan Craig, Willie Duncan, Hugh Fife, Andrew Haining, Tom Holden, Syd House, Kim Miller, Osbourne McMinn, Murdo Morrison, Mike Nelson, David Pollock, Ian Rose, Rosalind Smith, Bobby Smith, Derek Skilling, John Skilling, Sarah Wanless and Bernard Zonfrillo all of whom provided useful comment. Billy Gray and Rody Gorman advised me on the Gaelic and Scots names.

I owe much to Helen Main who coped with my original hand written draft and typed the manuscript and to Mandy Shaw and Stanley Hepburn who prepared the final text for publication.

A special debt is due to D Wilson Ogilvie, Past President, Burns Federation, not only for his Foreword but also for reading and commenting on the whole manuscript and to Jill Dick of Scottish Cultural Press whose professional expertise was invaluable.

None of the above have of course any responsibility for errors or misrepresentation. Omissions and interpretations within the text including the opinions expressed in it are entirely my own responsibility.

I appreciate that not all readers will share some of my views, but I trust they will at least acknowledge that, to cover such an emotional and intrinsically complex subject as Burns and Nature, that at the 'end of the day' it must become a very personal statement and opinions meant only to be constructive.

*The Complete Works of Robert Burns*; *The Complete Letters of Robert Burns* and *Burns A - Z: The Complete Word Finder*, all by James A Mackay, proved to be invaluable sources and my constant aid.

Photographs were either kindly donated by Bobby Smith, the late Jim Young, Brian Turner, or taken by the author. The map was drawn by Norman Young.

I am most grateful to Keith Brockie and Donald Watson who provided the main illustrations. The members of my family – Margaret, Lorna and Fiona – were supportive throughout the project.

# FLOWERS

Spear Thistle (Keith Brockie)

Ellisland Newyearday morning 1789:

*I have some, favourite flowers in Spring, among which are the mountain-daisy, the hare-bell, the foxglove, the wild brier-rose, the budding birk and the hoary haw-thorn, that I view and hang over with particular delight.*

Extract from a letter to Mrs Frances Anna Dunlop of Dunlop

## Introduction

Flowers eventually reach out and touch everyone's life, whether or not one claims to be at all interested in them, or in botany as a science. There are so many different aspects to plants, that will inevitably ensure a very personal contact.

They are brought to the ill, decorate our various churches, and are used to convey our symbolic messages of love, joy and, at times, sadness.

A relatively recent and laudable development, for example, has been the establishment of flower gardens for the blind, where the unsighted can experience the 'feel' and fragrance of such beautiful objects whose vast range of colours are unfortunately denied them.

Flowers are now regarded as 'essential products' and used commercially to provide manufacturing industry with the basic raw materials to provide delicate perfumes and healing drugs; and, of course, they provide a food source – not only for many species of insects but subsequently man – from their honey-producing nectars.

The demand for blooms to decorate the home or to stock gardens has led to the establishment of a vast international industry employing many thousands of people in culture laboratories, nurseries and retail outlets seeking to supply an increasing and indeed almost insatiable demand.

Plants are indeed beautiful, but in the wild – from where all the ancestors of the current domestic varieties emanated – they are now, unfortunately, no longer bountiful. Many species yet remain, either undiscovered or under-researched, with the potential to produce life saving drugs. Others, the delicate lichens for example, now act as indicators to environmental destruction through air pollution.

Without fundamental knowledge of soils and plants it is quite impossible for ecologists to understand, manage, and thus conserve the higher plants and the birds and other animals that depend on them.

All are interdependant, with flowers and plants not only beautiful, decorative and useful to man but indeed vital to our future well being on earth.

There are over 2,500 different plants known to be growing in the wild in Britain and the scientific standing of British botanists is now beyond dispute. Plants in Britain have arguably been more thoroughly surveyed and studied than anywhere else in the world.

Originally only studied and gathered by herb collecting apothecaries seeking a 'magical potion to cure all ills', the study of plants gradually became more and more scientifically orientated.

The first notable figure – often called 'the Father of British botany' – was in fact a medical man, William Turner, Dean of Wells and a fiery Protestant controversialist. Before he died in 1568 he was able to produce a list of some 300 species.

By the middle of the seventeenth century several notable botanists were active – none more so than Thomas Johnston whose remarkable publication *Mercurius Botanicus* of 1641 listed some 700 known plants. There followed onto the botanical scene the greatest influence ever known in British botanical history – John Ray, a blacksmith's son born in Essex. During an illustrious career – culminating in the publication of his *Catalogus Plantarum Angliae* in 1670 – he toured Scotland and collected many specimens which are detailed in his diaries.

The period from Ray's death in 1704 up to 1760 was considered to be botanically 'lean'. His work, written in Latin, was not readily available; there were in fact only eight other books published up to 1760 depicting local flora, and none of these specifically covered either Ayrshire or Dumfries. William Dunbar, 'rattlin roarin Willie', presented Burns with a copy of 'Spencer', a favourite source of reference to flower names. Burns, an avid collector of books, still had little hope of learning about local plants from published sources.

There followed an active period which saw a further 40 national and local floras published between 1760 and 1820. Most of these pertained to English regions, and in turn led to what became known as the 'Romantic Revival', with more floras, both national and local, being written and a virtual spate of popular books appeared on wild flowers.

The plant list that we can glean from Burns' work, with only some 240 specific references to some thirty seven species must be considered in the light of two aspects. Firstly, the lack at that time of informed written material; and secondly, would he have used such additional knowledge in his poetry and songs even if he had known the names of many more plants.

My personal view is that his botanical knowledge and appreciation mirrors his ornithological expertise, in that it greatly exceeded the lists that can be produced from his writings. He was a poet and songwriter – and a romantic one to boot. He continually used short, single-syllable words that suited the metre and rhyme of his individual works rather than attempt to show off his natural history knowledge by accommodation. For example, 'rose' fits rather better than 'dandelion' into any verse whether set to music or not. His references to Dog Rose alone were in the order of 26% of his total botanical references. Rose, Heather and Lily species combined make up a very significant 48% of all known mentions he made of flowering plants.

Such a brief 'bare bones' type of analysis does not, of course, truly reflect the Poet's undoubted love for and affinity with flowers. Often, naturally enough, he uses it in the vernacular referring to the 'ladies'. His referrals are more accurately gauged by his non-specific statements where he mentions variants of flowers, blossom, buds and stems. On a quite staggering 206 occasions, a rather grand total of 446 references, which quite significantly proves the point:

> The simple Bard, unbroke by rules of art,
> He pours the wild effusions of the heart:
> And, if inspired, 'tis Nature's pow'rs inspire;
> Hers all the melting thrill, and hers the kindling fire.

In the following species' notes, the English and scientific names are followed by any local ones that were extensively used. An abbreviated checklist with the Scots and Scottish Gaelic may be found in Appendix 1.

I have omitted all Burns' references to exotic and garden fruits, such as peach and gooseberry. Similarly, farm crops and vegetables do not fall within the remit of this particular review.

In conclusion, I can confess that I am not a trained botanist, but I do care passionately for plants and must invoke my perogative here with a personal and special plea.

Many people, when they find wild flowers, still like to pick them, perhaps to have a pressed collection from which to draw or paint, dry them out as a winter decoration or simply to decorate a room for the duration of their short 'vase life'.

If, when I was younger and starting out 'in the field' anyone had said that relatively common species – for example the Primrose – would become so scarce in my lifetime as to warrant legal protection, I would have literally laughed them 'out of court', but alas, it is now sadly a trueism.

Picking, uprooting or the collection of very scarce wild flowers or seed, other than under a specific scientific licence granted by Scottish Natural Heritage, and without permission of the landowner, is in my view, rather like egg collecting by young boys – it belongs in the Victorian era and has no place now in the ecologically-threatened final decade of this century.

Surely, all responsible adults, parents and especially educationalists – including authors of botanical works – should now firmly discourage the practice.

I do not suggest, of course, that anyone should be discouraged from botanical study. Quite the reverse – an appreciation of wild plants by the young student, the disabled or retired adult will undoubtably not only enhance their delight and understanding of nature but improve the whole quality of life itself.

Tutorials, night classes, holidays at field stations are all now within the financial range of most people. In addition, field guides and keys to identification are now readily available, reasonably priced and produced to such a high standard as to allow accurate determination in the field, without any need to resort to collection.

Conservation of wild plants can only be effective if people follow a voluntary code of conduct in the countryside and avoid damaging plants and their habitats without very good reason. The Wildlife and Countryside Act may well provide formal legal protection for most species, but without a change of *attitude* towards such aspects, little will be accomplished.

The great educational drive towards a green sympathetic ethic has indeed come full circle, to virtually haunt those whose task it is to protect plants in their natural environment.

It is now often the very rare specialised plants, living in vulnerable 'delicate' habitats that are most at risk, not always from the farmer or forester, but also at the hands and trampling feet of the quite learned, well informed but over enthusiastic botanist. Many actually wear the proverbial path to some of our most rare plants, 'garden' for photography then stick tripod legs through the earth and root system within inches of the plant.

I am privileged to currently work at Caenlochan National Nature Reserve in North Tayside and can say without fear of contradiction that some of the recent behaviour by visiting, so called botanists, has been absolutely disgraceful and totally irresponsible.

Without doubt, there is in operational existence within botanical circles, an unofficial but proficient 'grapevine' that allows enthusiasts to enter the field armed with location maps and lists – including six-figure map references – enabling them to locate stations of the rarest of plants, some in extremely vulnerable habitat. Other than within the Government Conservation Agencies, confidentiality is simply not now being observed by 'those in the know' who purport to lecture or write publicly on such aspects.

'Tis such as they who must now stand up and be counted, by acting quickly to put their own house in order, before they totally lose credibility and direct their undoubted expertise towards sharing responsibility for the future conservation of our rich botanical heritage.

### Behold, my love, how green the groves

> Behold, my love, how green the groves,
> The primrose banks how fair;
> The balmy gales awake the flowers,
> and wave thy flowing hair.
>
> The lav'rock shuns the palace gay,
> And o'er the cottage sings:
> For Nature smiles as sweet, I ween,
> To Shepherds as to Kings.
>
> Let minstrels sweep the skilfu strings,
> In lordly lighted ha':
> The Shepherd stops his simple reed,
> Blythe in the birken shaw.
>
> The Princely revel may survey
> Our rustic dance wi scorn;
> But are their hearts as light as ours,
> Beneath the milk-white thorn?
>
> The shepherd, in the flowery glen;
> In shepherd's phase, will woo:
> The courtier tells a finer tale,
> But is his heart as true?

These wild-wood flowers I've pu'd, to deck
That spotless breast o thine:
The courtier's gems may witness love,
But, 'tis na love like mine.

## WALLFLOWER  *Cheiranthus cheiri*

An introduced species of southern European origin now naturalised and cultivated for its clusters of yellow, orange, red or purple flowers, Wallflower produces a pleasant fragrance, grows on most types of soil and survives on old walls and cliffs. The plant was thought to have come over from France attached to building stone at the time of the Norman invasion.

Burns refers to it once, in a work formerly called **'A Vision'** (later revised, it was renamed **'As I Stood By Yon Roofless Tower'** – the roofless tower was in fact Lincluden Abbey, north of Dumfries situated on the banks of the river Nith):

As I stood by yon roofless tower,
Where the *wa'flow'r* scents the dewy air…

## BOG MYRTLE or SWEET GALE  *Myrica gale*

**Local:** Sweet Gale; Flea Wood

Reasonably large areas of endemic myrtle still survive in Scotland, where bogs and wet heathland have been conserved. A shrubby plant with sucker shoots, upright reddish twigs and growing to 24-54 inches (60-137 cm). The flowers are borne in short catkins. Yellow dots (glands) are scattered over the leaves which have a delightful eucalyptus-like aromatic smell. Known also as flea-wood since it is not attractive to insects (indeed the scent repels some species), it was used in the eighteenth century by country people to make flea-free beds and provided the basic ingredient in early attempts to produce, especially, a repellant for midges.

In the song **'Here Is The Glen'** it is probable that the Bard had myrtle in mind when he wrote:

'Tis not Maria's whispering call –
'Tis but the balmy-breathing *gale*,
Mixed with some warbler's dying fall
The dewy star of eve to hail!

He was quite specific when writing a tribute to Jean Armour which he entitled **'Their Groves O Sweet Myrtle'** and opened with the first lines:

Their groves o sweet *myrtle* let foreign lands reckon,
Where bright-beaming summers exalt the perfume!

Referring to myrtle growing abroad in groves in **'The Twa Dogs'**:

> Or down Italian vista startles,
> Whore-hunting amang groves o *myrtles*;

and in an earlier work entitled **'Poem On Pastoral Poetry'** (later renamed **'Sketch'**) he said 'Nae gowden stream thro' *myrtles* twines'.

## COMMON DOG VIOLET   *Viola riviniana*

Common and widespread throughout Scotland, it is small smooth perennial with unscented flowers. This violet has a leafy flowering stem, it can grow up to 8 inches (20 cm) and the flowers are usually blue-violet with a paler spur. There are several species of violet and its close relative the pansies. In his references it is most likely that Burns at least inferred this species. It is the more common and most widely distributed species found in meadows and woodlands in Ayrshire and Dumfries.

Burns refers to the 'violet' in the rather sad song **'And Maun I Still On Menie Doat'**: 'In vain to me the *vi'lets* spring', and in the song **'The Posie'** he attributes the traditional meaning or language of the flowers with: 'The *violet*'s for modesty, which weel she fa's to wear'.

In an additional stanza to the lines **'Adown Winding Nith'** which was later omitted, he wrote:

> The primrose is o'er for the season,
> But mark where the *violet* is blown;
> How modest it peeps from the covert,
> So modesty sure is her own.

The popular song **'My Nanie's Awa'** has a rather fine botanical couplet with:

> The snawdrap and primrose our woodlands adorn,
> And *violets* bathe in the weet o the morn…

An early version of the song **'O Were My Love'** commences with:

> O, were my love you *vi'let* sweet,
> That peeps frae 'neath the hawthorn spray;

In the 1793 revision, Burns changed the first two lines to -

> O, were my love you lilac fair
> Wi purple blossoms to the spring…

Then writing to Thomson, he declared: 'I produced (the first lines), far inferior to the foregoing, I frankly confess.'

The bawdy song **'Una's Lock'** has as its opening lines:

> 'Twas on a sweet morning
> When *violets* were a-springing...

### BLUEBELL  *Hyacinthus Endymion non-scriptus*

**Scotland:** Wild Hyacinth
**Local:**     Craw taes

The bluebell is now unfortunately scarce in south-west Scotland, although where protected from collecting and especially trampling may still form a 'spectacular blue carpet' in some woodlands; it also continues to feature in hedgerows, on scrub land, sea cliffs and on the higher hills.

Bluebell grows to some 8 to 20 inches (20-50 cm). The flower stems are surrounded at the base by long, strap-shaped leaves from which the flower spike is curved, drooping at the tip with all the blooms hanging to one side. Blossoms are not in fact always blue; pink and white flowers are not infrequent.

In the mid-eighteenth century, sap taken from the bluebell was used to produce a glue, used to bind books.

In the song **'The Posie'** the Poet refers to it thus: 'The *hyacinth*'s for constancy wi its unchanging blue...'

### HAREBELL  *Campanula rotundifolia*

**Scotland:**    Bluebell
**Local:**        Fairy bells, Witches thimbles, Old man's bells

Widespread and reasonably common throughout mainland Scotland. A slender perennial with creeping underground stems, the hairless stems are bent at the base then straighten up, the distinctive pale blue flower has a broad five-lobed petal tube in the form of a bell. The harebell, which grows on to 6-16 inches (15-40 cm) prefers dry grassy sites, often on poor soil.

In his **'Elegy on Captain Matthew Henderson'** Burns mentions the species specifically: 'Mourn, little *harebells* o'er the lea...', and in the song **'Their Groves O Sweet Myrtle'** he refers to the Scots:

> Far dearer to me are you humble broom bowers,
> Where the *blue-bell* and gowan lurk lowly, unseen;

## LADIES SMOCK   *Cardamine pratensis*

**Local:** Cuckoo flower; Pink

A perennial with smooth stems about 12-18 inches (30-80 cm) high with pink flowers and commonly found in damp meadows and by burns.

In his rewording of the air **'The Posie'** Burns wrote:

> The primrose I will pu, the firstling of the year,
> An I will pu, the *pink*, the emblem o my dear.

Some authorities have suggested that 'pink' referred to a garden carnation. The whole scene was set in the spring and in the scenario of the woodland walk beside a river. I prefer to suggest that this would almost certainly refer to Ladies' Smock or Cuckoo Flower, known locally as Pink in Dumfriesshire.

## SPEAR THISTLE   *Cirsium vulgare*

**Local:** Scotch Thistle; Burr

A common and widespread thistle throughout Scotland growing in field margins, wood edges, river and road sides and flourishing on waste ground. A biennial with robust stems, it can grow up to 5 feet tall (1.5m) partly winged by prickly leaves. The purple flower heads are either carried singly or in groups of two or three on short stalks.

It is this species 'Spear' – not the oft illustrated Cotton Thistle *Onopordun acanthium* – that is the National Emblem of Scotland. Early Scottish Kings used a thistle as their personal heraldic device; it then became generally accepted as the national emblem by 1503 when the poet William Dunbar wrote the 'Thistle and the Rose' to celebrate the marriage of James III of Scotland to Princess Margaret of England; and was ratified in 1687 when James VI instituted the Order of the Thistle as a Scottish order of knighthood.

In the reworking of the Jacobite song **'Awa, Whigs, Awa'**, Burns has as the first verse:

> Our *thrissles* flourish'd fresh and fair,
> And bonnie bloom'd our roses;
> But Whigs cam like a frost in June,
> An wither'd a our posies.

Replying to a verse-epistle sent to him by one Mrs Scott in 1787, Burns sent verses which he called **'To the Guidwife of Wauchhope House'**. In the second verse he produced a very significant quote:

> The rough burr-*thistle* spreading wide
> Amang the bearded bear,
> I turn'd the weeder-clips aside,
> An spar'd the symbol dear.

'Burr' refers to the jagged edges of the leaves; 'bearded bear' is the fruited barley.

His reference in **'The Author's Earnest Cry and Prayer'** is similarly nationalistic:

> Paint Scotland greetin owre her *thrissle*;
> Her mutchkin stowp as toom's a whissle;

and in his famous **'Address To A Haggis'**, completed while in Edinburgh in 1786:

> But mark the Rustic, haggis-fed,
> The trembling earth resounds his tread,
> Clap in his walie nieve a blade,
> He'll make it whissle;
> An legs an arms, an heads will sned,
> Like taps of *thrissle*.

## BRACKEN *Pteridium aquilinum*

**Local:** Brake; Fern

A common and widespread fern occurring all over mainland Scotland. Invasive in field margins, in woodland and especially on gently sloping hills where heather is burned. Growing at times to 5-6 feet tall (2m) it has large green fronds with spore cases and extensive underground rhizomes. In former times, when dried it was used extensively as a low grade fodder, as bedding for both people and animals, as an additive to dung in the production of manure, and especially as a roof thatch.

Burns refers to the plant in **'Their Groves O Sweet Myrtle'**, a song written in 1790 as a tribute to Jean Armour:

> Far dearer to me yon lone glen o green *breckan*,
> Wi the burn stealing under the lang, yellow broom;

and again in **'Halloween'**:

> Amang the *brachens*, on the brae,
> Between her an the moon,
> The Deil, or else an outler quey,
> Gat up an gae a croon.

## CLOVER *Trifolium repens/pratense*

White (or Dutch) Clover *T. repens* is widespread and common throughout Scotland. The stems creep along the ground and take root, the leaves with three leaflets are on upright stalks growing on to 20 inches (50 cm) and the flowers, white coloured are carried in heads on long stems. Clover produces a relatively large volume of nectar and is thus valuable to bees and other long-tongued insects.

Similarly, Red Clover *T. pratense* is common and widespread in southern Scotland. Growing up to 24 inches (60 cm) it has pointed leaflets with a pale V-band. The reddish-purple flower heads rise stalkless from a pair of leaves at the end of a stem.

Of the several clover species, white and red are the most likely to have been present during the mid-eighteenth century. In fact, of the three references available, one was of white, the others unspecified.

Red Clover was certainly preferred by farmers of that era, being harvested for fodder or ploughed in to enrich the soil and interestingly, there is ample evidence of an early 'agricultural revolution', which included seed selection for fodder crops that Burns farmed. In addition, Red Clover was used during the period to make wine and to produce a thick syrup for the relief of throat and chest complaints. In a song entitled **'The Country Lass'** the Poet was quite specific:

> In simmer, when the hay was mown
> And corn wav'd green in ilka field,
> While *claver* blooms white o'er the ley
> And roses blaw in ilka bield.

The **'Elegy on Captain Matthew Henderson'** includes:

> Mourn, clam'ring craiks, at close o day,
> 'Mang fields o flow'ring *clover* gay!

and recalls an era when corncrakes were present in most hayfields; which Burns refers to again in an old song entitled **'Bessy And Her Spinnin-Wheel'** in which he has the line 'The craik amang the *claver* hay'.

## FOXGLOVE  *Digitalis purpurea*

**Local:** Dead Man's Bells; Fairy thimbles

A common plant, widely distributed throughout Scotland, found in woodland, field margins, bankings, waste ground and even in rocky conditions. A tall, stately biennial it grows to between 2-5 feet (100-152 cm) with 20 to 80 purple, sometimes white, flowers hanging from a single stem.

Foxglove is very poisonous, yet it yields the drug digitalis which is used in small doses for the treatment of some heart disorders. The drug was in fact discovered in 1785, although the way in which it stimulated the heart was not understood at that time.

Burns mentions the plant in his **'Elegy On Captain Matthew Henderson'**:

> Ye stately *foxgloves*, fair to see;
> Ye woodbines, hanging bonile,
> In scented bowers;
> Ye roses on your thorny tree,
> The first o flowers!

Of course he also refers to it in his famous letter of 1789 to Mrs Frances Anna Dunlop of Dunlop.

## SNOWDROP  *Galanthus nivalis*

**Local:** Snow piercer; Snowflake; Snawdrop

A reasonably common and widespread plant which is often found growing in impressive clumps in woodland. Prefers a south-facing aspect and becomes relatively scarcer further north in Scotland. It grows to about 6 to 10 inches (15-25cm) with strap-shaped leaves at the base of each stem, which bears a single drooping blossom. The generic name *Galanthus* describes it aptly, from the Greek meaning 'milk' and 'flower'. One of the earliest of flowering plants to appear it provides a vital first new source of nectar for bees. Other than the aesthetic, the only connection with man is that it was once gathered and worn as garlands by village maidens as a symbol of purity, connected with the Feast of Purification of St Mary.

Burns refers to it in the rather sad song **'My Nannie's Awa'** 'The *snawdrap* and primrose our woodlands adorn'; and in **'The Kiss'**: 'Love's first *snow-drop*, virgin kiss!'

These verses were accepted by most authors but not by Maria Riddell in 1802.

## STINGING NETTLE  *Urtica dioica*

**Local:** Stinging Jenny

A very common and widespread perennial plant found in woodland, hedgerows, neglected land and invasive of agricultural land. It may form into dense clumps and reach a height of up to 60 inches (152 cm). It produces upright leafy stems and the whole plant bristles with stinging hairs.

The nettle has had a long and mainly useful association with man. Detested by some as a difficult weed, it was used as an instrument of torture, often self inflicted in monastic orders. It was harvested to produce a primitive type of cloth, used in Scotland as shrouds or bed linen during the eighteenth century.

Young nettle leaves were eaten, boiled as a vegetable and when dried made a type of 'tea'. Nettle soup was common in southern Scotland and persists to this day. Rich in chlorophyll it was used in early medicines, and also to produce a green dye.

In his **'Monody'** on a lady famed for her caprice, Burns wrote:

> We'll search through the garden for each silly flower,
> We'll roam thro' the forest for each idle weed,
> But chiefly the *nettle*, so typical, shower,
> For none e'er approach'd her but rued the rash deed.

## BROAD-LEAVED DOCK  *Rumex obtusifolius*

**Local:** Dock; Dockins

A large plant growing at times up to 3 feet (90 cm) with large oblong leaves. Very common and widely distributed in Scotland. It favours bare or disturbed ground and grows on most soils including damp, waste areas, or in shade. The leaves have long been used by country people to keep food moist, cool and insect free. Butter and newly caught fish, for example, were regularly wrapped in the large fresh leaves. They were also used either as a wound dressing, or boiled as a poultice, and rubbing of the dry leaves were reputed to lessen the pain of nettle stings.

Clearly, Burns identified another use in his revision of an old popular ballad **'There Was Twa Wives'**:

> She farted by the byre-en',
> She farted by the stable;
> And thick and nimble were her steps
> As fast as she was able:
> Till at yon dyke-back the hurly brak,
> But raxin for some *dockins*,
> The beans and pease cam down her thighs,
> And she cackit a' her stockins.

> 'Hurly' is the Scots for diarrhoea.

## PRIMROSE  *Primula vulgaris*

A well known 'harbinger of spring', primroses grow throughout Scotland, especially in the west, and are to be found in woodlands and hedgerows before the canopy forms a shady cover. Often found, too, on open grassy bankings, the flowers are a delicate pale yellow and the plant rarely exceeds 5 inches (130 mm) in height. Sadly now, becoming quite scarce, largely due to collecting. The plant's generic name *Primula* is from the latin, meaning 'forest rose', *vulgaris* means common. Used in primitive medicines, it was thought to ease rheumatism and nervous headaches. Clearly the flower was well known to Burns and he mentions it in several works.

In **'The Chevalier's Lament'** Burns uses a direct reference, when he words his lament as if spoken by Charles Edward Stuart after the battle of Culloden -

> The small birds rejoice in the green leaves returning,
> The murmuring streamlet winds clear thro the vale,
> The *primroses* blow in the dews of the morning,
> And wild scatter'd cowslips bedeck the green dale:
> But what can give pleasure, or what can seem fair,
> When the lingering moments are number'd by care?
> No flow'rs gaily springing, nor birds sweetly singing,
> Can soothe the sad bosom of joyless despair!
> The deed that I dar'd, could it merit their malice,
> A king and a father to place on his throne?
> His right are these hills, and his right are those valleys,
> Where the wild beasts find shelter, tho I can find none!
> But 'tis not my suff'rings this wretched, forlorn-
> My brave gallant friends, 'Tis your ruin I mourn!
> Your faith prov'd so loyal in hot bloody trial,
> Alas! can I make it no better return?

The beautiful and sensitive song **'Sweet Afton'** contains:

> How pleasant thy banks and green vallies below,
> Where wild in the woodlands the *primroses* blow…

In another lament **'Lament Of Mary Queen of Scots'** he wrote 'The *primrose* down the brae'; and in the song **'The Posie'** – a well known air in the west country – 'The *primrose* I will pu, the firstling o the year'.

In the song **'By Allan Stream'** he not only mentions the plant but demonstrates once more his familiarity of it with: 'The haunt o Spring's the *primrose*-brae.'

Burns revised the song **'The Primrose'** originally written by Robert Herrick in the mid-seventeenth century:

> Dost ask me, why I send thee here,
> This firstling of the infant year?
> Dost ask me, what this *primrose* shews,
> Bepearled thus with morning dews?

His song **'Lassie Wi The Lint White Locks'** has the line 'the *primrose* bank, the wimpling burn,' and rather similarly, the song **'Behold, My Love, How Green The Groves'** has 'The *primrose* banks how fair.'

In the beautiful but sad lines of **'My Nannie's Awa'**:

> The snawdrap and *primrose* our woodlands adorn,
> And violets bathe in the weet o the morn,
> They pain my sad bosom, sae sweetly they blaw;
> They mind me o Nannie - and Nannie's awa!

His letter of 1787 to William Nicol contains the description 'as sweet and modest's a new blawn *plumrose* in a hazel shaw'. The song **'Adown Winding Nith'** had at one time an additional stanza that had as its opening line 'The *primrose* is o'er for the season...'; and the song **'Una's Lock'**, which Burns revised, has the comment:

> And the *primrose*, that then blows,
> Bespangled nature's verdant gown.

## COMMON POPPY *Papaver rhoeas*

**Local:** Corn Poppy; Corn Rose; Field Poppy

A widespread, common flower but decreasing, typically and traditionally found in association with cornfields and on disturbed land. In the mid-eighteenth century, prior obviously to the use of selective weedkillers, one would expect that many fields would be a virtual 'blaze of red'. A tall upright plant growing to some 24 inches (20-60 cm) it has a distinctive large, solitary, red flowerhead.

Poppies have long been used in old medicines and feature in folklore as a test of fidelity.

Burns refers to the species in his famous epic **'Tam O Shanter'**:

> But pleasures are like *poppies* spread:
> You seize the flow'r, its bloom is shed;

## COWSLIP *Primula veris*

Closely related to the primrose, they in fact hybridise at times. The yellow flowers of the cowslip, in comparison to the primrose, are drooping and their petals more cupped. Longer stemmed it reaches up to 12 inches (30 cm). Very attractive to insects, the delicately perfumed flowers have long been used to produce a very potent wine. Reasonably common and widespread in southern Scotland in pastures, field margins, wood edges and on some river banks, it becomes progressively scarcer further north.

In his song **'The Lass Of Cessnock Banks'** written for Alison Begbie, who rejected his proposal of marriage, Burns wrote:

> She's stately like yon youthful ash,
> That grows the *cowslip* braes between...

and the song written during his period in Edinburgh **'And Maun I Still On Menie Doat'** contains: 'In vain to me the *cowslips* blaw.'

**'The Chevalier's Lament'**, already alluded to, has both the *Primula* species in successive lines -

The primroses blow in the dews of the morning,
And wild scatter'd *cowslips* bedeck the green dale:
But what can give pleasure, or what can seem fair,
When lingering moments are number'd by care?

The lengthy **'Elegy On Captain Matthew Henderson'**, so full of natural history delights, includes:

Mourn, Spring, thou darling of the year!
Ilk *cowslip* cup shall kep a tear:

## COMMON RAGWORT *Senecio jacobaea*

**Local:** Ragwood; Ragweed; 'stinking Billy'; Mougart

This striking plant, with contrasting dark green leaves, is a common and widespread biennual or perennial found throughout Scotland, especially on waste ground or in pastures, and is often indicative of ground disturbance or overgrazing by either stock or, more usually, rabbits. Growing up to 4 feet tall (1.2 m) it sports a conspicuous rosette of divided leaves at its base, and numerous flower heads, each with some fifteen bright yellow florets.

'Ragwort' refers to the ragged edged leaves; and in Scotland, the local name of 'stinking Billy' alludes to the unpleasant odour emitted when crushed; 'Billy' is William, the vile and ruthless Duke of Cumberland (butcher), who led the hated Hanoverians at Culloden.

Usually the plant is ungrazed, but when cut and dried its leaves contain an alkaloid poison, which if eaten may cause liver damage to animals. It was once mistakenly believed that the plant cured staggers in horses, hence the scientific name of *jacobaea* called after St James, the patron saint of these noble beasts.

Burns refers to the plant in his **'Address To The Deil'**:

Let warlocks grim, an wither'd hags,
Tell how wi you, on *ragweed* nags,
They skim the muirs on dizzy crags,
Wi wicked speed;

Writing to Captain Francis Grose in 1790 he describes: 'Among the many Witch Stories I have heard relating to Aloway Kirk, I distinctly remember only two or three. . .

As he passed the kirk, in the ajoining field, he fell in with a crew of men and women, who were busy pulling stems of the plant *ragwort*. He observed that, as each person pulled a *ragwort*, he or she got astride of it and called out, 'Up horsie!' on which the *ragwort* flew off, like Pegasus, through the air with its rider. The foolish boy likewise pulled his *ragwort*, and cried with the rest 'Up horsie!' and, strange to tell, away he flew with the company.

## HEATHER *Calluna vulgaris*

**Local:** Ling; Heath

The most common of the several species of heather that may grow on the Scottish moors; *Calluna* probably could be described as a small evergreen shrub. It is usually less than 2 feet high (60 cm) with branched stems rooting at the base. Occasionally white, the flowers are normally purple and in autumn may provide a continuous dense mass, indeed provide a rather spectacular 'show' of flowers.

The name probably originally derives from the Scots 'heath'; and the commonly used local name of ling – also used to describe rush or coarse grasses growing on moorland in Scotland – is from the Anglo-Saxon 'lig' meaning fire and recalls its importance as a fuel source. The scientific name *Calluna* is from the Greek meaning 'to brush'; heather stems were made to make house brooms and were also woven into baskets, fish traps, thatch bundles, beds and in the Highlands used for a variety of tasks ranging from roofing and wall construction to food straining.

Important to many forms of wildlife – heather honey for example is renowned for its flavour – it is probably best known as providing vital habitat for Red Grouse. Heather moorland is now typically managed by burning within a 12-year cycle to provide the optimum conditions for this valuable sporting bird, tender young shoots providing food while the older stems provide cover for nesting and shelter during winter. Unfortunately, in spite of its value for shooting, due to several other economic factors, especially reclamation for grazing and forestry, heather dominated moorland in Scotland has decreased alarmingly since the early 1950s.

Burns was very familiar with heather and the relationship with grouse, demonstrating that in the song **'Now Westlin' Winds'**:

> Now Westling Winds and slaught'ring guns
> Bring Autumn's pleasant weather;
> The moorcock springs on whirring wings
> Amang the blooming *heather*:

The beautiful song, **'As I Cam O'er The Cairney Mount'** contains 'And down amang the blooming *heather*'; and the popular Border song **'Braw Lads O Galla Water'** has 'They rove amang the blooming *heather*'. There are several versions of this song, all containing a similar reference.

Burns produced two versions of the traditional ballad **'Ca' The Yowes To The Knowes'** and although the texts were quite different he retained the same chorus in both.

> Ca' the yowes to the knowes,
> Ca' them where the *heather* grows,
> Ca' them where the burnie rowes,
> My bonnie dearie!

**'Elegy On Captain Matthew Henderson'** has another reference to both heather and grouse – 'Ye grouse that crap the *heather* bud' and for good measure includes the fact that grouse primarily eat the tender new buds.

An early Ayrshire folk song **'Brose And Butter'** has the lines -

> My daddie sent me to the hill
> To pu my minnie some *heather*;

and an undated fragment contains

> Jenny M'Graw, she has ta'en to the *heather*,
> Say was it the covenant carried her thither;

The song **'Montgomerie's Peggy'** has as its first lines

> Altho my bed were in yon muir,
> Amang the *heather*, in my plaidie,
> Yet happy, happy I would be,
> Had I my dear Mongomerie's Peggy.

The chorus in the song **'Broom Besoms'** contains:

> Buy broom besoms! wha will buy them now;
> Fine *heather* ringers, better never grew.

A further reference, combining red grouse with heather, is in the song **'My Lord A-Hunting He is Gane'**:

> Out o'er yon muir, out o'er yon moss,
> Whare gor-cocks thro the *heather* pass,

and in his famous **'Tam Samson's Elegy'**, penned on the hypothetical demise of a noted hunter,

> Yon auld grey stane, amang the *heather*,
> Marks out his head;

Later in the same work he refers again:

> When August winds the *heather* wave,
> And sportsmen wander by yon grave...

**'The Author's Earnest Cry and Prayer'**, written in protest at an Act which was aimed at restricting distillation of spirits, was given a postscript which ends:

> Scotland, my auld, respected mither!
> Tho whiles ye moistify your leather,
> Till whare ye sit on craps o *heather*,
> Ye tine your dam;
>
> Freedom an whisky gang thegither
> Tak aff your dram!

His verse – epistle **'To Alexander Findlater'** contains: 'I'd treated them wi caller *heather*', and the revised song **'The Bonie Moor-Hen'** opens with a first verse of -

> The *heather* was blooming, the meadows were mawn,
> Our lads gaed a-hunting ae day at the dawn…

and later in the same work:

> Sweet-bruising the dew from the brown *heather*-bells,
> Her colours betray'd her on yon mossy fells!

In a song he called **'Bonie Jean'** the subject of which was Jean McMurdo, daughter of the chamberlain of Drumlanrig, her proposal of marriage from a fictional 'Young Robbie' included the promise -

> At barn or byre thou shalt na drudge,
> Or naething else to trouble thee,
> But stray amang the *heather*-bells,
> And tent the waving corn wi me.

She accepted! -

> 'At length she blush'd a sweet consent'

In **'Epistle to William Simpson'** (the Ochiltree school master), Burns again demonstrated his nationalistic feelings with:

> We'll sing auld Coila's plains and fells,
> Her moors red-brown wi *heather* bells,
> Her banks an braes, her dens and dells,
>     Whare glorious Wallace
> Aft bure the gree, as story tells,
>     Frae Suthron billies.

His song of 1787 **'Yon Wild Mossy Mountains'** has again a very significant and descriptive ornithological line: 'Where the grouse lead their coveys thro the *heather* to feed.'

His **'Ode For General Washington's Birthday'** contains: 'Thee, Caledonia, thy wild *heaths* among'; and his **'Elegy on The Late Miss Burnet of Monboddo'** includes 'Ye *heathy* wastes immix'd with reedy fens.'

The 1794 song which he called **'Sleep'st Thou'** contains:

> Now to the streaming fountain
> Or up the *heathy* mountain
> The hart, hind, and roe, freely, wildly-wanton stray;

In the song **'The Gloomy Night Is Gath'ring Fast'**, apparently written when his emigration from Greenock to the West Indies was imminent, he included in the final verse:

Farewell, old Coila's hills and dales,
Her *heathy* moors and winding vales;

It was during his Highland Tour of 1787, when Burns came down the east shore of Loch Ness to Foyers, that he wrote while 'standing on the spot' **'Lines on the Falls of Fyers'** which opens with the lines -

Among the *heathy* hills and ragged woods
The roaring Fyers pours his mossy floods;

In the street ballad of about 1775, **'Charlie, He's My Darling'**, Burns in his revision uses the lines:

It's up yon *heathery* mountain
And down the scroggy glen…

## WILD THYME *Thymus drucei*

A common and widespread, usually prostrate, sweet mint-smelling perennial with long creeping stems often found on banks, heaths and in dry, grassy areas.

Burns refers to it in the ballad of **'Kellyburn Braes'**, possibly set and referring to the Kello water in Dumfriesshire:

(Hey, and the *rue* grows bonie wi *thyme*!)

And the *thyme* it is wither'd and the *rue* is in prime

**Rue:** *Ruta graveolens* is native to the Eastern Mediterranean. A small deciduous shrub, whose leaves produce an acrid volatile oil, was formally used medicinally as a narcotic or stimulant. More often cultivated in gardens from where it at times escaped.

## DAISY *Bellis perennis*

**Local:** Gowan; Oxeye; Mountain Daisy; Common Daisy; Wild Daisy

A widespread and common dwarf perennial growing in pastures, hay meadows, fields and wood edges. It can grow up to between 8 and 24 inches (20-60 cm) and flowers right through from March till October. The spoon-shaped leaves form a rosette at the base, the flower stalk is leafless and produces a single flower head which has a yellow disc surrounded by a ring of white rays.
The name daisy is derived from 'day's-eye' comparing the plant to a small sun, which opens in the morning and closes as light fades. The generic name

*Bellis* is from the Latin meaning 'beautiful'. It was used by primitive herbalists: 'boiled in asses milk, it is very effectual in consumption of the lungs'.

Burns was clearly not only familiar with the daisy but regarded it as one of his favourite flowers using the local name frequently too, as in the verses **'My Nannie O'**:

> Her face is fair, her heart is true;
> As spotless as she's bonie, O;
> The op'ning *gowan*, wat wi dew,
> Nae purer is than Nannie, O.

obviously demonstrating that he too was aware that the daisy opened in the morning.

His famous **'Epistle to Davie, A Brother Poet'** refers to the generic name in a rather pensive verse:

> Yet Nature's charms, the hills and woods,
> The sweeping vales, and foaming floods,
> Are free alike to all.
> In days when *daisies* deck the ground,
> And blackbirds whistle clear,
> With honest joy our hearts will bound,
> To see the coming year:

The composition simply titled **'The Vision'** includes the line: 'The lowly *daisy* sweetly blows'; and the song **'Their Groves O Sweet Myrtle'**, written as a tribute to Jean Armour, has the romantic couplet:

> Far dearer to me are yon humble broom-bowers,
> Where the blue-bell and *gowan* lurk lowly, unseen;

Within the epic tale of **'The Auld Farmer's New-Year Morning Salutation To His Auld Mare, Maggie'**, on giving her the accustomed ripp of corn to hansel in the New Year, he wrote:

> Tho now thou's dowie, stiff an crazy,
> An thy auld hide as white's a *daisie*,
> I've seen thee dappl't, sleek and glaizie,
> A bonie gray:

The song **'Adown Winding Nith'** includes:

> The *Daisy* amus'd my fond fancy,
> So artless, so simple, so wild:

and in his song **'And Maun I Still On Menie Doat'** he includes:

> And when the lark, 'tween light and dark,
> Blythe waukens by the *daisy's* side...

Burns had sympathies for the tragic heroine of Scottish history, and penned in 1790 his **'Lament Of Mary Queen of Scots'**, which commences with:

> Now Nature hangs her mantle green
> On every blooming tree,
> And spreads her sheets o *daisies* white
> Out o'er the grassy lea;

An old air that he revised, **'The Posie'**, which contains more references to flowers than any of his other writings, includes:

> The *daisy's* for simplicity and unaffected air -
> And a' to be a posie to my ain dear May!

In an old **'Poem on Pastoral Poetry'** (later changed to **'Sketch'**), he wrote: 'In *gowany* glens thy burnie strays'; and **'Death and Dr Hornbook'** produced:

> His braw calf-ward whare *gowans* grew
> Sae white an' bonie…

and in his very familiar 'classic' **'Auld Lang Syne'**, sung at the close of most organised events, and known by so many throughout the world, totally irrespective of colour, creed or politics:

> We twa hae run about the braes,
> And pou'd the *gowans* fine,
> But we've wander'd monie a weary fit,
> Sin auld lang syne.

In April of 1786, while ploughing at Mossgiel Farm near Mauchline in Ayrshire, Burns was clearly moved when he turned down a daisy with the plough. He penned the verses originally entitled **'The Gowan'** (later revised to **'To A Mountain Daisy'**). Of course the destruction of, and comments on, the flower triggered his thoughts and responses, alluding then to very personal problems he was experiencing at that time with the Armour family, over his association with their daughter, Jean.

He sent the completed verses to John Kennedy on 20th April 1786, with a letter describing the work 'as just the native querulous feelings of a heart which, as the elegantly melting Gray says, "Melancholy has marked for her own".'

## To a Mountain Daisy

*On turning one down with the plough, in April, 1786*

> Wee, modest, crimson-tippèd flow'r,
> Thou's met me in an evil hour;
> For I maun crush amang the stoure
> Thy slender stem:
> To spare thee now is past my pow'r,
> Thou bonie gem.

Flowers

Alas! it's no thy neebor sweet,
The bonie-lark companion meet,
Bending thee 'mang the dewy weet,
Wi spreckl'd breast!
When upward-springing, blythe, to greet
The purpling east.

Cauld blew the bitter-biting north
Upon thy early, humble birth;
Yet cheerfully thou glinted forth
Amid the storm,
Scarce rear'd above the parent-earth
Thy tender form.

The flaunting flow'rs our gardens yield,
High shelt'ring woods and wa's maun shield;
But thou, beneath the random bield
O clod or stane,
Adorns the histie stibble-field,
Unseen, alane.

There, in thy scanty mantle clad,
Thy snawie bosom sun-ward spread,
Thou lifts thy unassuming head
In humble guise;
But now the share uptears thy bed,
And low thou lies!

Such is the fate of artless maid,
Sweet flow'ret of the rural shade!
By love's simplicity betray'd,
And guileless trust;
Till she, like thee, all soil'd, is laid
Low i' the dust.

Such is the fate of simple Bard,
On Life's rough ocean luckless starr'd!
Unskilful he to note the card
Of prudent lore,
Till billows rage, and gales blow hard,
And whelm him o'er!

Such fate to suffering Worth is giv'n,
Who long with wants and woes has striv'n,
By human pride or cunning driv'n
To mis'ry's brink;
Till, wrench'd of ev'ry stay but Heav'n,
He, ruin'd, sink!

Ev'n thou who mourn'st the Daisy's fate,
That fate is thine - no distant date;
Stern Ruin's plough-share drives elate,
Full on the bloom,
Till crush'd beneath the furrow's weight,
Shall be thy doom!

## LESSER BURDOCK  *Arctium minus*

**Local:** Sticky Willie; Wild rhubarb; Rats rhubarb

Common and widespread throughout Scotland, flourishing in dryer woods, clearings and on waste ground. A vigorous plant growing to a height of 24-28 inches (60-120 cm). The red/purple florets flower in July to September.

The bur-like buds stick to clothing when thrown and are often used by small children at play. Burdock and its relatives have long featured in primitive medicine. The juice was said to soothe burns and improve the flow of urine. The leaves were applied to wounds and sores and the seeds were prescribed for sciatica.

The young stalks were collected for food; peeled and chopped they were used in salads or boiled and added to soups. The large green leaves have often led the plant to be mistaken for rhubarb.

Burns referred to Burdock when writing to the Rev. Archibald Alison in 1791:

> ...that the delicate flexure of a rose-twig, when the half-blown flower is heavy with the tears of the dawn, was infinitely more beautiful and elegant than the  upright stub of a *burdock*;

## DOG ROSE  *Rosa canina*

**Local:** Briar; Hip Rose; Wild Rose; Breer; Brier

A very common shrub, native to Scotland. It is widespread geographically, restricted only by higher ground and may be found on most types of soil on rough uncultivated land. It is present in woods, hedges, on river banks and thrives in field margins, especially where sheltered by dykes. The stems have sharp hooked prickles (thorns) and the sweetly-scented pink or white flowers produce pollen attractive to a diverse range of insects. Distinctive and attractive red hips are later formed at the top of the flower stalk. Although now known to be rich in vitamin C, there is no evidence to suggest that this fact was either known or utilised prior to the Second World War.

Garden or cultivated roses were first brought to Scotland in 1596 and known as Provence or Old Cabbage Rose. Thus present potentially in gardens during the Burns era, some of his non specific references 'my love is like a red, red rose' for example, could equally have referred to a cultivated variety. Although I prefer to assign all of his records to the wild. I have included here his references to brier. Locally this was at times also used to describe Bramble.

Burns listed the 'wild brier-rose' as one of his favourite flowers and with over sixty references he made that obvious. Arguably the most popular and finest love song ever written was:

**'My Luve is like a Red, Red Rose'**:
> O, my luve is like a red, red *rose*,
> That's newly sprung in June;

**'Awa, Whigs, Awa'** (song):
> And bonie bloom'd our *roses*;

**'Delia'** (poem):
> Fair the tints of op'ning *rose*;

**'On Capt. M. Henderson'** (elegy):
> Ye *roses* on your thorny tree,
> The first o' flowers.

**'Her Flowing Locks'** (fragment):
> Her lips are *roses* wet wi' dew!

**'The Banks of the Devon'** (song):
> And England, triumphant, display her proud *rose*;

**'The Blue-Eyed Lassie'** (song):
> Her lips like *roses* wet wi' dew,

**'The Country Lass'** (song):
> And *roses* blaw in ilka bield;

**'My Love's a Winsome Wee Thing'** (early version) (song):
> No chilly blast nor shower
> Shall blight this *rose* of mine.

**'My Peggy's Charms'** (song):
> The lily's hue, the *rose's* dye…

**'O Bonie Was Yon Rosy Brier'** (song):
> That crimson *rose* how sweet and fair;

**'O Kenmure's on And Awa, Willie'** (song):
> And here's the flower that I lo'e best -
> The *rose* that's like the snaw.

**'Philly and Willy'** (song):
> As on the brier the budding *rose*
> Still richer breathes and fairer blows…

**'O, Were My Love'** (song):
> O, gin my love were yon red *rose*…

**'On a Bank of Flowers'** (song):
> Her lips, still as she fragrant breath'd,
> It richer dyed the *rose*.

The following quotation is from **'Epitaph On the Poet's Daughter'**, hitherto thought to be by Burns; however, more recent analysts believe it to be by Shenstone:

25

Here lies a *rose*, a budding *rose*,
Blasted before its bloom;
She's from a world of woe relieved,
And blooms a *rose* in Heaven.

**'The Ronalds of the Bennals'** (poem):
While peaches and cherries, and *roses* and lilies,
They fade and they wither awa, man.

**'On the Death of John McLeod Esq'** (poem):
Sweetly deckt with pearly dew,
The morning *rose* may blow;

**'The Posie'** (song):
I'll pu' the budding *rose*, when Phoebus peeps in view…

**'The Vision'** (poem):
Yet, all beneath th' unrivall'd *rose*,
The lowly Daisy sweetly blows;

**'The Winter it is Past'** (song):
The *rose* upon the brier by the waters running clear,

**'To Daunton Me'** (song):
The blude-red *rose* at Yule may blaw…

**'To James Smith'** (epistle):
We eye the *rose* upon the brier,
Unmindful that the thorn is near,"
Among the leaves!

**'Young Jessie'** (song):
Fresh is the *rose* in the gay, dewy morning,
And sweet is the lily at evening close
But in the fair presence o lovely young Jessie,
Unseen is the lily, unheeded the *rose*.

**'The Lass O Ballochmyle'** (early version) (song):
The lilies hue, and *roses*' die Bespoke the
Lass o' Ballochmyle.

**'Wee Willie Gray'** (song):
The *rose* upon the brier will be him trouse an' doublet…

**'As I Went Out Ae May Morning'** (verses):
But among yon birks and hawthorns green,
where *roses* blaw and woodbines hing…

**'The Soldiers Return'** (song):
She gaz'd - she redden'd like a *rose*...

**'Where are The Joys'** (song):
No, no, the bees humming round the gay *roses*…

**'The Banks O Doon'** (song):
> Aft hae I rov'd by bonie Doon
> To see the *rose* and woodbine twine,
> And ilka bird sang o its luve,
> And fondly sae did I o mine.
>
> Wi lightsome heart I pu'd a *rose*,
> Fu sweet upon its thorny tree!
> And my fause luver staw my *rose*-
> But ah! he left the thorn wi me.

**'Sweet Are The Banks'** (song):
> Wi lightsome heart I pu'd a *rose*,
> Upon its thorny tree...

**'Ye Flowery Banks'** (song):
> Wi lightsome heart I pu'd a *rose*
> Frae aff its thorny tree...

an alternative second line gave:
> Upon a morn in June.

**'A Rose-Bud By My Early Walk'** (song):
> A *rose-bud*, by my early walk
> Adown a corn-inclos'ed bawk,
>
> So thou, sweet *rose-bud*, young and gay,
> Shalt beauteous blaze upon the day...

**'Adown Winding Nith'** (song):
> The *rose-bud*'s the blush o my charmer...

**'I Do Confess Thou Art Sae Fair'** (song):
> See yonder *rose-bud*, rich in dew,
> Amang its native briers sae coy...

**'O, Bonie Was Yon Rosy Briar'** (song):
> O, bonie was yon *rosy brier*
> That blooms sae far frae haunt o man...
>
> Yon *rose-buds* in the morning dew,
> How pure, amang the leaves sae green!...
>
> That crimson *rose* how sweet and fair!
> But love is far a sweeter flower
> Amid life's thorny hath a care...

**'Muirland Meg'** (song):
> Her *rose-bud* lips cry, kiss me now;

**'O, That's The Lassie O My Heart'** (song):
> In tears the *rose-buds* steeping!

**'Phillis the Fair'** (song):
>> Sweet to the opening day,
>> *Rosebuds* bent the dewy spray;…

**'To Miss Cruikshank'** (poem):
>> Beauteous *Rose-bud*, young and gay,
>> Blooming on thy early May,
>> Never may'st thou, lovely flower,
>> Chilly shrink in sleety shower!

**'To J Lapraik'** (epistle):
>> While *briers* an woodbines budding green…

**'O Tibbie, I Hae Seen The Day'** (song):
>> Ye'll fasten to him like a *brier*…

**'The Winter It Is Past'** (song):
>> The rose upon the *brier*, by the waters running clear

**'There Grows A Bonie Brier-Bush'** (song):
>> There grows a bonie *brier*-bush in our kail-yard,
>> And below the bonie *brier*-bush there's a lassie and a lad…

**'Young Jamie, Pride Of A' The Plain'** (song):
>> He strays amang the woods and *breers*;

**'On Captain M. Henderson'** (elegy):
>> Ye hazly shaws and *briery* dens!

**'Ye Flowery Banks'** (song):
>> And my fause luver staw my *rose*,
>> But left the thorn wi me.

**'Tam Lin'** (ballad):
>> She had na pu'd a double *rose*,
>> A rose but only tway,
>>> *(Repeated in same work)*

>> Why pu's thou the *rose*, Janet,
>>> *(Repeated in same work)*

**'To James Smith'** (epistle):
>> We wander there, we wander here,
>> We eye the *rose* upon the brier,
>> Unmindful that the thorn is near,
>> Among the leaves;

**'To The Woodlark'** (alternative line used)
>> Sing on sweet songster o the *brier*…

## My Luve is Like a Red, Red Rose

O, my luve is like a red, red rose,
    That's newly sprung in June.
O, my luve is like the melodie,
    That's sweetly play'd in tune.

As fair art thou, my bonie lass,
    So deep in luve am I,
And I will luve thee still, my dear,
    Till a' the seas gang dry.

Till a' the seas gang dry, my dear,
    And the rocks melt wi the sun!
And I will luve thee still, my dear,
    While the sands o life shall run.

And fare thee weel, my only luve!
    And fare thee weel, a while!
And I will come again, my luve,
    Tho it were ten thousand mile!

## FLAX *Linum usitatissimum*

**Local:** Lint

Cultivated flax has been used for making linen since time immemorial, its Latin name meaning 'flax that is very much used'. However, individual plants often escape and grow wild.

Wrapping for Egyptian mummies was produced some 5,000 years ago; indeed long before the Pharaohs of Egypt built the first pyramids, flax had been used in the Middle East. In later times it virtually clothed civilised people, until it was replaced by American cotton in the nineteenth century.

Linen is made by wetting, or soaking, the flax stems in water then beating and combing out the fibres.

The growing of flax played an important part in Burns' life while at Lochlea near Tarbolton in Ayrshire. From there he travelled to Irvine to learn flax dressing. After the flax was processed, it was spun and woven into cloth. The quality of their particular flax is indicated by a notice which appeared in the then *Glasgow Mercury* newspaper, with the title -

*Gainers of the Premium for Flax Raising Crop, 1781*
*Mr Robert Burns, Lochlie Farm, Tarbolton  Parish – £3.*

In an attempt to cash in on what was a profitable crop at that time, Burns went to live in Irvine to learn the flax trade and to heckle the flax himself ready for the spinners. He only stayed about six months during which time he became quite

29

depressed with his attempts to thus augment his income.

The end of his flax experiment came in the New Year when his shop 'burnt to ashes and left me, like a true poet, not worth a sixpence.'

Considering his interest in flax, it is rather surprising that he only mentioned the plant on eight occasions. In **'The Cotter's Saturday Night'**:

> The frugal wifie, garrulous, will tell,
> How 'twas a towmond auld, sin *lint* was i' the bell.

(meaning twelve months since flax was in flower).

In the ballad **'The Weary Pund O Tow',** he has the first line, 'I bought my wife a stane o *lint*', and writing to Alexander Findlater in 1794 he included the lines:

> I'll never forget while the *hollin* grows green,
> The bonnie sweet Lassie I kist yestreen.

('hollin refers to the good quality sheets made from flax; these lines were an alteration from Herd's *Ancient and Modern Scottish Songs*, 1776).

The verses entitled **'The Ronalds of the Bennals'** have the line, 'A ten-shillings hat, a *Holland* cravat'; and in **'The Rowin'T In Her Apron'** we have the repeated line, 'Her apron was o the *hollan* fine...'

The revised verses **'The Lass That Made The Bed To Me'** contain:

> She took her mither's *holland* sheets,
> An made them a' in sarks to me...

The old ballad **'When She Cam Ben, She Bobbed',** similarly refers to the material, 'Tho thou hast nae silk and *holland* sae sma'...

Burns' letter to William Niven, written on 29 July 1786, concludes: 'I have three acres of pretty good *flax* this season perhaps in the course of marketing it may come your way.'

## LILY *Lilium* spp

Burns refers to the lily no fewer than twenty-three times, in as many different works.

The white colour, as in the water-lily, has for centuries been regarded as a symbol of purity and not unexpectedly for such a notable romantic, Burns mentions or infers such a virtue in many of his quotations. These, of course, are not at all rela-ted in a strict botanical sense, but are at least flower-related, and on balance deserve to be included here.

He specifically mentions Water Lily, then the issue becomes rather confused when, without being precise, he refers to a land-based lily species too! In addition, some references are definitely of a lily, but non-specific to either an aquatic or terrestrial species.

Water Lily records are comparatively straightforward to determine, there being only one white and two yellow species in Scotland. The land-based lily family is quite large, although many – like Solomon's Seal *Polygonatum* species and the native Lily of the Valley *Convallaria majalis* for example – may be excluded largely on the grounds of geographical rarity; difficulty in identification; or, indeed, being so distinctive as would have certainly merited individual mention. Bluebell, and Ramson *Allium ursinum*, were two common and widespread members of the lily family, found in Scotland during this time, that could well have been in the 'poetic frame'.

In addition, it was the local practice, certainly in parts of Dumfriesshire, to call Daffodil *Narcissus pseudonarcissus* – those growing wild, outside gardens – either Lent Lily or singularly, lily.

In conclusion, other than those that are specifically acceptable as a species, one has simply to accept the poetic licence involved.

## Water Lily:

     Yellow - *Nuphar lutea*
     White - *Nymphaea alba*

Reasonably common on small lochs, slow flowing burns and ditches in southern Scotland. In all species the large flowers and nearly circular leaves float on the surface of the water. The plant is anchored by a stout underground stem as deep as 6 feet (1.8 m) below the surface. To poets, the bloom of the white water lily, the largest flower head of any native Scottish plant, has long been regarded as a symbol of purity of the heart. For the early apothecaries it produced oils and distillations of nenuphar, which they used to treat skin complaints, sunburn, baldness and feminine disorders.

The yellow water lily was called locally 'brandy bottle' – its flowers exude a distinct aroma of stale alcohol and its seed capsules have a remarkable resemblance to miniature bottles.

In the song **'The Posie'** he refers to it as signifying purity, which suggests he had 'alba' in mind.

> The *lily* it is pure, and the *lily* it is fair,
> And in her lovely bosom I'll place the *lily* there…

In the **'Ronalds of the Bennals'** he again refers to feminine beauty:

> While peaches and cherries, and roses and *lillies*,
> They fade and they wither awa, man

The renowned historical piece **'The Cotter's Saturday Night'** has the parents say in prayer:

> The parent-pair their secret homage pay,
> And proffer up to Heavan the warm request,
> That He who stills the raven's clam'rous nest,
> And decks the *lily* fair in flow'ry pride,
> Would, in the way His wisdom sees the best,
> For them and for their little ones provide;

Burns' famous tale **'The Brigs Of Ayr'** has the New Brig say:

> The Genius of the Stream in front appears,
> A venerable chief advanc'd in years;
> His hoary head with *water-lilies* crown'd,

and during the approach of spring, in his sad sympathetic **'Lament Of Mary Queen Of Scots'**:

> Now blooms the *lily* by the bank,
> The primrose down the brae…

('By the bank' is suggestive of being in water 'by the bank' rather than on terra firma.)

The song **'Adown Winding Nith'** also contains -

> How fair and how pure is the *lily*!
> But fairer and purer her breast.

and in the song **'The Banks of The Devon'** he has the lines -

> Let Bourbon exult his gay gilded *lilies*,
> And England triumphant display her proud rose!

(One might assume 'gay gilded' as a reference to Yellow Water Lilies. 'Bourbon' was a member of the European royal line that ruled in France for a period up to 1793.)

In the song **'Lady Mary Ann'** Burns wrote:

> And the longer it blossom'd the sweeter it grew,
> For the *lily* in the bud will be bonier yet.

and in the verses entitled **'The Lass That Made the Bed For Me'** the reference is, 'Her cheeks like *lilies* dipt in wine'; similarly in his **'Will Ye Go To The Indies, My Mary'** the oft quoted reference pertaining to 'white', 'And plight me your *lily*-white hand!'

In the summer of 1786, by which time Burns was resigned to emigrate to the West Indies, he wrote the verses **'On A Scotch Bard'** reflecting his mood at that time:

> Fareweel, my rhyme-composing billie!
> Your native soil was right ill-willie;
> But may ye flourish like a *lily*,
> Now bonilie!

The song **'To Daunton Me'** was from an old Jacobite ballad dating from 1715, about a lass forced to marry an old man:

> The blude-red rose at Yule may blaw,
> The simmer *lilies* bloom in snaw,

> The frost may freeze the deepest sea,
> But an auld man shall never daunton me.

(Daunton is to subdue or discourage.)

In a song about Jean Jaffray of Ruthwell, called **'The Blue Eyed Lassie'**, he refers thus, 'Her heaving bosom, *lily*-white;' and another song written in 1795 called **'My Lord A-Hunting He Is Gane'**, contains:

> Where wons auld Colin's bonie lass,
> A *lily* in a wilderness.

and **'On A Bank of Flowers'** produces:

> The springing *lilies*, sweetly prest,
> Wild-wanton kiss'd her rival breast:

A poem called **'On Sensibility'**, sent to his friend Mrs Dunlop, offering condolences, includes:

> Fairest flower, behold the *lily*
> Blooming in the sunny ray:

Burns wrote a song for Jessie Staig, the daughter of the Dumfries Provost, in 1775 which he called **'Young Jessie'** -

> Fresh is the rose in the gay, dewy morning,
> And sweet is the *lily* at evening close;
> But in the fair presence o lovely young Jessie,
> Unseen is the *lily*, unheeded the rose.

**'The Soldier's Return'** contains the couplet:

> She gaz'd, she redden'd like a rose,
> Syne, pale like onie *lily*...

and in the song **'Bonnie Jean'**:

> As Robie tauld a tale of love
> Ae e'ening on the *lily* lea?

The nursery jingle revised by Burns called **'Wee Willie Gray'** has in the second verse:

> Wee Willie Gray an his leather wallet,
> Twice a *lily*-flower will be him sark and gravat;

Old verses called **'Blue Bonnets'** (later altered to **'Wherefore Sighing Art Thou'**) and attributed to Burns:

> Hast thou found that beauty's *lillies*
> Were not made for aye to last

33

and the song **'My Peggy's Charms'**, 'The *lily's* hue, the rose's dye…' The song collected by Burns, probably during his Highland Tour, **'Geordie – An Old Ballad'**, contains, 'Till she wallow't like a *lily*…'

Finally, an early version of **'The Lass O Ballochmyle'** originally had the lines:

> The *lilies'* hue and rose's die
> Bespoke the Lass o' Ballochmyle.

His reference to lilies, in his letter to Charles Sharpe in 1791, was a biblical one referring to Solomon's Lilies: 'Toil not, neither do they spin.'

## Miscellaneous Botanical References

*VINE*

Burns' reference to Vines *Vitus vinifea* in **'Sketch'**, 'While nightly breezes sweep the *vines*,' was clearly meant to infer the grapevine of continental origin. Similarly, in **'Scotch Drink'**, ''Bout *vines*, an' wines, an' drunken Bacchus.'

*FIG*

His mention of Fig *Ficus caria* in **'The Jolly Beggars'**, 'A fig for those by law protected' was no more than the use of a well known figure of speech.

*HEMP*

The references to Hemp were not, in my view, of Hemp-agrimony *Eupatorium cannabinum*, but of Hemp as in *Cannabis satirva*, a strong smelling Asian moraceous plant, with very tough fibres grown to produce rough canvasses and rope. Whether or not they were used also to produce narcotic drugs remains a moot point, since these are normally produced from a variety known as Indian Hemp.

His references are suggestive of both. In his early **'From Esopus to Maria'** it was specific enough when he wrote, 'Beat *hemp* for others, riper for the string'; and when referring to the death of Mallie, his pet ewe, in **'The Death and Dying Words of Poor Mailie'**: 'Wi wicked string's o *hemp* or hair!'

The verses called **'The Bob of Dumblane'** has as its opening line, 'Lassie, lend me your braw *hemp*-heckle'; and in the **'Epistle To Dr. Blacklock'** a reference to male hemp, with 'Thou stalk o *carl-hemp* in man!'

Referring to seed in **'Halloween'**, Burns wrote:

> He gat *hemp*-seed, I mind it weel,
> An he made unco light o't;
> But monie a day was by himsel,
> He was sae sairly frighted.

('Was by himsel' clearly infers being out of one's mind.)

The same work goes on to describe the sowing of hemp seed, which could of course have been totally fictitious: 'That he could saw *hemp*-seed a peck'; 'And ev'ry now and then, he says, "*Hemp*-seed I saw thee".'

*HOP*

His references to Hop(s) *Humulus lupulus* are clearly in the context of using the female flowers to provide a bitter taste in the old ales and beers made from malt. In **'The Brigs of Ayr'**: 'Men wha grew wise priggin owre *hops* and raisins'; and when writing **'To John Syme of Ryedale'** (with a present of a dozen of porter):

> Or had the malt thy strength of mind,
> Or *hops* the flavour of thy wit…

**'Elegy On The Late Miss Burnet Of Monboddo'** produced almost certainly brief references to three species.

> Ye heathy wastes, immix'd with *reedy* fens;
> Ye mossy streams, with *sedge* and *rushes* stor'd.

*COMMON REED*

The Common Reed *Phragmites australis* was widespread throughout Scotland, in association with wet areas or fens. A tall robust plant, with stout, branchless stems and smooth grey-green leaves, it grew to some 60-120 inches (152-300 cms).

It was very well known to the country people of the eighteenth century. It made excellent thatch and was also collected and bundled as bedding for both the house and in the animal boxes. He refers to the plant again in **'And Maun I Still On Menie Doat'** when he says:

> The wanton coot the water skims,
> Amang the *reeds* the ducklings cry,

Other references to *reed* are from the Scots and refer to the vibrating reed, inserted in the chanter or musical pipes.

*MOSSES*

Burns mentions Mosses or *Mossy* on at least sixteen occasions, for example in **'Tam O Shanter'**:

> The *mosses*, waters, slaps, and styles,
> That lie between us and our hame…

and in **'The Twa Herds'**, 'By *mosses*, meadows, moors, and fells.'

In Scots these terms are used to describe a peat bog or marsh. There is no single reference that can be substantiated as specifically meaning a moss species, a bryophyte of the class *Musci*.

SEDGE

Sedge(s) *Carex sp.* are a grass-like plant differing in having solid, often three-sided stems. Many species growing on or near wet ground and have small flowers in spikes. Burns' reference is totally unspecific and does not warrant speculative discussion as to species.

Burns refers to 'rush' in his well known song **'Green Grow The Rashes O'** derived from an ancient ballad 'Cou thou me the *raschyes* grene', first published in 1549.

> Green grow the *rashes*, O;
> The sweetest hours that e'er I spend,
> Are spent among the lasses, O.

Similarly, in **'A Fragment'** of 1786 the line, 'Green grow the *rashes* O,' is repeated twice. His famous **'Address To A Haggis'** has the very descriptive:

> Poor devil! see him owre his trash,
> As feckless as a writher'd *rash*...

The song **'My Highland Lassie O'** mentions: 'Aboon the plain sae *rashy*, O,' in the chorus; and in the final verse, 'Farewell the plain sae *rashy*, O!'
    In **'Address To The Deil'**:

> Ye, like a rash-bush, stood in sight,
> Wi waving sugh...

('Bush' in this context is taken to refer to a clump.)

The famous poem, **'The Wounded Hare'**, sent to Mrs Dunlop, contains the verse:

> Seek, mangled wretch, some place of wonted rest,
> No more, of rest, but now of dying bed!
> The sheltering *rushes* whistling o'er thy head,
> The cold earth with thy bloody bosom prest.

The word 'rush' is derived from the Germanic meaning to 'bind' or 'plait' and naturally reflects the extent to which rushes have been used since time immemorial for various types of basket weaving. In Scotland, rushes, reeds and heather were all used to cover the earthen or stone floors to provide a crude form of insulation against the cold. Rushes were also used to make candle wicks and tapers; and at least one early herbalist maintained that, after being softened and mixed in wine, the resultant concoction could be recommended as a cough cure.

There are several rush species, but it is almost certain that the plant best known and referred to by Burns would be the Soft Rush *Juncus effusus*. Common and widespread throughout Scotland, it flourishes in wet places, especially on acid soils, in grassland, woods, and bogs. It grows to some 12-60 inches (30-152 cms). Typically in a clump or tuft, it produces cylindrical leaves that are stiff and upright.

GRASS

Grass *Gramineae* species is mentioned at least fifteen times by the Bard, and of these, five records refer to grasses that proverbially cover the 'grave', for example, in **'The Calf'**:

> And when ye're numer'd wi the dead,
> Below a *grassy* hillock…

Others are obviously meant to infer grass as a growing sward or species as in the song **'Young Peggy'**:

> The rosy dawn, the springing *grass*,
> With early gems adorning.

However, four of his references are sufficiently specific to classify as to species. In his song **'As I Cam O'er the Cairney Mount'** he writes -

> Now Phebus blinkit on the *bent*,
> And o'er the knowes the lambs were bleating:

There he clearly inferred Common Bent or Brown Top Grass *Agrostis tenuis*; and in the song **'Comin Through The Rye'**:

> She draigl't a' her petticoatie,
> Comin thro' the *rye*!

he was clearly referring to Common Rye *Secale cereale* which was widely grown at the time.

The bawdy song **'The Jolly Gauger'**, and similarly that of **'The Trogger'**, both refer to 'bent' as grass.

TOADSTOOL

In his **'Lament For the Absence Of William Creech, Publisher'**, Burns wrote

> Now gawkies, tawpies, gowks, and fools,
> Frae colleges and boarding schools
> May sprout like simmer *puddock*-stools
> In glen or shaw:

clearly referring to a Toadstool, which is a large group of basidiomycetous fungi with a capped, spore-producing body, that is often poisonous in Scotland.

SEAWEED

The **'Third Epistle To J. Lapraik'**, (composed in 1785 at harvest time) contains a reference to Seaweed *Fucas sp.*

> May Boreas never thresh your rigs,
> Nor kick your rickles aff their legs,
> Sendin the stuff o'er muirs an haggs
> Like driven *wrack*!

('Boreas' is the north wind; thresh is to strip the grain; and rigs are the 'corn rigs' set up to dry. 'Driven wrack' is storm-tossed seaweed. *Wrack* can be any of the seaweed species, *Fucus* or indeed any collection of marine vegetation cast ashore.)

Similarly, in **'The Brigs of Ayr'**: 'His manly leg with garter-*tangle* bound'; and in **'Despondancy - An Ode'**, 'The cavern, wild with *tangling* roots' ('tangle' was commonly used in the Scots to describe seaweed species).

Rush

Seek, mangled wretch some place of wonted rest,
No more, of rest but now of dying bed!
The sheltering *rushes* whistling o'er thy head
The cold earth with thy bloody bosom prest.
Extract from **The Wounded Hare**

# TREES

Hazel (Keith Brockie)

*That man shall flourish like the trees,*
*Which by the streamlets grow,*
*The fruitful top is spread on high,*
*And firm the roots below.*

## Introduction

In 1773, the notorious English conversationalist and would-be critic, Samuel Johnston, while travelling through Fife on his way to St Andrews, 'sneered' that, 'a tree in Scotland was as rare as a horse in Venice'.

It was certainly true that in Scotland – once thought to be 80% covered in woodland, of mainly native Scots pine, birch, oak and juniper – the forest area was greatly reduced by a continued felling policy. This was mainly because clearances for agriculture – and provision of timber for ship and other building – did not have a policy of conservation of existing stocks, either by replacement by replanting or of encouraging natural regeneration. All useable types of timber were ruthlessly exploited, as timber was also the main fuel source for cooking and heating in the home, especially where peat or coal were unavailable. In the main, the largest areas were cleared of trees principally in the cause of agricultural 'improvement'. Indeed, there are also records of deliberate wanton abuse – such as areas of forest being 'put to the torch to deprive wolves of shelter and hunting areas'. Even the scrub species were harvested in a haphazard manner, to provide hardwood for tools, wheels and the construction of primitive agricultural implements.

Johnston's outspoken first impressions were as usual inaccurate, although there were indeed large areas in the Borders almost completely denuded of significant stands of trees to accommodate the 'new economy' – sheep! There were still important remnants of the great Wood of Caledon in remote Highland glens. Meanwhile, following the work of the agricultural improvers, several large landowners had recognised the value of tree planting both for landscape enhancement and to provide timber. Indeed, not far from Boswell's estate at Auchinleck in Ayrshire, the biographer who in fact had made Dr Johnston famous, Burns' father William, had been employed by one Dr W Ferguson 'to plant out shrubberies and woods' at Doonholm near Alloway.

Elsewhere in Scotland, the Laird at Monymusk in Aberdeenshire had begun a programme to plant trees mainly 'spruce fir' and before he died no fewer than fifty million trees had been planted on his estate.

In 1727, the then Duke of Atholl had been given a present of larch plants from the Tyrol and from these propagated some 'twenty seven million for his own estate and countless millions others were sold on'.

When Burns visited the Bruar valley, some three miles from Blair Castle, he later wrote to the Duke via Josiah Walker (the tutor of the Marquis of Tulliebardine, the Duke's son). His classic verses **'The Humble Petition of Bruar Water'** were no more than a blatant plea by Burns to the Duke to plant more trees, both sides of the river –

Would, then, my noble master please
To grant my highest wishes,
He'll shade my banks wi tow'ring trees
And bonie spreading bushes.

Let lofty firs and ashes cool,
My lowly banks o'erspread,
And view, deep-bending in the pool,
Their shadow's wat'ry-bed:
Let fragrant birks, in woodbines drest,
My craggy cliffs adorn,
And, for the little songster's nest,
The close embow'ring thorn!

To his eternal credit, the Duke responded quickly and initiated a planting programme which, within a relatively short period, ensured that woodlands were established 'as requested'.

Elsewhere on their respective estates, Lord Moray had planted some twelve million oak, elm and beech between 1750 and 1760, and Lord Finlater, eleven million 'trees' from 1767. These somewhat dramatic examples, from one end of the spectrum at least, suffice as examples to demonstrate that the afore-mentioned era of wanton destruction had ended, with a few forward looking landowners appearing to recognise the need for tree conservation and a strategy of replanting (but not necessarily or usually of native species) to allow an eventual planned harvesting of a woodland resource.

So massive was the planting programme in some areas that the peasantry regarded the 'new planting of trees' as a threat. It was then thought that they would 'suck the heart out of the soil' and provide nesting areas for 'hordes of birds, that would eat their newly sown seeds'. For a time, organised gangs actually toured the countryside pulling out the newly planted seedlings to ensure that this did not occur. Gradually, with persuasion and practical example, attitudes changed, especially when it was demonstrated that trees could be beneficial in providing shelter to both crops and grazing animals.

In addition, trees assisted in drainage of surface water and, through transpiration, to keep the soil dry; they also provided valuable humus from leaf mould; useful thinnings; and some species augmented the restricted diet of the local population with nutritious edible fruits and berries.

Burns himself, largely influenced by his father, was an active tree planter and put in 'many trees at Ellisland'.

Considering the undoubted feudal nature of those times, he was considered 'brave' when he reputably firmly remonstrated with the then Duke of Queensberry (Buccleuch) on his destruction of the woodlands around Drumlanrig near Thornhill, Dumfriesshire, his ducal seat in Nithsdale:

The worm that gnaw'd my bonie trees,
That reptile wears a ducal crown.

By 1800, tree planting had become 'almost a cult' with both estate owners and farmers alike, as the first early plantations matured to produce a valuable source of income and demonstrated that agricultural crops and farm stock quality was significantly enhanced and improved.

In this chapter, I have included both trees and shrubs with some other associated plants.

The distinction between trees and shrubs is at best tenuous and retained more for convenience than for any strict botanical reasons.

It is usually considered that a tree is a mainly single stemmed plant from ground level and attains a height on maturity of over 20 feet (6 m), whereas a shrub may be multi-stemmed and can range in height from a mere few inches or less, to 20 feet (several cm to 6 m).

It is not in fact possible to categorise many species into either tree or shrub species. Obviously the way any plant grows is dependant on many ecological factors such as soil type, exposure, climatic conditions and interference by either browsing animals or 'management' by man. For example, the *Hawthorn* is often stunted by poor rocky soil, wind pruning or browsing. Left alone in sheltered sites with a rich soil substrate, it may attain a height of up to 29 feet (9 m).

I have therefore not made any distinction between a tree or a shrub and have included with the true trees, species like blackthorn and gorse. In addition, for convenience, plants associated with trees or shrubs, such as ivy and honeysuckle, are also included.

Specific records of the trees and shrubs mentioned by Burns are listed in Appendix 2, with their English, scientific, Scots and Scottish Gaelic names.

The following notes on the individual species includes any relevant local names. It is worthy of note that, in addition to the specific references to tree or shrub species, Burns used variants of the following allied terms:-

Boughs (9 times); bower (30); branch (5); bush (18); covert (5); forest (22); grove (26); glade (4); leafs (32); roots (10); sapling (1); shaw (17); trees (59); wood-fringed (2); woodland (7); woods (56) – a quite remarkable list of 303 related references bringing the grand total to 457 references.

### *Additional Notes*:

1. The reference to 'spruce' is not in the context of species, referring rather to 'neat and tidy'.

2. 'Furze' and 'thorn' were regularly used as figures of speech.

3. I have excluded the reference to Palm Tree species *Palmaceae*.

4. I have included in this section three tree species – beech, elm, and birch – all of which are included in the verses **'On Seeing His Favourite Walks Despoiled'**. Most authorities accept the verses as the work of Burns, although authorship was claimed by one Henry Mackenzie.

## POPLAR *Populus spp.*

There are several species of poplar in Britain although possibly only one, Aspen *P. tremula*, is native to Scotland and in his one reference to the species in **'The Tree of Liberty'**, Burns was referring to the sad political scene in Britain as opposed to his usual practice of being specifically Scottish:

> Let Britain boast her hardy oak,
> Her *poplar* and her pine, man,
> Auld Britain ance could crack her joke,
> And o'er her neighbours shine, man,
> But seek the forest round and round,
> And soon 'twill be agreed, man,
> That sic a tree can not be found,
> 'Twixt London and the Tweed, man.

This reference makes specific identification more difficult, although we can exclude the Lombardy Poplar *P. n. 'Italica'*, since this was only introduced to Britain from a single cutting in 1758 and could neither have been very well known, or widespread when Burns wrote his song in 1792. If this be accepted, the many hybrids later propagated to supply amenity trees can be eliminated too.

The White Poplar, *P. alba*, which was introduced to Britain would be present, with related trees like Grey Poplar *P. canescens*, but they were regarded as being rarer and planting was concentrated in sandy coastal areas.

My own view is that, it is more likely that the commonest, and thus probable, species would be the Black Poplar *P. nigra.* var. betulfolia.

This vigorous deciduous tree is remarkably resistant to air pollution and was widely planted, including lining town and city streets, and providing avenues to large town and country houses. It had very little value timber-wise and it was not until the Lombardy became available in large numbers that the poplar was used as a wind break for field crops. It remains rather surprising that Burns did not mention the Aspen *P. tremula* specifically as a tree species, it being the only poplar native to Scotland and being a more widespread and common tree during that era. One would have expected Burns to have referred to its main characteristic – 'the trembling leaf'– had he been familiar with the species as a tree. Nonetheless he did refer to it, at least obliquely, as a medical diagnostic feature in his letter to Peter Hill in 1790:

> ...And when many years and much port and great business have delivered them over to Vulture Gouts and *Aspen* Palsies...

## SILVER BIRCH *Betula pendula/B. pubescens*

**Local:** Birk; Silver tree (*pendula*); Downy (*pubescens*)

In mid-eighteenth century Scotland the 'birch' was, without doubt, the commonest tree. Both species are native to Scotland, and may hybridise; they grow well in open 'light' areas even on peat and *B. pubescens* regularly colonises open heather moorland. A graceful, widely distributed tree, it often forms thickets, with beautiful pendant catkins in April. As the name suggests, the bark becomes silvery white on maturity. *B. pubescens* is as common as *B. pendula* in west Aberfeldy, for example, while *B. pendula* is dominant in the Bruar.

Birch proved an extremely valuable tree in the mid-eighteenth century. It provided excellent firewood without requiring a long drying-out period. It was especially used by the military, particularly where peat and coal were not available, not only for fuel but with other species to produce charcoal – a main constituent of early gunpowder. It was also used in the construction of looms and furniture. The finer branches and twigs were made into brooms and the waterproof bark was used for roofing, tanning and as a wood dye. It proved quite unsuitable for building except for the most temporary of shelter as the timber rots quickly when cut, although it was used until recently by travelling people, being light, pliable and easily replaced. It proved to be ideal for building estuarine fish traps or stake nets; being buried in the tidal mud after seasonal use, the poles lasted for many years. The branches were trimmed to make flogging birches; and the sap used to produce a shampoo; also a very popular and potent country wine. Traditionally, oatmeal brose was eaten from a birch bowl. In keeping with ancient tradition, 'birk' continued to represent love, beauty and fertility, the birch wood being the place of love trysts. Burns often referred to the scent, which is particularly noticeable in early summer.

Perhaps the best known references are in the song **'The Birks of Aberfeldie'**, composed while standing under the falls of Aberfeldy in 1787:

> Now simmer blinks on flow'ry braes,
> And o'er the crystal streamlets plays,
> Come, let us spend the lightsome days
> In the *birks* of Aberfeldie!

He mentions the species again, in his **'The Humble Petition of Bruar Water'**:

> Let fragrant *birks*, in woodbines drest,
> My craggy cliffs adorn...

and in the same work:

> And *birks* extend their fragrant arms
> To screen the dear embrace.

The song **'Blythe Was She'** contains the line, 'On Yarrow banks the *birken* shaw;' and in the lovely sincere **'Sweet Afton'**:

> How pleasant thy banks and green vallies below,
> Where wild in the woodlands the primroses blow

> There oft, as mild Ev'ing weeps over the lea,
> The sweet-scented *birk* shades my Mary and me.

In his song **'Thou Lingering Star'** we find the lines:

> The fragrant *birch* and hawthorn hoar,
> 'Twin'd amorous round the raptur'd scene;

The verses of 1794 which he called **'Here is the Glen'** have as a first verse:

> Here is the glen, and here the bower
> All underneath the *birchen* shade...

A disputed work, formerly titled **'The Vowels'**, but now accepted as the Bard's with the title **'A Tale'**, provides an example of the birch twigs being used as a 'birch' (a flogging device):

> Twas where the *birch* and sounding thong are plyed,
> The noisy domicile of Pendant-pride;
> Where Ignorance her darkening vapour throws,
> And cruelty directs the thickening blows;

The verses **'On Seeing His Favourite Walks Despoiled'**, remonstrating with the Duke of Buccleuch on the destruction of woodlands near Drumlanrig in Dumfriesshire, contain:

> But now the cot is bare and cauld
> Its branchy shelter's lost and gane,
> And scarce a stinted *birk* is left
> To shiver in the blast its lane.

Verses collected for Johnston in 1792, entitled **'As I Went Out Ae May Morning'** include, 'But amang yon *birks* and hawthorns green,'; while the song **'Bonnie Peg-A-Ramsay'** has the verse:

> Cauld is the e'eving blast
> O Boreas o'er the pool
> An dawin, it is dreary,
> When *birks* are bare at Yule.

The epic ride of **'Tam O Shanter'** took him...

> ...past the *birks* and meikle stane,
> Whare drunken Charlie brak's neck-bane;

The 1794 song **'Behold, My Love, How Green The Groves'** – probably written for Chloris – has:

> The Shepherd stops his simple reed,
> Blythe in the *birken* shaw.

while the 'charming pastoral' of **'Bessy and Her Spinnin-Wheel'** contains:

> The scented *birk* and hawthorn white
> Across the pool their arms unite...

That well loved song **'The Lea-Rig'** contains the reference:

> Down by the burn, where scented *birks*
> Wi dew are hangin clear, my Jo,
> I'll meet thee on the lea-rig,
> My ain kind dearie, O!

and the song, **'Highland Mary'**, which Burns rewrote completely, produces 'How sweetly bloom'd the gay, green *birk*'.

In conclusion, Burns modelled the song **'The Bonie Lad That's Far Awa'** on a seventeenth century ballad 'The Unconstant Shepherd' or the 'Forsaken Lass's Lamentation'.

> O, weary Winter soon will pass,
> And Spring will cleed the *birken* shaw,
> And my sweet babie will be born,
> And he'll be hame that's far awa!

**Note**

The seven references to 'birkie' are in the Scots meaning of 'a person; a smart, insolent or conceited fellow'. As for example in:

> Ye see yon *birkie* ca'd 'a lord,'
> Wha struts, and stares, an a' that?
> Tho hundreds worship at his word,
> He's but a cuif for a' that.
> For a' that, an a' that,
> His ribband, star, an a' that,
> The man o independant mind,
> He looks an laughs at a' that...

and

> But faith! the *birkie* wants a manse...

## HAZEL *Corylus avellana*

A very common and widely distributed native shrub in woods, hedges and scrub, with distinctive yellow hanging catkins, highly prized for its edible nuts. The stems were traditionally cut for porridge spirtles, cask hoops, hurdles and especially walking sticks or shepherd's crooks. They were also harvested as roof spars when thatching, and for chairs or cradles. The forked twigs are still used as divining rods. The name 'hazel' is derived from the Anglo-Saxon 'haesl' meaning a rod or staff of authority. Strong and pliable, the smaller stems were used to support the traditional long nets used for rabbit and fish trapping.

Burns was obviously very familiar with the hazel and mentions it no fewer than fourteen times. In the song **'Now Westling Winds'** we find a direct quote: 'The *hazel* bush o'erhangs the thrush'; and in **'Halloween'**:

Below the spreading *hazel*
Unseen that night,

In the **'Sketch'** (eventually accepted as being by Burns): 'trots by *hazelly* shaws and braes'. **'The Brigs of Ayr'** produces the delicate lines:

Last, white-rob'd Peace, crown'd with a *hazel* wreath,
To rustic Agriculture did bequeath
The brocken, iron instruments of death:
At sight of whom our Sprites forgat their kindling wrath.

Verses composed while standing under the falls of Aberfeldy were called **'The Birks of Aberfeldie'** and contain:

The little birdies blythely sing,
While o'er their heads the *hazels* hing,

The first version of the famous song **'Ca' The Yowes To the Knowes'** has a rather splendid second verse:

'Will ye gang down the water-side,
And see the waves sae sweetly glide
Beneath the *hazels* spreading wide?
The moon it shines fu clearly.'

(In the second version of the song, the first line was altered to 'We'll gae down by Cluden side,' and 'Beneath' was changed to 'Thro'.)

His **'Elegy On Captain Matthew Henderson'** contains 'Ye *hazly* shaws and briery dens!'
In an old song which he called **'Waukrife Minnie'** – 'I pickt up this old song and tune from a country girl in Nithsdale. I never met with it elsewhere in Scotland' – it has the line:

And wi a meikle *hazel*-rung
She made her a weel-pay'd dochter.

The song **'Sleep'st Thou'**, composed in 1794, contains:

In twining *hazel* bowers,
His lay the linnet pours,

while an old version of the song **'The Contented Cottager'** (later renamed **'Bessy and Her Spinnin-Wheel'**) has, 'The lintwhites in the *hazel* braes'; an early version of **'A Vision'** (later renamed **'As I Stood By Yon Roofless Tower'**) apparently had the line, 'The burn adown its *hazelly* path.'
Finally in **'The Auld Farmer's New-Year Morning Salutation To His Auld Mare, Maggie'** Burns wrote:

Nae whip nor spur, but just a wattle
O saugh or *hazle*.

Burns' letter of May 1787, to Robert Ainslie, rather sarcastically described a woman's riding equipment to include '… a crooked meandring *hazle* stick'. Rather similarly, but in a complimentary mood, when writing to William Nicol also in 1787, he described one girl '…as sweet and modest's a new blawn plumrose in a *hazle* shaw.'

## BEECH *Fagus sylvatica*

A native to Europe and the southern half of England, it was an introduced species to Scotland.

At one time considered useful to farm stock, as it certainly affords good shade in summer and the mast provided food for pigs. It also produced very good firewood and was used in basket work and provided soles for clogs.

Burns mentions it once in the disputed work **'Verses'** (**'On Seeing His Favourite Walks Despoiled'**):

> There was a time, its nae lang syne,
> Ye might hae seen me in my pride,
> When a' my banks sae bravely saw
> Their woody pictures in my tide;
> When hanging *beech* and spreading elm;
> Shaded my stream sae clear and cool:

## OAK *Querus spp*

**Local:** Aik

There are two species in Scotland, *Q. robur* (English Oak) and *Q. petracu* (Sessile Oak). The latter is more commonly found in the West and in upland areas. It was regarded in folklore as a symbol of strength. Oaks were recorded as being first planted by the Druids. Acorns were also valued as a food source, especially for pigs. The tree is a native to Scotland and grows best on the heavy, fertile soils of the lowlands although there are significant remnants of native sessile oak woodlands on the thinner, more acid soils of Argyll and the upland valleys, together with natural English oak and hybrid forms. Nurtured in policies of country houses and later planted on a large scale, the oak was prized as the main timber in ship building. In Argyll the oak was felled for iron smelting in the sixteenth and seventeenth centuries, giving rise to such place names as Furnace in Argyll. In the eighteenth and nineteenth century, a profitable trade was established using oak bark for the tanning of hides.

The species is mentioned in **'Halloween'**, 'He taks a swirlie, auld moss-*oak*'; and in the song **'Blythe Was She'**, composed in 1784, includes, 'By Oughtertyre grow the *aik*…'

Burns composed **'Election Ballad'** soon after the general election of 1790 and wrote:

> The stubborn Tories dare to die:
> As soon the rooted *oaks* would fly
> Before th' approaching fellers!
> The Whigs come on like Ocean's Roar,
> When all his wintry billows pour
> Against the Buchan Bullers.

**'Ode On The Departed Regency Bill'** contains, 'In manner due, beneath this sacred *oak*...'; and alternative verses originally in **'A Lass Wi A Tocher'**:

> But see yon strappin *oaks* at the head o the shaw,
> Wi the whack! of an ax how stately they'll fa'.

His **'Lament For James, Earl of Glencairn'** contains

> He lean'd him to an ancient *aik*,
> Whose trunk was mould'ring down with years;

The song **'Lady Mary Ann'** has the descriptive reference:

> Young Charlie Cochran was the sprout of an *aik*,
> Bonie and bloomin and straucht was its make;

The controversial revolutionary song **'The Tree of Liberty'** is now generally accepted as being attributable to Burns. In it, he says, 'Let Britain boast her hardy *oak*...'; whilst his disputed **'Verses'** contain:

> And stately *oaks* their twisted arms
> Threw broad and dark across the pool;

The well known song **'I'll Ay Ca' In by Yon Town'** has the lines:

> She'll wander by the *aiken* tree,
> When trystin time draws near again;

while **'The Tither Morn'** (at least collected by Burns) quotes:

> When I forlorn,
> Aneath an *aik* sat moaning;

The old version of the song **'The Contented Cottager'**, (later renamed **'Bessy And Her Spinnin-Wheel'**) contains, 'On lofty *aiks* the cushats wail'; and an old verse, **'Adam Armour's Prayer'** has the rather odd reference that probably did refer to the tanin with oiled bark:

> And gie their hides a noble curry
> Wi' oil of *aik*!

Burns' correspondence to Margaret Chalmers of 1787 includes this description of himself on crutches:'It would do your heart good to see my bardship, not on my "poetic", but on my *oaken* stilts.'

The song **'Una's Lock'** from a collection of songs by Burns, includes:

> Beneath a lofty spreading *oak*
> She sat with can and milking pail;

## WYCH or SCOTS ELM  *Ulmus glabra*

**Local:** Coffin maker

It is safe to assume that the one species mentioned as simply 'elm' by the Bard was the Wych or Scots Elm, native or indigenous to Scotland where they can be found widely distributed in both woods and hedgerows. Hardy against frost, and firm against gales, they mature at 150 years old and some individuals have been recorded as living for 600 years. The common or English elm, introduced from Holland, was originally confined to southern Britain.

Wych produces a very fine, good tough timber, which was widely used during the mid-eighteenth century. Non-splitting, it was found suitable for some parts of ships, bridges, piles, tool handles, carts and carriages, with the finer cuts going to the furniture and undertaker trades. Sea chests and food boxes were known as wyches or hucches from the use of this wood and the leaves made excellent cattle fodder. The hollowed stems were used to make the first crude water pipes.

Known as the witch hassell in the middle ages, it was traditionally used to make long bows. Wych in fact means 'supple', and the tough bark was used to secure thatch. The other notable aspect is that the tree is liable, without warning, to shed major branches very suddenly and quietly, giving its local name – 'coffin maker' – a rather dubious dual meaning!

Considering the value placed on the tree at that time, it is surprising that Burns only mentioned it once, when he penned his '**Verses**' on the destruction of the woods near Drumlanrig, Dumfriesshire:

> When hanging beech and spreading *elm*;
> Shaded my stream sae clear and cool:

## WILD CHERRY  *Prunus avium*

**Local:** Gean

A native of temperate Europe including Scotland, Wild Cherry grows well on most substrates but prefers base rich soils. It survives well individually but may also occur in woodlands and in hedges.

All cultivated 'sweet' cherries – used to produce fruit for preserves, wines, liqueurs and baking – are descended from this tree. The timber was much in demand for furniture, walking sticks, and the construction of musical instruments, but especially to produce smokers' pipes.

Due to poor soil conditions, exposure and lower average temperatures, cherry orchards were never significantly conspicuous in Scotland. There is in addition no evidence to show that, during the mid-eighteenth century, fruit would have been imported from areas where cherries were cultivated. Similarly, with possibly the exception of some of the larger estates, there was no evidence of significant planting in Scotland of the related cherry trees – the so-called flowering cherries – many of Japanese origin. Bird Cherry *P. padus* is native to the north of Britain, but was not described as being particularly numerous or widespread in Scotland at that time.

In my view, we can thus be reasonably confident that Burns' references to 'cherries' can be ascribed, at least originally, to the Wild Cherry or Gean; although, since Burns was more preoccupied with the colour of the fruit in relation to the female lips, a cultivated variety cannot be excluded.

The verses penned on **'The Ronalds of the Bennals'** and referring to the daughters of the house include:

> The charms of the min', the langer they shine
> The mair admiration they draw, man;
> While peaches and *cherries*, and roses and lilies,
> They fade and they wither awa, man.

and in the song **'Young Peggy'** he relates thus: 'Her lips, more than the *cherries* bright'; similarly the song **'The Lass of Cessnock Banks'** contains:

> Her lips are like yon *cherries* ripe,
> That sunny walls from Boreas screen:
> They tempt the taste and charm the sight -
> An she has twa sparkling, rogueish een!

and are indicative of the fruit being grown in a sheltered walled garden.


## COMMON HAWTHORN *Crataegus monogyna*

**Local:** Haw; Grannies Tree; Thorn; May Flower

A native to Scotland, it was very common and widespread throughout southern areas, except on open moorland and on the higher hills; it was often planted at times to provide stockproof hedges and to provide shade for hill sheep. It was also used in primitive medicines, and the leaves were eaten in spring by children as a sweet (grannies biscuits) and also made into 'tea'. The hard timber was cut, polished and used for dagger handles and small tool shafts. There can be no doubt whatsoever of the Bard's familiarity with the hawthorn, for it is by far his most frequently quoted tree. In ancient tradition of 'feminine' character, it is a symbol of beauty and fertility.

In the song, **'The Lass of Cessnock Banks'** there is an early definite and accurate description:

> She's spotless like the flow'ring *thorn*,
> With flow'rs so white and leaves so green…

and in his verses **'The Vision'** he refers to:

> Yet green the juicy *hawthorn* grows,
> Adown the glade.

Verses simply called **'Green Sleeves'** were probably traditional but were included by Burns in letters and contain:

> Be it by the chrystal burn,
> Be it by the milkwhite *thorn*…

'Thorn' was also alluded to in the song **'Jenny Macraw'** published in *MMC* and attributed to Burns.

The **'Sketch'** provides us with:

> Or trots by hazelly shaws and braes
> Wi *hawthorns* gray,
> Where blackbirds join the shepherd's lays
> At close o day.

> (Gray may refer to the hawthorn being covered with lichens)

The old song **'The Contented Cottager'** (later renamed **'Bessy and her Spinnin-Wheel'**), has 'The scented birk and *hawthorn* white'.

Burns' very sad poem, **'Thou Lingering Star'** (formerly known as **'To Mary In Heaven'**) was composed around the third anniversary of the death of (Highland) Mary Campbell:

> Ayr, gurgling, kiss'd his pebbled shore,
> O'erhung with wild-woods, thickening green;
> The fragrant birch and *hawthorn* hoar,
> 'Twine'd amorous round the raptur'd scene;

> (Hoar may refer to hoarfrost, a grey lichen colour or to a tangled appearance)

His verses for Johnson, **'As I Went Out Ae May Morning'**, include: 'But amang yon birks and *hawthorns* green…'

A rather bawdry old song **'The Soldiers Return'** was revised by Burns and contains the line 'Sweet as yon *hawthorn*'s blossom.'

Burns rewrote one old song completely and called it **'Highland Mary'**. The poignant second verse begins :

> How sweetly bloom'd the gay, green birk,
> How rich the *hawthorn*'s blossom,
> As underneath their fragrant shade
> I clasp'd her to my bosom!

In his use of the adjective 'thorny' there is potential confusion; he also uses it to describe something difficult – as in a problem, for example, in the **'Epistle to Davie, A Brother Poet'**:

> Long since, this world's *thorny* ways
> Had number'd out my weary days...

Similarly, in his frequent use of the singular 'thorn(y)', it is not always evident whether or not he meant 'hawthorn' or the thorn-type stalk of the wild rose or brier, or even bramble. I have invoked my somewhat parochial prerogative to assign his references to one or another. Those that I believe relate more firmly to hawthorn are mentioned below.

In his famous songs **'Ye Flowery Banks'** and the extensive revision, **'The Banks O Doon'** he used thorny to describe firstly the wild rose, then in the latter, clearly refers to hawthorn with:

> Thou'll break my heart, thou warbling bird,
> That wantons thro the flowering *thorn*!

The song **'Lassie Wi The Lint-White Locks'** has the lovely verse:

> The primrose bank, the wimpling burn,
> The cuckoo on the milk-white *thorn*,
> The wanton lambs at early morn
> Shall welcome thee, my dearie, O.

In the well loved song **'Sweet Afton'**: 'Ye wild whistling blackbirds in yon *thorny* den'; and in the song **'Blythe Was She'**: 'She tripped by the banks o Earn, As light's a bird upon a *thorn*.'
**'Halloween'** has:

> But Rab slips out, an jinks about
> Behint the muckle *thorn*:

The song **'Now Spring Has Clad the Grove in Green'** has a delightful verse describing a hawthorn beside a stream:

> The trout within yon wimpling burn
> Glides swift, a silver dart,
> And, safe beneath the shady *thorn*,
> Defies the angler's art:

With the song **'Now Westlin Winds'**, it was clearly the hawthorn that was intended:

> The hazel bush o'erhangs the thrush,
> The spreading *thorn* the linnet...

and later in the same work:

> The rustling corn, the fruited *thorn*,
> and ilka happy creature.

Similarly, in the famous **'Tam O Shanter'**, with -

> And near the *thorn*, aboon the well,
> Whare Mungo's mither hang'd hersel.

From the other epic **'The Cotter's Saturday Night'** comes 'Beneath the mild-white *thorn* that scents the ev'ning gale'.

Burns' successful plea to the Duke of Atholl to plant trees, in **'The Humble Petition of Bruar Water'**, contains the lines:

> And, for the little songster's nest,
> The close embow'ring *thorn*!

The 'winter' reference in the song **'Up in the Morning Early'** is arguably best assigned to the hawthorn, 'The birds sit chittering in the *thorn*.'

The song **'The Soldier's Return'** infers a permanent tree rather than a brier, with the lines:

> At length I reach'd the bonie glen,
> Where early life I sported.
> I pass'd the mill and trysting *thorn*,
> Where Nancy aft I courted.

The renowned **'The Brigs of Ayr'** gives us -'Hailing the setting sun, sweet, in the green *thorn* bush'; and in his **'Address to Edinburgh'** the fourth verse begins with:

> Thy daughters bright thy walks adorn,
> Gay as the gilded summer sky,
> Sweet as the dewy, milk white *thorn*,
> Dear as the raptur'd thrill of joy!

On 20th August 1788, Burns wrote the song **'The Banks of Nith'**. In a letter to Mrs Dunlop the following day, he wrote: 'The following is the first compliment I have paid the Nith and was the work of an hour as I jogged up his banks yesterday morning…' The second verse commences with:

> How lovely, Nith, thy fruitful vales,
> Where bounding *hawthorns* gayly bloom…

Alternative lines in a later manuscript include:

> And richly wave thy fruitful vales,
> Surrounded by the *hawthorn*'s bloom:

The '**Elegy on Captain Matthew Henderson**' states:

> Ye roses on your *thorny* tree,
> The first of flowers!

Although he uses the term 'roses', in this case I feel he is actually describing the flower heads as such; the fact that he uses 'tree', then describes it as 'the first of flowers' tips the balance in favour of hawthorn rather than the wild rose.

In his collection of the song '**The Posie**' – where he described the old words as 'trash' – he reworded the line, 'The *hawthorn* I will pu, wi its locks o siller gray…'

The song '**Behold, My Love, How Green The Groves**', allegedly written for Chloris in 1794, has a lovely fourth verse:

> The Princely revel may survey
> Our rustic dance wi scorn;
> But are their hearts as light as ours,
> Beneath the milk-white *thorn*?

In '**Lament of Mary Queen of Scots**': 'The *hawthorn*'s budding in the glen'; and the song '**Logan Braes**' has the descriptive:

> Within you milk-white *hawthorn* bush,
> Amang her nestlings sits the thrush:

In an early version of the song '**O, Were my Love**' Burns used in the first two lines:

> O were my love yon vi'let sweet,
> That peeps frae 'neath the *hawthorn* spray;

> (In the revision of 1793 'vi'let sweet' was changed to 'lilac fair' and the second line altered to 'Wi purple blossoms to the spring'.)

In a letter to Mrs Dunlop in 1789, Burns included an epistle which included the line, 'Mild as the maiden blushing *hawthorn* blows'; and in a letter to William Nicol he penned: 'as blythe's a lintwhite on a flowrie *thorn*.'

While submitting the song '**O, Wat Ye Wha's In Yon Town?**' to George Thomson in 1795, he suggested the lines:

> O sweet to me yon spreading tree,
> Where Jeanie wanders aft her lane;
> The *hawthorn* flower that shades her bower,
> Oh, when shall I behold again! –

An additional stanza, later omitted from the revised song, has:

> O sweet to me yon spreading tree,
> Where Jeanie wanders aft her lane;
> The *hawthorn* flower that shades her bower,
> Oh, when shall I behold again!

## HOLLY *Ilex aquifolium*

Long associated with religious and superstitious beliefs, this tree was often planted near homesteads 'to ward off lightning and witches'. Native to Scotland it was common, especially in the milder west of the country, where it was also used to provide stockproof hedges. The young leaves made a tea-like beverage and the boiled bark was used originally to produce bird-lime, a tacky substance traditionally used to catch song birds in Scotland. The stems of hard white wood were used for decorative work with furniture, smaller household objects and for tool handles.

Burns was obviously familiar with the tree, and quoted it in **'The Vision'**, 'Green, slender, leaf clad *holly*-boughs,'; and later in the same work:

> 'And wear thou *this*' - She solemn said,
> And bound the *holly* round my head:
> The polish'd leaves and berries red
> Did rustling play;

Alternative verses included:

> Not rustic Muses such as mine,
> With *holly* crown'd.

Burns also included the species in the instructions for his heraldic device:

> On a field, azure a *holly* bush, seeded proper…

A full quotation of the heraldry is given on page 145.

## ASH *Fraxinus excelsior*

Native to Scotland, it readily forms both scrub or forest and is equally to be found in hedges on riversides and at times on rocky outcrops, crags and in wooded gorges with base rich soils.

The ash was the subject of a great deal of legend and superstition and the bark and fibre was used in primitive medicines. The ash provided excellent firewood, made good charcoal and the hard timber was light, strong and shock resistant, making it excellent for cart shafts, wheel spokes and tool handles.

In the song **'The Lass of Cessnock Banks'** Burns opens the third verse with the descriptive 'She's stately like yon youthful *ash*'; and in **'The Humble Petition of Bruar Water'**:

> Let lofty firs and *ashes* cool,
> My lowly banks o'erspread…

## BAY *Laurus nobilis*

Also called Sweet Bay or Poet's Laurel, *L. nobilis* was known to the Ancient Greeks as Daphne, who in mythology turned into a Bay to escape from Apollo, the Greek god of music, poetry and healing. Man has since held the Sweet Bay in special regard. Romans called it *laurus* from which 'laurel' derives. They used it to award their conquering warriors and poets – warriors being crowned with leaves; poets being presented with branches of fruit. The modern position of Poet Laureate originates from this ancient custom.

Writing to one A Cunningham in 1794, with details of his own intended heraldic device, Burns inscribed his own design and text, which included 'A woodlark perching on a sprig of *bay-tree.*'

This inclusion of bay has no obvious natural history explanation; it is a Mediterranean laurel, a lauraceous evergreen tree with small, blackish berries, the glossy, aromatic leaves of which were used to flavour cooking.

In verses to the tune of 'Maggy Lauder' which only has the title **'Song'**, he includes:

> Did warlike laurels crown my brow,
> Or humbler *bays* entwining -
> I'd lay them a' at Jeanies feet,
> Could I but hope to move her...

In Burns' letter to Mrs Dunlop in 1790, he again refers to 'the *laurel* will prove a very defenceless shade'. This is a figure of speech and not meant to refer to the tree.

## HONEYSUCKLE *Lonicera periclymenum*

**Local:** Woodbine

Native to Scotland, honeysuckle is a deciduous woody climber which grows up to 6 metres high, and is widely distributed on a variety of soil types and present in both hedges and woods. A striking feature is the creamy flowers, often becoming orange or buff and reddish, with a distinctive, strong but very pleasant fragrance, often wafted for some distance in gentle breezes. It climbs by twining round a variety of 'host' trees.

In the song **'Adown Winding Nith'**, about one Phillis McMurdo, Burns states:

> Her breath is the breath of the *woodbine*,
> Its dew-drop a diamond her eye.

He rewrote the words of **'By Allan Water'** for George Thomson in 1793, renamed it **'By Allan Stream'** and included:

> 'O, happy be the *woodbine* bower,
> Nae nightly bogle make it eerie!

and in his **'Elegy On Captain Matthew Henderson'**:

> …Ye *woodbines*, hanging bonilie,
> In scented bowers…

aptly, simply and succinctly described the honeysuckle.

In the second version of his **'Elegy On The Late Miss Burnet of Monboddo'** Burns penned a sensitive final verse:

> The parent's heart that nestled fond in thee,
> That heart how sunk, a prey to grief and care!
> So deckt the *woodbine* sweet yon aged tree,
> So, rudely ravish'd, left it bleak and bare.

The pastourelle dialogue **'As I Went Out Ae May Morning'** includes 'Where roses blaw and *woodbines* hing'. His outstanding verse epistle **'Epistle to J Lapraik'** opens with the line 'While briers and *woodbines* budding green'; and the **'Epistle to Robert Graham, Esq. of Fintry'** contains references in both versions. The final one contains:

> She cast about a standard tree to find;
> In pity for his helpless *woodbine* state…

In the song **'Lassie Wi The Lint-White Locks'** a rather charming verse has:

> And when the welcome simmer shower
> Has cheer'd ilk dropping little flower,
> We'll to the breathing *woodbine*-bower
> At sultry noon, my dearie, O.

The renowned song **'Sweet Are The Banks'** has a distinctive passage:

> Aft hae I rov'd by bonie Doon,
> To see the *woodbine* twine,
> And ilka bird sang o its luve,
> And sae did I o mine.

and the song **'Philly and Willie'** has the verse:

> The *woodbine* in the dewy weet,
> When ev'ning shades in silence meet
> Is nocht sae fragrant or sae sweet
> As is a kiss o Willy.

In the extensive revision of the song **'Ye Flowery Banks'**, which contains the line 'To see the *woodbine* twine', the revision was renamed and became the well-loved **'The Banks O Doon'**, in which the alteration became:

> Aft hae I rov'd by bonie Doon
> To see the rose and *woodbine* twine…

**'The Humble Petition of Bruar Water'** contains the plea:

> Let fragrant birks, in *woodbine* drest,
> My craggy cliffs adorn…

and in the song **'The Posie'**: 'The *woodbine* I will pu, when the e'ening star is near'.


# IVY  *Hedera helix*

Ivy is a woody stemmed evergreen climber. Native to Scotland, it does not seem to require any special soil conditions and grows in woods, hedges, on trees, rocks and on some buildings.

It featured in Greek and Roman mythology, where soldiers adorned their armour with its foliage and poets were awarded crowns of ivy as a token of high esteem. In the so-called Romantic Period, ivy was associated with owl-haunted ruins and thus became a symbol for solitude and melancholy.

It is one of the preferred food items of Roe Deer and very often the uniform cropping of ivy to a height of four feet is the first good indication of that animal frequenting a given area.

When writing fragments while at Friars Carse Hermitage, Dumfries, Burns included 'This *ivied* cot was dear' and 'This *ivied* cot rever.'
In **'The Vision'**, an early version had the line 'Where th' howlet mourns in her *ivy* bower'; and his **'Elegy on Captain Matthew Henderson'** has the quotation 'Ye houlets, frae your *ivy* bower.'


# GORSE  *Ulex europaeus*

**Local:** Furze; Whin

A dense evergreen shrub, native to Scotland, gorse grows commonly but prefers light, acid substrates, from coastal sites to quite high stations in sheltered glens. It produces beautiful, fragrant, canary-yellow flowers.

There is no apparent value in the stems, although they burn well. Formerly, the foliage was cut, dried and crushed as fodder for cattle and horses but especially goats.

Stands of gorse were extremely valuable as a wildlife habitat, especially for insects and small song birds and were often planted round rabbit warrens to deter predation by birds, foxes and dogs.

In **'Halloween'**, Burns describes 'Leesie' getting a fright and:

> ...She thro the *whins*, an by the cairn,
> An owre the hill gaed scrievin;

whilst in the famous **'Tam O Shanter'**:

> Tam skelpit on thro dub and mire,
> Despising wind, and rain, and fire;

> ...And thro the *whins*, and by the cairn,
> Whare hunters fand the murder'd bairn;

## BRAMBLE *Rubus fruticosus*

**Local:** Blackberry; Thorn; Brier; Sweet brier

Bramble is common and widespread throughout Scotland and can be found on a variety of soils in woodland, hedges, field margins and within scrub. There are several hundred species and they hybridise; it is thus a very complex family of plants. Bramble has stems which can either climb by use of prickles over hedges or bushes or may trail along the ground sending out shoots where the tips come in contact with the earth. Leaves often persist into winter, the fruit changes colour from green, through to red and black when ripe.

Country people have long harvested the blackberry. It makes excellent wine and jelly and was used to produce a comforting drink for sufferers of the common cold. In some areas it was crushed and used to produce a dye.

Burns mentioned it specifically only once, although it must have been a very common and well known plant to him. He may well have been referring to it at times when he used the local names of thorn and briar.

When writing to Robert Ainslie in 1789, he included the observation on men as: '...While two of those that remain either neglect their parts, as flowers blooming in a desert or mispend their strength, like a bull goring a *bramble*-bush.'

## WILLOW *Salix spp*

**Local:** Saugh; Sauchie; Sallow

Some species are native to Scotland and widespread in distribution. Willow and their related trees, the sallows, are now recognised as a very complex group. There are, for example, over 300 willow species and many hybrids worldwide. The name Saugh, from the Gaelic *Seileach*, was more commonly used in Scotland referring more specifically to the Great Sallow or Goat Willow *Salix capraea*. It is now, however, quite impossible to be more precise.

The branches were used to make sweeping brushes (besoms), and being pliable were often used where hoops were required. They were also cut as whips for driving cattle and as a crop for a horse. Some old water diviners preferred the willow wand.

In **'The Auld Farmer's New-Year Morning Salutation To His Auld Mare, Maggie'**:

> Nae whip nor spur, but just a wattle
> O *saugh* or hazle.

Burns' **'Epistle To Dr Blacklock'** contains the line:

> But I'll sned besoms, thraw *saugh* woodies,
> Before they want.

and his **'Elegy on Captain Matthew Henderson'** has:

> Thou, Autumn, wi thy yellow hair,
> In grief thy *sallow* mantle tear!

The poem **'Prayer under the Pressure of Violent Anguish'** was annotated with the non-specific: 'I hung my harp on the *Willow* tree, except in some lucid intervals, for which I composed the following...'; and in the revised nursery rhyme **'Wee Willie Gray'**: 'Peel a *willow-wand* to be him boots and jacket!'


## LILAC *Syringa vulgaris*

An introduced ornamental shrub which has occasionally become naturalised. Some specimens grow into small trees and produce large sprays of either white or purple flowers, well known for their fragrance. Clearly, it was at least known to Burns when he revised the verses of the song **'O, Were My Love'**. He opened the first verse with:

> O, were my love you *lilac* fair
> Wi purple blossoms to the spring,
> And I a bird to shelter there,
> When wearied on my little wing.


## BROOM *Cytisus scoparius*

Native to Scotland, broom is a tall deciduous shrub with spectacular yellow flowers. Widespread and common on drier soils, it is often wind-pruned or prostrate on coastal sites. It is attractive to insects, preferred by nesting songbirds and the flowers can be used to make wine. The stalks were cut and bound, fitted with a shaft, traditionally of hazel, and the resultant 'tool' used as a sweeping brush – hence, broom! – which was also used to assist in the game of curling, being played then, of course, on natural ice. As a low grade fodder it was often chopped and used to supplement the winter diet of wild rabbits.

In the song **'Their Groves of Sweet Myrtle'** Burns leaves us in no doubt, with the lines:

> Far dearer to me yon lone glen o green breckan,
> Wi the burn stealing under the lang, yellow *broom*;

An early version of the well known song **'Braw Lads O Galla Water'** (later revised), contains the lines:

> Down amang the *broom*, the *broom*,
> Down amang the *broom*, my deary,

The ancient ballad of **'Tam Lin'** produces:

> Out then spak the queen o Fairies,
> Out of a bush of *broom*;
> Them that has gotten young Tom-lin,
> Has gottan a stately groom.

**'The Banks Of Nith'** has alternative lines:

> Fair spread, O Nith, thy flowery dales,
> Where rove the flocks amang the *broom*;

while the song **'The Banks Of Nith'** contains:

> How lovely, Nith, thy fruitful vales,
> Where bounding hawthorns gayly bloom,
> And sweetly spread thy sloping dales,
> Where lambkins wanton through the *broom*!

In the song **'O, Wat Ye Wha's In Yon Town?'**, written by Burns while trapped at Ecclefechan by a snowstorm:

> The sun blinks blythe in yon town,
> Among the *broomy* braes sae green;
> But my delight in yon town,
> And dearest pleasure is, my Jean.

and the song **'Their Groves O Sweet Myrtle'** has the lines:

> Far dearer to me yon lone glen o green breckan,
> Wi the burn stealing under the lang, yellow *broom*;
> Far dearer to me are yon humble *broom* bowers,
> Where the blue-bell and gowan lurk lowly, unseen;

The song **'The Jolly Gauger'** is now attributed to Burns, and the rather bawdy version contains:

Amang the *broom* he laid her, amang the *broom* sae green,
An he's fa'n to the begger, as she had been a queen.

In a letter to Mrs Dunlop of 1790, he clearly was in a joyful mood when he described '…out skipt I among the *broomy* banks of Nith to muse over my joy.'


## BLACKTHORN *Prunus spinosa*

**Local:** Sloe; Slae

Native to Scotland and widely distributed, blackthorn grows almost anywhere on the lower ground except in permanently wet areas. Although it can tolerate damp conditions, it does not like very acidic sites. Often found in woods or as part of a hedge, but on its own it does not make a particularly good stock barrier.

The leaves were at times added to tea, and the ripe berries made into preserves, later being used to flavour gin or fermented into a potent wine known as 'winter pick'.

The timber is exceedingly hard and dense, and longer stems were used for walking sticks, but the main use was for hand clubs, carried by poachers and bailiffs alike.

Lines entitled **'On Chloris:- Requesting me to give her a sprig of blossomed thorn'** (Chloris was one Jean Lorimer) contain:

From the white-blossom'd *sloe* my dear Chloris requested
A sprig, her fair breast to adorn:
No, by Heaven! I exclaim'd, 'let me perish for ever
Ere I plant in that bosom a thorn!

In his **'Lament Of Mary Queen of Scots'**, Burns includes the line 'And milk-white is the *slae*.'

In **'The Holy Fair'**:

Their visage wither'd, lang and thin,
An sour as onie *slaes*:

The song **'There's A Youth In This City'** (the music for which was written by the famous fiddler, Niel Gow, as a lament for his brother), was given new words by Burns which include, 'His hose they are blae, and his shoon like the *slae*…'


## ELDER *Sambucus nigra*

**Local:** Bourtree; Boortree; Boortries; Bower tree; Bore tree

Native to Scotland and capable of growing well in almost any situation, it is very variable in size, often no larger than a good 'bush', whilst in other circumstances develops into a substantial tree of at least 6 metres high. Seldom used as fuel, the timber was very hard, heavy and close grained and was thus more suitable for wooden tools and vessels such as bowls, spoons, tool handles and, in southern Scotland, soles for clogs. It also features significantly in eighteenth century religious beliefs and superstitions.

Referred to as the 'Bower tree' from the structure which develops as the plant matures; and 'Bore tree' from boring out the broad soft pith to make early water pipes, and pea shooters as a boys' toy.

Traditionally it is thought to be the tree species from which Judas hanged himself and from which Christ's cross was made, although some authorities believe that the timber actually used was the Cedar of Lebanon *Cedrus libani*, known to the Romans as 'cedrus'. The carpenters of that time made crucifixion crosses only under duress, and they are known to have used cedar for other tasks – it was readily available, light, and strong. Greek legend insists that the Judas Tree is *Cercis siliquastrum*. It was certainly widely used in the building of King Solomon's Temple, and King Hiram of Tyre traded it for saffron with the people of northern Iraq.

In the past, highly prized for healing powers (and still used today) there is no doubt that the flowers and fruit are rich in vitamin C. Both were also used to make wine, and the crushed leaves were used to poultice sores and wounds.

Burns mentions the species in his **'Address To the Deil'**:

> Or, rustlin, thro the *boortries* comin,
> Wi heavy groan.

## CRAB APPLE  *Malus sylvestris*

Native to Scotland and parent to many cultivated orchard apples, it was found in both hedgerows and small woods. The fruit although small and sour, was collected for preserves, sauces and to mix with other fruits in early wine making.

The wood was prized for carving and engraving, being used to form dagger handles and gun stocks.

In his **'Heron Election: Ballad Forth'** the Bard uses the line 'The crest, a sour *crab-apple* rotten at the core'.

Other references to 'apple' are at least worthy of mention. They infer, since fruit was not imported, the existence of other types of apple trees able to produce a sweeter fruit. It would be convenient to call them *M. domesticus* since there were at least twenty-five possible species and, later, innumerable hybrids.

The verses on **'On Glenriddell's Fox Breaking His Chain'** contain, 'As sleek's a mouse, as round's an *apple*'; and in his **'Halloween'**:

> I'll eat the *apple* at the glass,
> I gat frae uncle Johnie…

and in the same work

...She gies the herd a pickle nits,
An' twa red cheekit *apples*...

The old song, **'My Tochars The Jewel'**, has 'It's a' for the *apple* he'll nourish the tree.'
Writing to William Nicol on 28 May 1790 he added, 'I expect little Neddy is a good boy, and that I shall have him here to gather *apples* and nuts against harvest...'; and writing to his wife Jean Armour from Ellisland, Dumfries on 14 October 1788, before she joined him there: 'The *apples* are all sold and gone... I am extremely happy at the idea of your coming to Nithsdale.' The latter records rather infer that he had a walled garden, as the area is not renowned for its capacity to produce fruit unaided.

# ROWAN  *Sorbus aucuparia*

**Local:** Mountain Ash

A native to Scotland, there is in fact no relationship at all with the ash family. Rowan is a very hardy tree, found naturally on mainly acid or base rich substrates, often high on mountainsides, in rocky areas, or clinging to narrow, ungrazed ledges.

The timber is of little use and does not even burn well, although the berries make an excellent tangy jelly, especially when mixed with crab apple. The shoots were used to make birdlime.

Considered a sacred tree by the Celts even up to 1950, it was difficult to find a farmhouse, gamekeeper's or shepherd's cottage which did not have a rowan planted nearby, in the belief that it warded off all witches, fairies and other evil spirits.

In the parody **'Grim Grizzel'** he writes -

His bonnet and his *rowantree* club
Frae either hand did fa';

# SCOTS PINE  *Pinus sylvestris*

**Local:** Pine; Scots Fir

Native to Scotland and at one time wide-spread over much of the country north of the Highland Boundary fault. A hardy tree, not susceptible to wind blow, it was used extensively for building, fence timber and coffins. A medicinal oil was extracted from the needles and the tree also yielded pitch tar, resin, and turpentine.

Several other pine species have been introduced: prior to mid-eighteenth century these were rare and mainly planted in England. The majority of non-native pines were introduced to Scotland in the late nineteenth and twentieth centuries, thus we can be reasonably sure that Burns was referring to the native 'Scots' in the following references.

In **'The Tree of Liberty'**:

> Let Britain boast her hardy oak,
> Her poplar and her *pine*, man...

The very popular song **'The Lass O Ballochmyle'** has the verse:

> Give me the cot below the *pine*,
> To tend the flocks or till the soil;
> And ev'ry day have joys divine
> With the bonie lass o Ballochmyle.

Burns mentions 'and the apple on the *pine*' in his verses **'To Mary'** but he was clearly describing the 'Indies' and thus not worthy of inclusion here as a tree record in Scotland; indeed he may have been referring to pineapples.

## COMMON YEW  *Taxus baccata*

A native to Scotland, the yew is an evergreen growing to a height of 70 feet (21 m). Some specimens have huge girths up to 35 feet (10 m) round, usually hollow. Some of these very old trees are believed to be over 1,000 years old, but when with age they hollow out, it becomes impossible to count the annual growth rings and to be absolutely accurate.

Generally regarded as poisonous – a great deal of confusion exists, however with some authorities insisting it is highly toxic, whereas elsewhere it has been known to have been fed to farm stock as winter feed.

The timber is fine-grained, heavy, hard, but pliable. The oldest known weapons discovered by archaeologists and attributable to Palaeolithic times (10,000 years ago) were made of yew. Its elastic nature made it a traditional wood for long-bow making and that practice continued up till the seventeenth century, although English archers preferred imported or Irish yew. Other uses were in furniture and hand tool manufacture.

Many of the ancient trees are to be found in churchyards. If they are indeed over 1,000 years old, they obviously pre-dated Christianity in parts of Scotland and originally may well have marked sites of pagan worship – later to have churches built on the site – and thought by some to represent the forces of good over evil. Yew has remained a symbol of everlasting life and sprigs are still buried with the dead; a practice which should not be confused with the Masonic tradition of placing a sprig of Acacia *mimosaceous sp.* at the head of the grave.

Burns referred to Yew when writing to Peter Hill on 1 October 1788. He was giving his views on an **'An Address to Loch Lomond'** by James Cririe, 1788.

...The following perspective of a mountains blue – the imprisoned billows beating in vain – the wooded isles – the digression of the *yew-tree* – Benlomond's lofty cloud - enveloped head, and etc are beautiful...

### The Humble Petition of Bruar Water

My lord, I know, your noble ear
   Woe ne'er assails in vain;
Embolden'd thus, I beg you'll hear
   Your humble slave complain,
How saucy Phoebus' scorching beams,
   In flaming summer-pride,
Dry-withering, waste my foamy streams,
   And drink my crystal tide.

The lightly-jumping, glowrin trouts,
   That thro my waters play,
If, in their random, wanton spouts,
   They near the margin stray;
If, hapless chance! they linger lang,
   I'm scorching up so shallow,
They're left the whitening stanes amang
   In gasping death to wallow.

Last day I grat wi spite and teen,
   As poet Burns came by,
That, to a Bard, I should be seen
   Wi half my channel dry;
A panegyric rhyme, I ween,
   Ev'n as I was, he shor'd me;
But had I in my glory been,
   He, kneeling, wad ador'd me.

Hear, foaming down the skelvy rocks,
   In twisting strength I rin;
There high my boiling torrent smokes,
   Wild-roaring o'er a linn:
Enjoying large each spring and well,
   As Nature gave them me,
I am, altho I say't mysel,
   Worth gaun a mile to see.

Would, then, my noble master please
   To grant my highest wishes,
He'll shade my banks wi tow'ring trees
   And bonie spreading bushes.
Delighted doubly then, my lord,
   You'll wander on my banks,
And listen monie a grateful bird
   Return you tuneful thanks.

Let lorty firs and ashes cool,
  My lowly banks o'erspread,
And view, deep-bending in the pool,
  Their shadows' wat'ry-bed:
Let fragrant birks, in woodbines drest,
  My craggy clifrs adorn,
And, ror the little songster's nest,
  The close embow'ring thorn!

So may, old Scotia's darling hope,
  Your little angel band
Spring, like their fathers, up to prop
  Their honour'd native land!
So may, thro Albion's farthest ken,
  To social-flowing glasses,
The grace be - 'Athole's honest men
  And Athole's bonie lasses!'

The sober laverock, warbling wild,
  Shall to the skies aspire;
The gowdspink, Music's gayest child,
  Shall sweetly join the choir;
The blackbird strong, the lintwhite clear,
  The mavis mild and mellow,
The robin, pensive Autumn cheer
  In all her locks Or yellow.

This, too, a covert shall ensure,
  To shield them from the storm;
And coward maukin sleep secure,
  Low in her grassy form:
Here shall the shepherd make his seat
  To weave his crown Or flow'rs;
Or find a shelt'ring, safe retreat,
  From prone-descending show'rs.

And here, by sweet, endearing stealth,
  Shall meet the loving pair,
Despising worlds with all their wealth,
  As empty idle care:
The flow'rs shall vie, in all their charms,
  The hour of heav'n to grace;
And birks extend their fragrent arms
  To screen the dear embrace.

Here haply, too, at vernal dawn,
  Some musing Bard may stray,
And eye the smoking, dewy lawn
  And misty mountain grey;
Or, by the reaper's nightly beam,
  Mild-chequering thro the trees,
Rave to my darkly dashing stream,
  Hoarse-swelling on the breeze.

*Additional Notes*

1.  Other records which include the term/word *pine*, refer to the Scots – 'pine' has a dual meaning as in 'pain', 'uncomfortable' or 'uneasy'; and 'to pine'; 'waste away'.

    His mention of 'Fir' in **'The Humble Petition Of Bruar Water'**:

    > Let lofty *firs* and ashes cool,
    > My lowly banks o'erspread...

    would in my view refer to Scots Pine rather than any of the now familiar fir family. The 'firs' are native to mainland Europe and western north America, from British Columbia south to Mexico. As far as one can ascertain, seeds were not sent to Britain until 1824.

    In many old writings, Scots Pine was often called Scotch Fir. Another misnomer is that Norway Spruce was often called Norwegian Fir. It is thus more than likely that all eighteenth century records of 'Firs' were in fact *P. sylvestris* – Scots Pine.

2.  Sycamore *Acer pseudoplatanus* was known to have been widely planted, especially in Ayrshire, and was often called 'Scotch Plane'. There is no spelling variation to infer that Burns knew it. His references to 'Plain' were clearly geographically meant to infer a large, open, treeless tract of land.

3.  Burns' references to 'Lime' either refer to lime as in mortar, or to the exotic lime. There is in my view, nothing to indicate reference to the Lime Tree – *Tilia x vulgaris*.

4.  The reference to '*broom*-stick' is not in a natural history context but of a superstitious nature: 'A broom-stick o' the *witch* of Endor...'

5.  Burns wrote a group of couplets called **'Broom Besoms'** in which the chorus had the lines:

    > Buy *broom besoms*! wha will buy them now;
    > Fine heather ringers, better never grew.

    Although 'broom besoms' is a correct term for a broom sweeping brush, 'buying brooms' was apparently a euphemism for female sexual adventures.

6.  His reference to 'Laurel-boughs' in the **'Espistle To James Smith'** does not allude to the species specifically but to the practice in classical times, for a wreath of laurel to be placed on the head, as an emblem of victory or honour.

    > Then farewell hopes o *laurel-boughs*,
    > To garland my poetic brows!

7.  Although some of the woodlands and probably individual trees known to the Bard may still survive, being less permanent features and liable to significant change or modification, I have not listed them.

8.  The word/term 'sallow' is also used to describe an unhealthy or pale colour in the human skin complexion.

# MAMMALS

House Mouse (Keith Brockie)

*...truly sorry man's dominion*
*Has broken Nature's social union,*
*An justifies that ill opinion,*
*Which makes thee startle*
*At me, thy poor, earth-born companion,*
*An' fellow-mortal!*

## Introduction

In the following species' notes on the mammals mentioned by Burns, I have excluded domestic pets, working dogs and all references to farm animals. Although these are especially interesting, in that his comments demonstrated his almost passionate concern for their welfare – and he was clearly in advance of his time in abhorring all forms of cruelty to working or farm stock – nonetheless, they are strictly outwith the intended scope of this present review.

Similarly, I have excluded his references to exotic or non-native animals, such as ass, lion, tiger and rhinoceros. They, too, are not without academic interest, at least in demonstrating his wide knowledge of animals in an era prior to zoological gardens or substantive available literature on mammals.

I looked especially closely at his mention of bear, boar and goat, since these species formerly occupied southern Scotland in either a wild or feral state. On balance, these too were not thought to warrant inclusion in this work, which seeks only to explore his precise natural history knowledge. The mammals have been listed in Appendix 3.

In addition, his use of the word 'seal' was not in the context of a sea mammal, and reference to 'Scandinavian Boar' was of invading Vikings.


## HEDGEHOG  *Erinaceus europaeus*

**Local:**  Hurcheon; Urchin; Hedgepig

Historically abundant in southern Scotland especially in proximity to hedges, woods and rough grazing up to the tree line, hedgehogs were regularly collected, baked, and eaten by country people in the mid-eighteenth century.

Burns used both the proper and local names in his works. For example, in **'To Robert Graham, Esq. of Fintry'**: 'The Priest and *hedgehog* in their robes, are snug; and in his **'Elegy on Captain Mathew Henderson'** he wrote:

> Haurl thee hame to his black smiddie,
> O'er *hurcheon* hides…

'*Hurchin*' is also found in the song **'Bonie Mary'**; in Scots it was also used to describe an uncouth or slovenly person, and often applied to a mischievous child.


## MOLE  *Talpa europaea*

**Local:** Moldwarp; Moudie; Moudiewart

Historically described as 'common' in both Ayrshire and Dumfriesshire, moles are seldom seen above ground, the usual sign of their presence is in the fresh mole hills – round circular mounds of soil deposited on the ground following excavation of underground runways or tunnels.

Long associated with the farming community, there was, and remains, a great deal of dispute about the mole's activities in relation to agriculture. While some authorities decry the numbers of earthworms taken in its diet, others maintain that moles aerate the soil and thus assist drainage with construction of their burrows.

Burns mentions the species in **'The Twa Dogs'**: 'Whyles mice and *moudieworts* they howkit'; and referred to an old Scots air **'The Moudiewort'** in a letter to George Thomson in 1794. A song with this title was published in *MMC* and has as its opening line, 'The *modiewark* has done me ill'; and in the song **'Brose and Butter'**: 'The *Moudiewort* want the een'; the latter, of course, referring to the fact that moles are practically blind.

## BAT sp. Order chiroptera

**Local:** Baukie-bird

During the period under review, three bat species were in all probability equally common in both Ayrshire and Dumfries-shire: *Pipistrelle, Daubentons* and *Long-eared* bat. However, they were not scientifically described by science until: *Pipistrelle* [1774 in France; 1825 in England]; *Daubentons* [1839, Britain]; *Longeared* [1754, Sweden; 1829, England]. Other less common species, that may conceivably have been flying during the period were *Noctule* [first described in 1784] and *Natters* bat, not named until 1818.

From the two references available, it is, of course, quite impossible to be in any way specific, and Burns would be totally unaware of any scientifically named species.

In the **'Jolly Beggars - A Cantata'** we find the quotation, 'Or, wavering like the *bauckie-bird*'.

In his letter of 1793 to Deborah Duff Davies, Burns makes a very remarkable and biologically significant comment: 'their wildest ire is charmed into the torpur of the *bat*, slumbering out the rigours of winter in the chink of a ruined wall'.

Although not part of the Scottish fauna, it is at least worthy of note that Burns referred knowingly either to Vampire Bat *Desmondus rotundus* – found in the tropical regions of central and south America – or to Vampire (as in European superstitous folklore). In his **'To Robert Graham, Esq. of Fintry'** he insults Creech, the bookseller, thus: '*Vampyre* booksellers drain him to the heart'.

## RABBIT *Oryctolagus cuniculus*

**Local:** Bunny

Introduced to Britain by the Normans following the conquest, they were first taken to Scotland by the monks who were established on the Isle of May and they were also on Ailsa Craig by 1612. Widely distributed artificially, especially by religious orders and the military as a source of fresh meat, they were certainly present but scarce and strictly protected in Dumfriesshire during Burns' lifetime.

In his admirable *Burns Lore of Dumfries and Galloway*, James A Mackay includes an account of 'Jock' Brodie a local worthy and suspected poacher, who as a young man certainly knew Burns. One of his stories – which cannot now be verified – concerned Burns staying with a gamekeeper and, when asked to say grace before his last meal (by which time Burns had been apparently served with rabbit at every sitting) gave:

> Rabbits young and rabbits old,
> Rabbits hot and rabbits cold,
> Rabbits black and rabbits grey,
> Thanks the Lord I'm gaein away.

In my view there are two social aspects to be considered. Had Burns accepted an invitation to spend several days with a gamekeeper, one might assume that his host would not have insulted a respected visitor with such a monotonous diet. Even during the eighteenth century it would have been well within the compass of a keeper to have a variety of meat or fish available to his table. Similarly, I find it difficult to believe that, having accepted the invitation and the available hospitality, that on a final grace Burns would have insulted his host.

Although these comments are obviously speculative, in my view the episode is doubtful.

## BROWN HARE *Lepus capensis*

**Local[1]:** Poosie; Maukin

There were no records in Britain prior to the Roman occupation, and it is only from game-bag records, maintained on large estates, that we can be certain that the brown hare was common and widely distributed throughout Scotland – except on the higher mountains – up till the end of the nineteenth century. Although some old records show a presence of the Blue or Mountain Hare *L. timidus* in Dumfries-shire, these are misleading; the species cannot be substantiated until 1863 when it was then the subject of an attempted

---

[1]These, and other local names, were derived from 'slang', and transferred to hare (and other game) due to the severity of the Game laws in the 18th century, and subsequent punishment of perceived violation.

introduction.

In his **'Epistle to John Rankine'**, Burns first mentions it with 'It pits me ay as mad's a *hare*', demonstrating as well his knowledge of at least one aspect of their biology when referring to 'mad'. Following that, in **'Epistle to J Lapraik'**:

> An paitricks scraichin lound at e'en
> An morning *poussie* whidden seen,
> Inspire my Muse…

In **'The Vision'**, he uses a local name in a very descriptive winter scenario:

> The sun had clos'd the winter day,
> The curlers quat their roaring play,
> And hunger'd *maukin* taen her way,
> To kail-yards green,
> While faithless snaws ilk step betray
> Whare she has been.

The first mention of the hare as a shooting quarry is in **'The Twa Dogs'**, where he has Luath saying: 'Or shooting of a *hare* or moor-cock'. Referring to hunting in **'Tam Samson's Elegy'** he wrote 'Ye *maukins*, cock your fud fu braw'.

He returns to a more pensive mood in the **'Elegy On Captain Matthew Henderson'**:

> Ye *maukins*, whidden thro the glade,
> Come join my wail!

On 21 April 1789, Burns wrote **'The Wounded Hare'** to Mrs Dunlop, on seeing a wounded hare limping past. The verses do not specifically name the species (*see* pp. 192-3) but it was clearly intended.

The Jacobite song **'Awa, Whigs, Awa'**, lampoons the exponents of the 1688 Revolution:

> Gude help the day when Royal heads
> Are hunted like a *maukin*!

The poem (possibly by Burns) called **'On The Duchess Of Gordon's Reel Dancing'** contains:

> Gordon, the great, the gay, the gallant,
> Skip't like a *maukin* owre a dyke:

The **'Epistle to William Simpson'** of Ochiltree in 1785, further demonstrates his feeling for this animal:

> O, sweet are Coila's haughs an woods,
> Where lintwhites chant amang the buds,
> And jinkin *hares*, in amorous whids,
> Their loves enjoy;
> While thro the braes the cushat croods
> With wailfu cry!

A suppressed song entitled **'Ode To Spring'** refers to the maukin: 'When *maukin* bucks, at early fucks.'

Also written in 1785 **'The Holy Fair'** contains:

> The rising sun, owre Galston Muirs
> Wi glorius light was glintin;
> The *hares* were hirplin down the furs,
> The lav'rocks they were chantin
> Fu sweet that day.

**'The Brigs of Ayr'** has: 'Swift as the Gos drives on the wheeling *hare*' – a record discussed more fully under Peregrine Falcon; and in the song **'Dainty Davie'** we find:

> When purple morning starts the *hare*
> To steal upon her early fare...

lines that are repeated in his revision of the old song **'The Gard'ner Wi His Paidle'**.

In **'The Humble Petition of Bruar Water'**:

> This, too, a covert shall ensure,
> To shield them from the storm;
> And coward *maukin* sleep secure,
> Now in her grassy form:

Burns was clearly distressed on seeing a wounded hare limp by after being shot, and he wrote at some length in 1789 on this incident to Patrick Miller of Dalswinton, and to Alexander Cunningham. Writing on the same event to Mrs Dunlop he added: 'whatever I have said of shooting *hares*, I have not spoken one irreverend word against coursing them.' (Coursing is to hunt by dogs, usually hounds, relying on sight rather than scent.) Writing to Peter Hill (who lived in Edinburgh) on 5 February 1792, he concluded with, 'My best compliments to Mrs Hill. – I sent you a *Maukin* by last week's Fly, which I hope you received.'; and to the same person in October, 1794: 'Moreover, by last Saturday's Fly, I sent you a *hare*; which I hope came and carriage free, safe to your hospitable mansion.' (A 'Fly' is a light, one-horse, covered carriage.)

## HOUSE MOUSE *Mus musculus*

**Local:** Mousie; Moose; Field Mouse; Brown Mouse

Burns wrote his classic, oft quoted poem **'To A Mouse'**, 'on turning her up in her nest with the plough, November, 1785'. The 'mousie' field which sets the scene of this famous poem is on Mossgiel Farm, one kilometre north of Mauchline in Ayrshire. There seems little doubt that Burns, while as always sensitive and observant, used the poignant moment to reflect on the human situation of 'home' eviction with all the tragedy and trauma that that evokes.

But *Mousie*, thou art no thy lane,
In proving foresight may be vain:
The best-laid schemes o *mice* and men
Gang aft agley
An lea'e us nought but grief and pain,
For promised joy!

His other references include in **'The Twa Dogs'**, 'Whyles *mice* and moudieworts they Howkit'; in the song **'Brose and Butter'** he wrote 'The *Mouse* is a merry wee beast'; and in a fragment called **'On Glenriddell's Fox Breaking his Chain'**, 'As sleek's a *mouse*, as round's an apple'. In a letter to Peter Hill in 1789, he referred to a 'plundered *Mouse*-nest'.

Virtually since the first publication of this poem, there has been a general assumption by students and artistic illustrators that the specific mouse species involved was the Harvest Mouse *Micromys minutus*. This has largely been perpetuated because the 'scene' evolved in the 'harvest field' and that it described the destruction of a nest chamber constructed of fragments of leaves and stubble: 'That wee bit heap o leaves an stibble.'

In fact the Harvest Mouse remained undescribed to science in Britain until 1767; and it was not generally known till publication by Gilbert White in 1789 – four years after Burns wrote his verses.

In my view, therefore, identification of the species as Harvest Mouse cannot be substantiated from what Burns wrote, and can no longer therefore be supported. Even if Burns had actually claimed to have seen the mouse well, and had called it a 'harvest mouse', the animal would have moved so quickly – 'Thou need na start awa sae hasty' – as to defy acceptable, specific, identification in the field.

We are thus left to consider whether or not 'harvest mouse' could possibly have been present, in a field nest, in Ayrshire, during November in 1785.

Three different mouse species could conceivably have been involved: Harvest Mouse *M. minutus*; Wood Mouse (Long-Tailed Field Mouse) *Apodemus sylvaticus*; and House Mouse *M. musculus*. Contrary to popular belief, there is no such species as a 'field mouse' – only mice that live in fields!

The Harvest Mouse, although capable of living at a relatively high density where it occurs, has always been more restricted in geographical distribution, the main elements of the population being to the south and east of Britain. In addition, it has been reliably recorded that, for over a substantial period of time, there has been a retraction of geographical range towards the south.

In more recent years, for example, although recorded in Aberdeenshire in 1913 and in Angus, Fife and Perth during the 1800s, there are no acceptable records of the species in Scotland, except for one group near Edinburgh. Writing in 1912, the eminent Dumfries-shire naturalist, Sir H S Cladstone, refused to accept that 'minutus' had ever occurred in that county. Thus, bearing in mind that its distribution in Britain is of a southerly disposition, it is even less likely that it ever lived at Mauchline in Ayrshire.

Harvest Mouse is well known as the only mouse species that builds an elevated nest, well above ground in the 'stalk zone' of vegetation. These are predominantly in corn (oats) fields and breeding starts in May, peaks in July and may even continue to December (from English records). Obviously, during harvest these later active elevated nests and the remains of old and used ones would quite simply be destroyed. During the winter months, harvest mice live in burrows just below ground level, but there is no evidence at all of the construction of new winter nests underground as non-breeding havens, and it is much more likely that the animals disperse from the open field situation.

Wood Mouse, as its name infers, is predominantly a woodland mouse, living in runways in and below the forest litter. They have been known to occupy areas with less cover, such as hedgerows and gardens, but rarely in fields; and like the harvest mouse, there are no winter records of underground field nests.

House Mouse, in comparison, was, as one might expect, exceedingly common and widely distributed throughout Scotland. They lived in open fields, chiefly in arable areas and used drystone walls and hedges – especially those adjacent to grain-fields (with a preference for wheat and oats). They are, of course, catholic and were also to be found in all types of buildings.

A major point is that, although much reduced in winter, field-based populations of *M. musculus* continue to breed throughout the year. Therefore, they obviously continue to build nest chambers underground all year round. I have concluded that – when ploughing in the stubble in Ayrshire during November month, in a small field adjacent to human habitation and a farm steading – it is almost certain that Burns turned over the nest of a House Mouse *musculus*. Two vital biological facts are also worthy of note. The houses and steadings during Burns' era were all rat-infested. A small shy mammal by comparison, *musculus* would have found it extremely difficult to live safely beside *R. rattus*. By remaining predominantly 'in the field' the mouse would have largely avoided direct predation and competition from rats, thus improving its chances of survival. It also could have exploited more efficiently the all important available food supply, in the form of spilled grain.


## BEAVER *Castor fiber*

Now extinct in Britain but it survives in other areas of Europe, western and central Siberia. Subfossil remains are common in Britain especially in the peat of the Fens and in East Anglia. Records suggest it became extinct in Wales by the twelfth century and perhaps later in Scotland.

Burns was aware of the animal and in a letter to John Arnot in 1786, described: 'Religion, a feebly-struggling *beaver* down the roaring of Niagara'.


## SHIP RAT *Rattus rattus*

**Local:** Black rat; Roof rat; House rat; Ratton

The Ship Rat, better known in southern Scotland as the Black Rat, was carried by shipping all round the world, reaching Britain in Roman times.

In Britain, it was widespread both in towns and on farmland, living in roof spaces, walls, on rafters and in thatch. They do not live outdoors. It remained the common resident town and farm rat until 1728, when the Brown Rat first arrived from Russia. They rapidly increased and spread, till by 1912 it was common, ousting the Black Rat. Brown Rat *Rattus norvegicus* is known to kill Black Rats, which are now restricted to the vicinity of sea ports, where they are probably maintained by escapees from ocean-going shipping. Native to India and Egypt, they could not tolerate cold conditions and were extinct in Dumfries-shire by 1870. Brown Rat success is linked to its ability to withstand cold and hunt food in adverse conditions.

It was, thus, the Ship or Black Rat that lived in both Ayrshire and Dumfries-shire during Burns' lifetime. This was the species that carried bubonic plague – contracted from the bite of a rat flea, infected with the bacterium *Pasteurella pestis* – and which caused the death of fifty million people in Europe during the fourteenth century.

Burns mentions the species in **'The Vision'**:

> An heard the restless *rattons* squeak
> About the riggin.

and again in his **'Halloween'**:

> A *ratton* rattl'd up the wa'
> An she cri'd Lord preserve her!

In his Poem on Life, **'Epistle to Colonel De Peyster'**, he says 'Watches, like baudrons by a *ratton*' (baudrons is a cat); and in **'The Jolly Beggars - A Cantata'**:

> He ended; and the kebars sheuk
> Aboon the chorus roar;
> While frighted *rattons* backward leuk,
> An seek the benmost bore:

Peter Esslemont (1934) records an early incident in the life of Burns, when 'during the day his mother had hung washing from the rafters of the livingroom. At evening worship, a rat appeared on the roof and decended the rope to the floor.' Burns, then a mere child, is reputed to have written his first rhyme:

> A *rat* a *rat*, for want of stairs,
> Ran down a rope to say its prayers.

Unfortunately Esslemont does not provide any reference or source to support what would be a fascinating historical record.

Similarly, an amusing anecdote which cannot be verified was included by Tom Wilson (1904) in his booklet *Burns and Black Joan*:

Riding out of Sanquhar one day on his road to Ayrshire, Burns noticed a group of boys behind the Council House, and curious to learn what they were after rode close up to them, when he discovered that the youths had got hold of a *rat*, which, with a string tied to one of its legs, they were dragging about and poking with sticks. Instantly jumping from his horse, Burns, with a blow from his riding whip, put an end to the torments of the suffering rodent; and turning to the lads soundly rated them on their cruel conduct.

'It's only a *ratton*,' said one of the boys.

'Ay,' replied Burns, 'it's only a *ratton*. But ye maun min', laddies, that the same gude God that made you an' me put life as weel into that wee beast. Dinna let me hear tell o'ye daein' onything sae cruel again.'

Burns' reference to the rat in the alternative lines to the **'Election Ballad for Westerha' '** was obviously a political comment:

> The *rattan* ran wi a' his clan
> For fear the house should fa', man.

In **'The Brigs of Ayr'**, Burns has the Auld Brig say: 'And from Glenbuck down to *Ratton*-Key,' referring to the seaward course of the river Ayr ('key' is often used for quay in Scotland and 'Ratton-Key' infers a typically rat infested quay). The Ratton-Key was in fact a small landing stage a little upstream from the main harbour area at the mouth of the Ayr.

## Fox  *Vulpes vulpes*

**Local:** Red fox; Tod

Abundant in fragmented country-side offering a diversity of cover and hence food, the fox is found in woodlands and on higher hills and moorland, and was widespread and numerous in both Ayrshire and Dumfries-shire during the mid-eighteenth century. Later, organised hunting and shooting was in vogue as a sport and thought necessary as a form of 'pest control' to protect livestock, especially sheep, lambs, kids, free range poultry and game from direct predation by fox.

Burns kept one pet yowe (ewe) which he had called Mailie. When it was clear that she was dying, he penned the verses **'The Death and Dying Words of Poor Mailie'** ('An unco mournfu tale'); in it we find:

> O bid him save their harmless lives,
> Frae dogs, and *tods*, and butcher's knives!

In his **'The Twa Herds: Or, The Holy Tulzie'** (another described by Burns as

'An unco mournfu tale', according to his footnote), Burns gives a satirical account of a row between two ministers of the church:

> O a' ye pious godly flocks,
> Weel fed on pastures orthodox,
> Wha now will keep you frae the *fox*,
> Or worrying tykes?
> Or wha will tent the waifs an crocks,
> About the dykes?

and in the same work, he later includes the line 'The thrummart, wilcat, brock, and *tod*.'

In the song **'My Hoggie'** he identified the farmer's concern for his stock from attack by both fox and dogs (a hoggie is a young sheep).

> But the houlet cry'd frae the castle wa',
> The blitter frae the boggie,
> The *tod* reply'd upon the hill:
> I trembled for my hoggie.
> An unco tyke lap o'er the dyke,
> And maist has kill'd my hoggie.

In **'On Glenriddell's Fox Breaking his Chain'**, a fragment written in 1791, Burns displayed his dislike of animals being kept in captivity, and took the opportunity to record his views – with the theme of Liberty – using the poetic name for a fox.

> The staunchest Whig Glenriddell was,
> Quite frantic in his country's cause;
> And oft was *Reynard*'s prison passing,
> And with his brother – Whigs canvassing
> The rights of men, the powers of women,
> With all the dignity of Freemen.

His verses on **'To Robert Graham Esq. of Fintry'** also had a political theme:

> In all th' omnipotence of rule and power.
> *Foxes* and statesmen subtile wiles ensure;

In presumably an old version of **'A Vision'**: 'the *fox* was howling on the hill'; and in his **'The Kirk's Alarm'** of 1789, again in satirical mood, when his friend, the Rev. Mr McGill of Ayr was forced to apologise to the Presbytery following an enquiry by the General Assembly of the Church of Scotland:

> Daddie Auld! Daddie Auld, there's a *tod* in the fauld,
> A tod meikle waur than the clerk;

I have excluded all other references to 'fox' where they more specifically referred either to proper names or to behavioural aspects.

## STOAT (Ermine) *Mustela erminea*

**Local:** Weasel; Stot; White Stoat; Whittret

A great deal of confusion existed with the early field identifications of *stoat* and *weasel*, especially outwith the winter months, when the stoat completes a second moult to become completely white except for a black tip to the tail, known as 'ermine condition' or 'Royal Fur'.

That it was common in southern Scotland during Burns time is not in dispute. It is expected that it would have occupied a wide range of habitats from lowland agricultural land, marshes, and woods including also the higher moorlands and hills. It came into contact with man, mainly as a result of its exaggerated habit of killing poultry.

Burns refers to ermine – as in the 'skin of the stoat' – used to decorate a cloak, in **'To The Guidwife of Wauchope House'**:

> Than onie *ermine* ever lap,
> Or proud imperial purple.

## WEASEL *Mustela nivalis*

**Local:** Mouse weasel; Grass weasel; Whatrick; Whittrick; Wittret

Although often confused with the stoat, the weasel was common and widespread throughout southern Scotland during Burns' tenure. It is a small-bodied carnivore, generally smaller than a stoat, and with no black tip to the tail.

The animals posture and cunning often leads to the name being alluded to human behaviour and speech.

Mentioned in **'Libel Summons'**, a mock summons to a fictional Court of Equity:.

> See, ev'n himsel – there's godly Bryan,
> The auld *whatrek* he has been trying;

## BADGER *Meles meles*

**Local:** Brock (from the Gaelic 'Broc'); Grey; Pate; Bawson; Badget

Formerly regarded as fairly common and widespread, the badger had apparently decreased in southern Scotland to the extent that, by the end of the eighteenth century, they were considered as rare. Writing in 1912 Sir H S Gladstone could only cite one record of a single animal 'taken' at Dalswinton in 1887.

Burns refers to it in **'The Twa Dogs'**, where he has Caesar say:

> They gang as saucy by poor folk,
> As I was by a stinking *brock*;

and in **'The Twa Herds: or, The Holy Tulzie'**:

> The thrummart, wildcat, *brock* and tod,
> Weel kent his voice thro' a' the wood;

In a letter to Peter Hill, written at Ellisland in 1789, he was quite specific when he said, 'MAGISTRACY – how they hunt down a house breaker with the sanguinary perseverance of a bloodhound – how they outdo a terrier in a *badger*-hole.'

## POLECAT  *Mustela putorius*

**Local:** Foumart; Thrummart; Whumart

Thought to have been widespread in southern Scotland at one time. The last specimens in Dumfriesshire were obtained at Jardine Hall near Lochaben in 1853 and at Mountainhall near Dumfries in 1864. Some confusion exists with escaped polecat ferrets to which the original wild stock were originally ancestral. Polecats mark their territory with secretion from an anal gland mixed with urine, which obviously produces a distinct foetid smell. Hence the local name *foumart* or *foulmart*, meaning foul smell.

Burns mentions it three times; in his verses **'To Robert Graham Esq., of Fintry'**: 'The cit and *polecat* stink and are secure' (cit is meant to infer a city dweller); in **'Waukrife Minnie'**: 'And the *foumart* lay his crawin!'; and in the **'The Twa Herds: or, The Holy Tulzie'**:

> The *thummart*, wilcat, brock and tod
> Weel kent his voice thro a' the wood;

## WILDCAT  *Felis silvestris*

**Local:** Cat; Baudrons; Wilcat

Formerly widely distributed throughout Britain, although never considered very numerous in either Ayrshire or Dumfriesshire, the Wildcat became extinct by 1813, when the last known local cat was shot at Middlebie, Dumfriesshire.

The only mention is again in **'The Twa Herds: or, The Holy Tulzie'**: 'The thrumanart, *wilcat*, brock and tod.

## ELK  *Alces alces*

At one time widespread throughout Europe and Asia, it is also known as the Moose, in North America. Remains have been found in Dumfriesshire.

It has large flattened palmate antlers which have often given rise to mistaken identity and historical confusion. Some British deer species, especially where they are living in parks, do grown enormous, adnormal antlers, that are described as '*elk*-like.'

Writing to John Arnot in 1786, describing his own feelings at that time, he powerfully commented : 'Reason, a screaming *elk* in the vortex of a Moskae storm.'

## FALLOW DEER *Dama dama*

Unknown in southern Scotland until twelve animals were introduced to Raehills in Dumfries-shire during 1780, they obviously bred very successfully and became so numerous that they were ordered to be destroyed in 1844 because of the damage they were inflicting on crops and trees. A further introduction took place at Drumlandrig in 1860.

I can only find one specific mention in the old ballad entitled **'Hughie Graham'**:

> Our lords are to the mountains gane,
> A hunting o the *fallow deer*;

Other useages of the word 'fallow' refer to untilled land and to 'a fellow'.

## RED DEER *Cervus elaphus*

Remains of red deer have been found partly preserved in several of the peat mosses of southern Ayrshire and in Dumfries-shire indicating at least a post-

glacial presence. In the mid-eighteenth century, the hills between Dumfries-shire and Lanark were a famous haunt for red deer. Place names such as Hartfell and Harthope near Moffat are almost certainly indicative of, and derived from, the former presence of deer. It was in fact near Moffat in 1754, that 'the last hart was killed'. The large herds in southern Ayrshire and Galloway were thought mainly to have derived from survivors of ancient origin.

In the song composed in 1794, **'Sleep'st Thou'**, Burns includes:

> Or up the heathy mountain
> The *hart, hind,* and roe, freely wildly-wanton stray;

and in the song **'My Heart's in The Highlands'** the chorus has:

> My heart's in the Highlands, my heart is not here
> My heart's in the Highlands, a-chasing the deer,

A-chasing the *wild deer*, and following the roe -
My heart's in the Highlands, wherever I go!

In the above, 'a-chasing' clearly refers to red deer as in stalking, while 'following the roe' is self-explanatory of tracking through woodland cover.

Similarly, in the well known song **'The Lea-Rig'**, we find:

The hunter lo'es the morning sun,
To rouse the *mountain deer*, my jo
At noon the fisher takes the glen
Adown the burn to steer, my jo:

One can safely regard 'mountain deer' as a reference to red deer. Quite clearly the Poet was aware of the different species involved and whereas although both fallow and roe can now be found in a 'hill situation', they were predominantly animals of the lower ground and living preferably in wooded areas.

Other references to the words 'stag' and 'staggie' is meant in the context of a male of any species for example a horse (a colt) or a person.

## ROE DEER *Capreolus capreolus*

Roe deer have probably inhabited some areas in southern Scotland since post-glacial times, and remains from the Pleistocene period have been found at Shaw in Dumfries-shire. The smallest of the native deer, roe have been present in Britain since records were kept. In the Middle Ages it was widespread and common but not given protection by royal decree, being less favoured as a 'beast of the chase'. It decreased elsewhere, confronted by an increasing human population and destruction of the ancient forests until by the eighteenth century its main stronghold was in Scotland. They were the subject of introductions to Annandale in 1854 and Drumlandrig in 1860. Place names like Raehills and Raeclough Rig testify to a long presence in the country. It has maintained a steady recovery in parallel with increased afforestation.

The two references to the species in the works of Burns are already referred to in the species account of red deer (above). His use of the term 'buck' is not intended as referring to the male of the roe deer.

## WOLF *Canis lupus*

Now extinct in Britain, it was in historic times geographically widespread, with some ten specific 'Wolf' place names in the Borders, Dumfries and Galloway, but none in Ayrshire. It was found for example in Eskdale in the thirteenth century and the place names Wolfgill (Dumfries); Glenmaddie – Glen of the Wolf – (Sanquhar); and Braco are noteworthy. Wolves survived in the more remote areas of Scotland, the last one being killed about 1740.

Burns would therefore be more familiar with the wolf than we are today, although it is to be expected that the animal by then was featuring more in folklore and superstition than in biological fact.

He mentions the wolf in **'A New Psalm for the Chapel of Kilmarnock'**:

> Even as two howling, rav'ing *wolves*
> To dogs do turn their tail...

and in an early version of the song **'The Poor Thresher'**: 'We still keep the ravening *wolf* from the door.'

## *To a Mouse*

*On Turning Her Up In Her Nest With The Plough November 1785*

Wee sleekit, cow'rin, tim'rous beastie,
O, what a panic's in thy breastie!
Thou need na start awa sae hasty,
  Wi bickering brattle!
I wad be laith to rin an chase thee,
  Wi murdering pattle!

I'm truly sorry man's dominion
Has broken Nature's social union,
An justifies that ill opinion,
  Which makes thee startle
At me, thy poor, earth-born companion,
  An fellow mortal!

I doubt na, whyles, but thou may thieve;
What then? poor beastie, thou maun live!
A daimen icker in a thrave
  'S a sma request;
I'll get a blessin wi the lave.
  An never miss't!

Thy wee-bit housie, too, in ruin!
Its silly wa's the win's are strewin!
An naething, now to big a new ane,
  O foggage green!
An bleak December's win's ensuin,
  Baith snell an keen!

Thou saw the fields laid bare an waste,
An weary winter comin fast,
An cozie here, beneath the blast,
  Thou thought to dwell,
Till crash! the cruel coulter past
  Out thro thy cell.

That wee bit heap o leaves an stibble,
Has cost thee monie a' weary nibble!
Now thou's turn'd out, for a thy trouble,
  But house or hald,
To thole the winter's sleety dribble,
  An cranreuch cauld!

But Mousie, thou art no thy lane,
In proving foresight may be vain:
The best-laid schemes o mice an men
    Gang aft agley,
An lea'e us nought but grief an pain,
    For promis'd joy!

Still thou art blest, compar'd wi me!
The present only toucheth thee:
But och! I backward cast my e'e,
    On prospects drear!
An forward, tho I canna see,
    I guess an fear!

# RIVERS, LOCHS AND HILLS

River Nith at Sanquar(Edward Whitton)

*How lovely, Nith, thy fruitful vales,*
*Where bounding hawthorns gayly bloom,*
*And sweetly spread thy sloping dales,*
*Where lambkins wanton thro the broom!*
*Tho wandering now must be my doom,*
*Far from thy bonie banks and braes,*
*May there my latest hours consume,*
*Amang my friends of early days!*

## Rivers

Burns mentions an astonishing number of rivers in his collective works, including specific reference to some 33 of the major river systems in Scotland. These range from the Highland Spey to the Sark, which partly forms Scotland's most southerly national boundary with the 'auld enemy'.

In addition to these, reference is made to no fewer than 26 major rivers – including others in Scotland, several within England, mainland Europe and two other continents (see Appendix 4b).

He also mentions non-specifically the 'running water' habitat, as opposed to static water, with the use of:

> Broo (water) as applied to a river (1); burn/burnie (30); ditch (4); floating (3); floods (21); flow (19); rill (as in a brook or stream) (5); rin (to run, as applied to a stream) (6); rivulet (2); stream (44); rivers (non specific) (15) – a total of 150 references.

These, added to the list of 164 specific references to rivers, presents an impressive total of some 314 related comments on running water.

I have not listed every reference to each river in the descriptive notes. The total number of specific references to each are given in parenthesis after the title.

One is left in no doubt that Burns actually enjoyed being beside water and that he was intimately familiar with many of these rivers and streams. By inference, one can safely assume that a considerable amount of his leisure time must have been spent either walking on the banks, sitting in quiet contemplation at some favourite stretch, pool, or falls; or in fishing, a pastime that he particularly enjoyed.

To the artistic, rivers and streams have long been a catalyst to stimulus, demonstrating a scenario of differing lights and moods in association with the prevailing season and local conditions – the wild uncontrollable dramatic surges and passion of the winter flood or the contrasting placid serene calm beauty of the normal summer and autumnal flow, meandering on flat bedforms or tumbling and cascading through rocks or over falls.

To a very sensitive but observant country-wise poet, the continually and rapidly changing river scene can be a great joy. There is always the potential thrill of viewing, at reasonably close quarters, some aspect within the vast range of associated aquatic wildlife, which being in the main rather shy and retiring, are often more readily seen when the watcher is sitting quietly and alone. This allied to the engendered feeling of peace and solitude undoubtedly induced by such surroundings, the moving waters would certainly provide for Burns a marked degree of tranquillity, verging on the therapeutic, and perhaps acting in his case as a release, either to elicit relaxation of the mind or to stimulate further creative thoughts.

## SIGNIFICANT SCOTTISH RIVERS KNOWN TO BURNS

### *Afton Water* (8)

Rises 2 km south of Afton Reservoir, then flows north through the reservoir to join the River Nith at New Cumnock.

When writing to Mrs Frances Anna Dunlop of Dunlop on 5 February 1789, Burns wrote -

> There is a small river, *Afton*, that falls into Nith near New Cumnock, which has some charming, wild, romantic scenery on its banks. I have a particular pleasure in those little pieces of poetry such as our Scots songs, etc., where the names and landskip-features of rivers, lakes, or woodlands, *that one knows* are introduced. I attempted a compliment of that kind, to *Afton,* as follows:

#### *Sweet Afton*

Flow gently, sweet *Afton*, among thy green braes!
Flow gently, I'll sing thee a song in thy praise!
My Mary's asleep by thy murmuring stream -
Flow gently, sweet *Afton*, disturb not her dream!

Thou stock dove whose echo resounds thro the glen,
Ye wild whistling blackbirds in yon thorny den,
Thou green-crested lapwing, thy screaming forbear-
I charge you, disturb not my slumbering Fair.

How lofty, sweet *Afton*, thy neighbouring hills,
Far mark'd with the courses of clear, winding rills!
There daily I wander, as noon rises high,
My flocks and my Mary's sweet cot in my eye.

How pleasant thy banks and green vallies below,
Where wild in the woodlands the primroses blow
There oft, as mild Ev'ning weeps over the lea,
The sweet-scented birk shades my Mary and me.

Thy crystal stream, *Afton*, how lovely it glides,
And winds by the cot where my Mary resides!
How wanton thy waters her snowy feet lave,
As, gathering sweet flowerets, she stems thy clear wave!

Flow gently, sweet *Afton*, among thy green braes!
Flow gently, sweet river, the theme of my lays!
My Mary's asleep by the murmuring stream-
Flow gently, sweet *Afton*, disturb not her dream!

## *Allan Water* (1)

Rises near Blackford in Tayside then runs southwest down Strath Allan to Dunblane and south to join the River Forth.

There is a second Allan Water in the Borders. Fortunately the reference to Ben Ledie (879 metres) in the song **'By Allan Stream'** (Tune - 'Allan Water') avoids any confusion.

> By *Allan* stream I chanc'd to rove,
> While Phoebus sank beyond *Benledi.*

## *Ayr River* (17)

Rises to the east of Muirkirk, flowing west through Sorn and Catrine to enter the Firth of Clyde at Ayr (from the Scandinavian *eyrr*, a beach).

Burns was, of course, intimately familiar with the river. In the poem **'The Brigs of Ayr'** he describes its course from its rise to the estuary, listing first the four tributaries:

> When from the hills where springs the brawling *Coil*,
> Or stately *Lugar*'s mossy fountains boil,
> Or where the *Greenock* winds his moorland course,
> Or haunted *Garpel* draws his feeble source...
>
> *Auld Brig*
> Men three-parts made by tailers and by barbers,
> Wha waste your weel-hain'd gear on damn'd
> *New Brigs and harbours!*

Other major references to the river include:

**'Address to Edinburgh'**
> As on the banks of *Ayr* I stray'd (repeated)

**'The Vision'** (poem):
> Auld hermit *Ayr* staw thro his woods,
> On to the shore;

**'The Brigs of Ayr'** (poem):
> Auld *Ayr* is just one lengthen'd, tumbling sea...

**'The Braes o Ballochmyle'** (song):
> Fareweel the bonnie banks of *Ayr*!

**'The Fête Champetre'** (song):
> On th' bonie banks of *Ayr* to meet...

**'Man Was Made To Mourn'** (song):
> Along the banks of *Ayr*...

**'The Gloomy Night is Gath'ring Fast'** (song):
> Far from the bonnie banks of *Ayr*...

**'Thou Lingering Star'** (song):
> Can I forget the hallow'd grove,
> Where, by the winding *Ayr*, we met...
>
> *Ayr*, gurgling, kiss'd his pebbled shore...

**'Young Jessie'** (song):
> And fair are the maids on the banks of the *Ayr*;

**'One Night As I Did Wander'**
> Auld *Ayr* ran by before me,
> And bicker'd to the seas;

**'Epistle to William Simpson'** (song):
> While Irwin, Lugar, *Ayr* and Doon
> Nobody sings.

## *Bruar Water* (1)

Rises in Tayside running down Glen Bruar to join the River Gary, 5 km west of Blair Atholl.

**'The Humble Petition of Bruar Water'**, a significant poem 'To The Noble Duke of Atholl' describes the river and its wildlife.

> The sober laverock, warbling wild,
> Shall to the skies aspire;
> The gowdspink, Music's gayest child,
> Shall sweetly join the choir;
> The blackbird strong, the lintwhite clear,
> The mavis mild and mellow,
> The robin, pensive Autumn cheer
> In all her locks of yellow.

## *Cairn Water* (2)

Rises near Moniaive then flows southeast to join and form Cluden Water some 10 km north of Dumfries. From **'The Whistle-A Ballad':** 'Till Robert, the lord of the *Cairn* and the Scaur'; and **'Elegy on Willie Nicol's Mare':**

> But now she's floating down the Nith,
> and past the mouth o *Cairn*.

## *River Cart* (1)

Rises near Johnstone and flows through Paisley to join the River Clyde. From the song: **'The Gallant Weaver':**

> Where *Cart* rins rowing to the sea
> By mony a flower and spreading tree...

*Cessnock Water* (4)

Rises some 5 km south of Darvel then runs circuitously northwest to join the River Irvine between Galston and Kilmarnock. The river was first referred to twice by Burns in the song **'The Lass of Cessnock Banks'**:

> On *Cessnock* banks a lassie dwells…

> Her voice is like the ev'ning thrush,
> That sings on *Cessnock* banks unseen…

Alternative stanzas of the same title have:

> On *Cessnock* banks there lives a lass,
> Could I describe her shape and mien;

Similarly, alternative lines from the poem: **'The Vision'** (later removed): 'Where *Cessnock* flows with gargling sound'.

*Coyle (Coil) Water* (2)

A tributary of the River Ayr (see above).
  Also referred to in the song **'The Soldiers' Return'**:

> I thought upon the banks o *Coil*,
> I though upon my Nancy…

*Clyde* (2)

Rises in Lanarkshire south of Abington and west of Moffat; flowing northwest through to Glasgow and to join the Firth of Clyde near Dunbarton.
  Burns refers to this major river in two songs – **'Yon Wild Mossy Mountains'**: 'That nurse in their bosom the youth o' the *Clyde*'; and **'The Bonny Lass of Albanie'**: 'In the rolling tide of spreading *Clyde'*.

*Cluden Water* (2)

Flows east from Cairn Water to join the River Nith just north of Dumfries. It is mentioned in a song: **'Ca' The Yowes To the Knowes'**: 'We'll gae down by *Clouden* side'; and from verses **'Grim Grizzel'**: 'Along the banks o *Clouden* fair'.

*River Dee* (2)

Issues from Loch Dee in Glentrool and flows southeast through Clatteringshaws

Loch to Loch Ken, hence south to Kirkcudbright Bay.

From the collection **'Ballads on Mr Heron's Election'**:

### Ballad Third - John Bushby's Lamentation

> Twas by the banks of bonie *Dee*,
> Beside Kirkcudbright's towers...

### Ballad Fourth: The Trogger (Chorus)

> Buy braw troggin frae the banks o *Dee*!

*River Devon* (5)

Rises some 5 miles (8km) east of Dunblane; flows east down Glen Devon then southeast to the Crook of Devon, turning sharply to run almost due west towards Menstrie, then south to join the River Forth, west of Alloa.

**'Fairest Maid On Devon Banks'** (song):

> Fairest maid on *Devon* banks!
> Crystal *Devon*, winding *Devon*.

**The Banks Of The Devon** (song):

> How pleasant the banks of the clear winding *Devon*...

> Where Devon, sweet *Devon*, meand'ring flows...

*River Doon* (18)

Issues from Loch Doon and flows northwest through Bogton Loch, Patna and Dalrymple to enter the Firth of Clyde, near Alloway.

Immortalised by Burns in poem and song, the best known quotations are certainly:-

**'Tam o' Shanter'** (poem):

> Thou would be found, deep drown'd in *Doon*...

> Before him *Doon* pours all his floods;

**'Halloween'** (poem):

> Among the bonie, winding banks,
> Where *Doon* rins, wimpling, clear:

**'Poor Mailie's Elegy'** (poem):

> O, a' ye Bards on bonnie *Doon*!

**'Sweet Are The Banks'**

> Sweet are the banks-the banks o *Doon*,
> The spreading flowers are fair...

Aft hae I rov'd by bonie *Doon*,
To see the woodbine twine…

**'Scenes Of Woe'** (song): (disputed)
Bonie *Doon* whare early roaming,
First I weav'd the rustic sang…

Bonie *Doon*, sae sweet at gloaming…

**'Ye Flowery Banks'** (song):
Ye flowery banks o bonie *Doon*…

Aft hae I rov'd by bonie *Doon*…

**'The Banks O Doon'** (song):
Ye banks and braes o bonie *Doon*…

Aft hae I rov'd by bonie *Doon*…

**'The Vision'** (poem):
Here, *Doon* pour'd down his far-fetch'd floods;

**'Epistle To William Simpson'**
While Irwin, Lugar, Ayr and *Doon*
Naebody sings.

### The Banks o Doon

Ye banks and braes o bonie *Doon*,
How can ye bloom sae fresh and fair?
How can ye chant, ye little birds,
And I sae weary fu o care!

Thou'll break my heart, thou warbling bird,
That wantons thro the flowering thorn!
Thou minds me o departed joys,
Departed never to return.

Aft hae I rov'd by bonie *Doon*
To see the rose and woodbine twine,
And ilka bird sang o its luve,
And fondly sae did I o mine.

Wi lightsome heart I pu'd a rose,
Fu sweet upon its thorny tree!
And my fause luver staw my rose-
But ah! he left the thorn wi me.

*Earn* (2)

Rises in Tayside and flows east from Loch Earn down Strath Earn to join the River Tay southeast of Perth.

Mentioned by Burns in **'Blythe Was She'**, a song he composed in 1787 while staying at Ochtertye:

> Blythe was she butt and ben,
> Blythe by the banks of *Earn*...

> She tripped by the banks of *Earn*...

*Eden* (1)

Rises on Black Fell Moss, Cumbria, flowing southwest then north to Appleby and Carlisle into the Solway Firth.

**'Address To The Shade of Thomson'**, penned by Burns at the request of Erskine, 11th Earl of Buchan, to commemorate James Thomson of Ednam near Kelso contains:

> While virgin Spring by *Eden*'s flood
> Unfolds her tender mantle green...

*Ettrick Water* (1)

Rises east of Moffat, then flows northeast through Ettrick Forest to the River Tweed near Selkirk. In **'Lament For the Absence of William Creeh, Publisher':**

> And *Ettrick* banks, now roaring red
> While tempests blaw...

*Fail(e) River* (2)

Rises near Redrae then flows south near Failford, to join the River Ayr west of Mauchline.

It is referred to in the poem **'The Brigs of Ayr'** as, 'From where the *Feal* wild-woody coverts hide.'

The historic parting of Burns and his Highland Mary Campbell is generally accepted to have occurred at the meeting of the waters of Fail and Ayr at Failford. Here Burns and Mary exchanged bibles across running water and it is thus inferred in the poem **'The Tarbolton Lasses'** as his 'sequestered spot': 'Gae down by *Faile*, and taste the ale'.

*Forth* (7)

It is formed by two main headstreams – the Duchray Water and Kelty Water – which meet near Aberfoyle. It flows east by Stirling and Alloa to Kincardine, where it widens into the Firth of Forth.

**'Here's a Health to Them That's Awa'** (song):
> Here's friends on baith sides of the *Firth*

**'On The Late Captain Grose's Peregrinations'** (song):
> Or drownèd in the River *Forth*?

**'The Battle of Sherramuir'** (song):
> I saw mysel, they did pursue
> The horseman back to the *Forth*, man!

**'Epistle To William Simpson'**
> Ramsay and famous Ferguson
> Gied *Forth* and Tay a lift aboon;

**'Out Over The Forth'** (fragment):
> Out over the *Forth*, I look to the north...

**'Yon Wild Mossy Moutains'**
> Not Gowrie's rich valley nor *Forth*'s sunny shores
> To me nae the charms o yon wild, mossy moors;

**'When First I Saw'** (song):
> 'Twixt *Forth* and Tweed all over...

*Gala Water* (4)

Rises on Hunt Law, flows south then east through Galashiels to join the River Tweed. Made famous by the very popular song in the Borders **'Braw Lads O Galla Water'**:

> But Yarrow braes nor Ettrick shaws
> Can match the lads of *Galla Water*...

> ...The bonie lad of *Galla Water*...

> ...Yet, rich in kindest, truest love,
> We'll tent our flocks by *Galla Water*...

*Garpal* (1)

A tributary of River Ayr (see above) which it joins near Muirkirk. From the poem **'The Brigs of Ayr'**: 'Or haunted *Garpal* draws his feeble sourse...'

*Girvan River* (1)

Rises near Bargan then flows southwest and enters the Firth of Clyde at Girvan. Burns visited Girvan, and up to 1794 he gave as the first line of his song **'My Nannie, O',** as 'Beyond the hills where Stinchar flows'. In a letter to George Thomson (song collector), in 1792 Burns wrote, 'The name of the river is horribly prosaic - I will alter it'. He then gave the choice of the rivers *Girvan* and/or *Lugar*. Thomson chose the latter.

*Greenock Water* (1)

Rises in Priesthill Height then flows southwest to join the River Ayr some 4 miles (7 km) west of Muirkirk: 'Or where the *Greenock* winds his moorland course' – **'The Brigs of Ayr'.**

*Irvine River* (3)

Rises near Dreghorn, and runs west to enter the Clyde Estuary, south of the town. Burns was familiar with parts of the river, having lived at both Irvine and at Fairlie Estate, Dundonald.

**'Epistle To William Simpson'**
> While *Irwin*, Lugar, Ayr, an Doon
> Naebody sings...

**'The Vision'** (poem):
> There, well-fed *Irvine* stately thuds:

**'Lord Gregory'** (verses):
> Lord Gregory, mind'st thou not the grove
> By bonie *Irwine* side...

*Jed Water* (2)

Rising in the Borders, and flowing north through Jedburgh to join the River Teviot, Burns visited the Jed area during his Borders tour, and wrote in his diary: 'Eden scenes on crystal *Jed*'. '*Jed* – Pure be thy crystal streams, and hallowed thy sylvan banks.'

*Logan Water* (3)

Rises near Auchingilloch and runs east to join the River Nethan, some 2 miles (3 km) southwest of Lesmahagow.

**'Logan Braes'** (song):
> O *Logan*, sweetly didst thou glide...

And years sin syne has o'er us run,
Like *Logan* to the simmer sun…

**'Willie Wastle'** (song):
Her face wad fyle the *Logan* Water…


*Lugar Water* (5)

Rises west of Lugar and continues to flow west to Cumnock and Ochiltree, thence to join the River Ayr near Mauchline.

**'My Nanie, O'** (song):
Behind yon hills where *Lugar* flows,
'Mang moors an mosses many, O…

**'Lament for James Earl of Glencairn'**
That wav'd o'er *Lugar*'s winding stream.

**'The Brigs of Ayr'** (poem):
Or stately *Lugar*'s mossy fountains boil,

**'Epistle To William Simpson'**
While Irwin, *Lugar*, Ayr an Doon
Naebody sings.

**'The Vision'** (poem):
Where *Lugar* leaves his moorland plaid
(an additional stanza)


*River Nith* (12)

Rises east of Dalmellington and flows through New Cumnock, Sanquhar and Thornhill to Dumfries and then to the Solway Firth.

Living and working in Ayrshire and then in Dumfriesshire – and travelling between Dumfries, Sanquhar and New Cumnock regularly during his Excise duties – Burns became very familiar with the River Nith. The Ayr and Nith are naturally the two major river systems mainly associated with Burns.

**'As I Stood By Yon Roofless Tower'**
Hasting to join the sweeping *Nith*…

**'Adown Winding Nith'** (song):
Adown winding *Nith* I did wander…

**'Does Haughty Gaul Invasion Threat?'** (song):
The *Nith* shall run to Corsincon…

**'Elegy On Willie Nicol's Mare'**
But now she's floating down the *Nith*,
And past the mouth o Cairn…

But now she's floating down the *Nith*,
For Solway fish a feast...

**'O, Were I on Parnassus Hill'** (song):
But *Nith* maun be my Muse's well,

**'The Wounded Hare'** (verses):
Oft as by winding *Nith* I, musing wait

**'The Banks of Nith'** (song):
But sweeter flows the *Nith* to me.

How lovely, *Nith*, thy fruitful vales...

**'Election Ballad for Westerha' '** (song):
The Laddies by the banks o'*Nith*
Wad trust his Grace wi' a', Jamie.

**'Young Jessie'** (song):
...by the sweet side of the *Nith*'s winding river...

**'Epistle To Hugh Parker'**
Dowie she saunters down *Nithside*...

### *O Were I on Parnassus Hill*

O, were I on Parnassus hill,
Or had o Helicon my fill,
That I might catch poetic skill
To sing how dear I love thee!
But *Nith* maun by my Muse's well,
My Muse maun be thy bonie sel,
On Corsincon I'll glowr and spell,
And write how dear I love thee.

Then come, sweet Muse, inspire my lay!
For a' the lee-lang simmer's day
I couldna sing, I couldna say,
How much, how dear I love thee.
I see thee dancing o'er the green,
Thy waist sae jimp, thy limbs sae clean,
Thy tempting lips, thy roguish een-
By Heav'n and Earth I love thee!

By night, by day, a-field, at hame,
The thoughts of thee my breast inflame,
And ay I muse and sing thy name-
I only live to love thee.
Tho I were doom'd to wander on,
Beyond the sea, beyond the sun,
Till my last weary sand was run,
Till then - and then - I'd love thee!

*Sark* (2)

Rises in Dumfriesshire and runs south to form the border between Scotland and England to enter the Solway Firth near Gretna.

**'Such A Parcel Of Rogues In A Nation'**
> Now *Sark* rins o'er the Solway sands…

**'The Vision'** (poem):
> The Chief on *Sark* who glorious fell,
> In high command…


*Scaur Water* (1)

Rises in hills west of Sanquhar running southeast to join the River Nith some 2 miles (3 km) south of Thornhill. From the song **'The Whistle'** – 'Till Robert, the lord of the Cairn and the *Scaur*…'


*Spey River* (1)

Rises in Corrieyairack Forest, Highland, and flows northeast to Kingussie down Strathspey by Aviemore and Rothes, to Spey Bay on the Moray Firth. In a Cantata, **'The Jolly Beggars':** 'We rangèd a'from Tweed to *Spey*…'


*Stinchar* (1)

Rises in Glentrool Forest, flows north then west through Carrick, then southwest by Barr and Colmonell to Ballantrae Bay.

**'My Nannie O'** (song):
> Behind yon hills where *Stinchar* flows
> 'Mang moors an' mosses many, O…

In an alternative version of this song, the name of the river (Stinchar) – thought by Burns to be 'horribly prosaic' – was changed to *Lugar*.


*Tay* (3)

Rises on Ben Lui and flows east down Strath Fillan to Loch Tay. Issues as River Tay, flows past Dunkeld and Perth to the Firth of Tay and Dundee to the east coast.

**'Bonie Dundee'** (song):
> Whare *Tay* rins wimplin by sae clear;

**'Epistle To William Simpson'**
> Ramsay an' famous Ferguson
> Gied Forth an *Tay* a lift aboon;

**Verses Written With a Pencil**
> The *Tay* meand'ring sweet in infant pride...


*Tweed River* (12)

Rises in Scotland at Tweed's Well, some 10 km north of Moffat, and then flows by Peebles, Kelso and Coldstream to enter the North Sea at Berwick-upon-Tweed, England.

**'Address To The Shade of Thomson'**
> While Autumn, benefactor kind,
> By *Tweed* erects his aged head,

**'Caledonia'** (song:)
> From *Tweed* to the Orcades was her domain...

> Oft, prowling, ensanguin'd the *Tweed*'s silver flood...

**'Here's a Health of Them That's Awa'** (song):
> And friends on baith sides o the *Tweed*...

**'Poor Mailie's Elegy'** (verses):
> For her forbears were brought in ships,
> Frae 'yont the *Tweed*:

**'The Jolly Beggars'** (a cantata):
> We rangèd a' from *Tweed* to Spey,

**'The Tree of Liberty'** (song):
> That sic a treet can not be found,
> 'Twixt London and the *Tweed*, man.

**'Such A Parcel Of Rogues In A Nation'**
> An *Tweed* rins to the ocean,

**'Lament for William Creech'**
> Up wimpling, stately *Tweed* I've sped...

**'Epistle To William Simpson'**
> Yarrow an *Tweed*, to monie a tune,
> Owre Scotland rings;

**'When First I Saw'** (song):
> Twixt Forth and *Tweed* all over...

**'Willie Wastle'** (song):
> Willie Wastle dwalt on *Tweed*,


*Yarrow Water* (5)

Issues from St Mary's Loch then flows eastwards through Ettrick Forest to join Ettrick Water some 2 miles (3 km) southeast of Selkirk.

**'Address to The Shade of Thomson'**
>The hills whence classic *Yarrow* flows…

**'Blythe Was She'** (song):
>On *Yarrow* banks the birken shaw…

>But Phemie was a bonier lass
>Than braes o' *Yarrow* ever saw.

**'Epistle To William Simpson'**
>*Yarrow* an' Tweed, to monie a tune,
>Owre Scotland rings;

**'Young Jessie'** (song):
>True hearted was he, the sad swain of the *Yarrow*…

### *Epistle to William Simpson* (an extract)

>Ramsay an famous Fergusson
>Gied Forth an Tay a lift aboon;
>*Yarrow* and Tweed, to monie a tune,
>Owre Scotland rings;
>While Irwin, Lugar, Ayr and Doon
>Naebody sings.

>Th' Illissus, Tiber, Thames, an Seine,
>Glide sweet in monie a tunefu line:
>But, Willie, set your fit to mine,
>And cock your crest!
>We'll gar our streams an burnies shine
>Up wi the best!

## Lochs

*Typical Scottish hill loch*

Compared with his extensive references on rivers and streams, Burns' comments on the static or still waters are scarce indeed and probably best serve to emphasise that he did indeed prefer to be beside the flowing waters. Historically, early roadways – and subsequent human settlements – tended to follow and be near to river courses. Natural valleys acted as lines of communication, with areas nearer to lochs being colonised later. This was especially so in South West Scotland, which has notably fewer areas of standing or static waters than other parts of Scotland; thus it is only to be expected that Burns would be more familiar with the river systems.

He used the terms lake (8 times); loch (3) and stank (1) – a total of only twelve records; other references to a 'stank' were not in a natural history context, and his use of the word 'pool' infers a pool as an integral part of a river.

In **'Ballad On The American War'** Burns mentions, 'Then thro the *lakes* Montgomery takes' (clearly referring to the Great Lakes of Canada and the USA); and in his **'Verses Written With A Pencil'** – 'Over The Chimney-Piece, In The Parlour of the Inn at Kenmore, Taymouth', he wrote:-

> Th' outstreching *lake*, inbosomed 'mong the hills,
> The eye with wonder and amazement fills:
> The Tay meand'ring sweet in infant pride
> The palace rising on his verdant side,

Similarly, he clearly refers to Loch Tay without being absolutely specific.

His piece of 1787, while touring Clackmannanshire, was entitled **'On Scaring Some Water-Fowl In Loch Turit'** and started:

> Why, ye tennants of the *lake*,
> For me your wat'ry haunt forsake?

The song **'The Campbells Are Comin'** includes

> Upon the Lomonds I lay, I lay,
> I looked down to bonie *Lochleven.*

Other than these, his references were either non-specific, or of very minor water bodies.


## Hills

Burns used only four definitions to describe higher ground: brae(s) (47 times); hills (92); knowe (hillock) 15; and mountains (27) – a total of some 181 records, of which 25 were specific to named braes, hills or mountains.

The Scots 'brae' is synonomous with the accepted definition of a 'hill' as a conspicuous, often rounded natural elevation of the earth's surface, less high and craggy than a mountain. A mountain is simply regarded as higher and steeper than a hill, often with a rocky summit. Some authorities have suggested the purely arbitrary altitude of 3000 feet or 914 metres as to constitute a mountain proper but that is not generally accepted.

The song **'Sweet Afton'** for example, uses both terms thus: 'Flow gently, sweet Afton, among thy green *braes*!' and to start the third verse, 'How lofty, sweet Afton, thy neighbouring *hills*,'

Similarly, the equally famous and well loved song **'The Lass O Ballochmyle'**:

> In ev'ry glen the mavis sang,
> All Nature list'ning seem'd the while,
> Except where greenwood echoes rang,
> Amang the *braes* o Ballochmyle.

and in the sad, but poignant **'The Braes O Ballochmyle'**:

The Catrine woods were yellow seen,
The flowers decay'd on Catrine lea,
Nae lav'rock sang on *hillock* green,
But nature sicken'd on the e'e.
Thro faded groves Maria sang,
Hersel in beauty's bloom the while,
And aye the wild-wood echoes rang:-
Fareweel the *braes* o Ballochmyle!

Low in your wintry beds, ye flowers,
Again ye'll flourish fresh and fair;
Ye birdies, dumb in with'ring bowers,
Again ye'll charm the vocal air;
But here, alas! for me nae mair
Shall birdie charm, or floweret smile;
Fareweel the bonie banks of Ayr!
Fareweel! fareweel! sweet Ballochmyle!

The song **'The Banks Of The Devon'** contains:

But the boniest flow'r on the banks of the Devon
Was once a sweet bud on the *braes* of the Ayr.

The title of an old disputed song – **'Coming o'er the Braes O Couper'** (also known as **'Donald Brodie'**) – is certainly specific, although rather odd in such a flat area. The revised version of the song **'The Banks O Doon'** has the first line 'Ye banks and *braes* o bonie Doon'; and the well known old Jacobite song of **'Killiecrankie'** mentions the braes in both the chorus and the verse:

An ye had been whare I hae been,
Ye wad na been sae cantie, O!
An ye had seen what I hae seen,
On the *braes* o Killiecrankie O!

But I met the Devil an Dundee,
On the *braes* o Killiecrankie, O.

The song called simply **'The Trogger'** has 'Bedown the bents o Bonshaw *braes*'; and a ballad collected by Burns in Dumfries – **'The Rowin 't In Her Apron'** – which deals with the story of the aftermath of the 1715 Rebellion, has the alternative lines of 'In Edinburgh *braes* there is a well…'

His satirical ballad on the Battle of Sherriffmuir (1715) – **Up And Warn A' Willie'** – contains reference to the Earl of Mar who led the Jacobites:

When we gaed to the *braes* o Mar,
And to the weapon-shaw, Willie…

It is presumed that 'the braes' referred to the area occupied by the troops of Mar.

Burns devotes a song to **'Logan Braes'**, which mentions the braes on four separate occasions, the last of which ends the poem:

> But soon may peace bring happy days,
> And Willie hame to Logan *braes*!

while his compliment to the River Nith, sent to Mrs Dunlop in 1788, contains:

> Tho wandering now must be my doom,
> Far from thy bonie banks and *braes*…

The revised song **'Braw Lads O Galla Water'**, so popular in the Borders, also mentions the braes twice. In the first verse he opens with:

> Braw, braw lads on Yarrow *braes*,
> They rove amang the blooming heather;
> But Yarrow *braes* nor Ettrick shaws
> Can match the lads o Galla Water.

In his revised version of a traditional ballad **'Kellyburn Braes'**, it is thought probable that Burns was referring to braes within the catchment area of the Kello Water, which rises in the Cumnock hills, flows south via Kelloholm and enters the Nith near Sanquhar.

Very appropriately, his list of named braes ends with the quotation from his famous **'The Banks o Doon'**:

> Ye banks and *braes* o' bonie Doon.
> How can ye bloom sae fresh and fair?

*The green hills of Dumfriesshire*

Specific references to hill locations are contained in his **'Address To the Shade of Thomson'**: 'The *hills* whence classic Yarrow flows'. The beautiful song **'Sweet Afton'** opens the third verse with: 'How lofty, sweet Afton, thy neighbouring *hills*'. In the final version of the song **'My Nanie O'**, Burns uses the first line: 'Behind yon *hills* where Lugar flows'. (An earlier alternative to the river mentioned in the line was Stinchar, which Burns regarded as 'horridly prosaic' the rivers Afton, Girvan and the Lugar were even later alternatives.)

His famous satire on quacks offering medicines and spurious medical advice was inspired by just such a person – John Wilson, Tarbolton's parish dominie. **'Death and Doctor Hornbook'** contains:

> The rising moon began to glowr
> The distant Cumnock *Hills* out-owre:

**'The Brigs of Ayr'** has the line, 'from the *hills* where springs the brawling Coil', which may be included as sufficiently geographically located. Similarly, in his **'Epistle to William Simpson'** he wrote:

> Or frosts on *hills* of Ochiltree
> Are hoary gray;

Ochiltree is an Ayrshire village near Cumnock and should not be confused with his reference to the Ochils, a range of hills extending from Bridge of Allan to the Firth of Tay at Newburgh. He refers to these hills in the song entitled **'Where, Braving Angry Winter's Storms'**:

> Where, braving angry winter's storms,
> The lofty *Ochils* rise,

while his song **'Godly Girzie'** includes the lines:

> Wi godly Girzie met belyve,
> Amang the Cragie *hills* sae hie.

The Craigie Hills lie between Kilmarnock and Tarbolton in Ayrshire.

Burns composed the song **'Logan Braes'**, which includes 'Far far frae me and Logan *braes*' (*see also* Logan Water).

The verses called **'O, Were I on Parnassus Hill'** contain reference to Corsincon – 'On *Corsincon* I'll glower and spell'; and again in **'Does Haughty Gaul Invasion Threat?'**:

> The Nith shall run to *Corsincon*,
> and *Criffel* sink in Solway...

Corsincon (1554 ft; 472 m) is a major hill near New Cumnock in Ayrshire, very prominent and visible from the roadway between New Cumnock and Sanquhar, on which Burns regularly travelled .

Similarly, Criffel (1866 ft.; 569 m) is a well known outstanding landmark on the Stewartry side of the Nith Estuary, equally visible to the traveller on the coastal road south of Dumfries.

'Parnassus' refers either to Mount Parnassus, a mountain in central Greece with classical associations, or metaphorically to the world of poetry or the centre of poetic or other creative activity.

The **'Epistle to Davie, A Brother Poet'** commences with a very apt first line: 'While winds frae aff *Ben-Lomond* blaw'. Ben Lomond is a well known mountain (3192 ft; 973 m) near Rowardennan on the east shore of Loch Lomond. Ben Lomond should not be confused with the reference to the Lomond Hills in the song **'The Campbells Are Comin'**. The Lomond Hills are a range in Kinross, south of Loch Leven. In the song **'By Allan Stream'** the first verse starts with:

> By Allan stream I chanc'd to rove,
> While Phoebus sank beyond *Benledi*;

Ben Ledi (2883 ft:879 metres) is near Callander.

Burns refers to landscape features on 835 occasions. These are detailed in Appendix 7b.

# THE SEASONS

Eagles and Hills (Donald Watson)

*And doubly welcome be the **Spring**...*

*While corn grows green in **summer** showers...*

*How cheery, thro' her short'ning day
Is **autumn** in her weeds and yellow!...*

*And lang's the night frae e'en to morn-
I'm sure it's **winter** fairly...*

## Introduction

Burns was many things to many people – poet, correspondent, song writer and collector. Although latterly an exciseman, without doubt for the most significant part of his short life he was a farmer! In my view, had he not been 'a son of the soil', forced by circumstances into long, hard days of outdoor toil, he would not have come into such close contact with, and developed an affinity for, all of the aspects of natural history that clearly *did* inspire him in so many of his works, and to some of his most delicate lines. Every passing season brought a new scenario within his poetic view and every leaf, twig, branch, flower or bird had the potential to stimulate his fertile imagery.

While still a boy, he helped his father at their Alloway small-holding until 1766; later at Mount Oliphant, while still in his youth, he was expected to carry out the full range and workload of a grown man. The family later moved to Lochlie near Tarbolton, where with brother Gilbert and his by now ailing father, they again laboured long and hard on a difficult farm. Following their father's death, the brothers moved to Mossgiel, near Mauchline, where they shared the work and tenancy on yet another unfertile farm until 1788; after which Robert moved to Ellisland Farm, just north of Dumfries, where he had, for the first time, sole tenancy and responsibility for the farm's success.

In September 1789, to augment his income, he commenced work as an Excise Officer. The combination of his excise duties and maintaining the farm clearly proved onerous, and by the end of 1791 he was forced to rescind the lease of Ellisland, due largely to failing health and exhaustion. He then moved his family into a house in Dumfries. He died in the town on 21 July 1796.

Thus, although for this relatively short period he had the dual role of farmer-cum-excise officer, for the most part of his life he laboured on the land to earn his living and to sustain his family. The reality of farming and family life was starkly simple during this era. If one did not work, there was nothing to eat, and without food, people died! His appreciation of this basic fact was amplified in his obvious appreciation of food when it was made available.

> Some have meat and cannot eat.
> Some cannot eat that want it:
> But we have meat, and we can eat,
> Sae let the Lord be thankit.

There is ample evidence that Burns was regarded as a good and progressive farmer. Similarly, his attitude towards his farm stock, both sheep and cattle, was one of innovation. Above all it is abundantly clear, too, that he cared sincerely, almost passionately, for the welfare of his stock, horses and working dogs. He viewed them more as fellow creatures on earth, sharing the traumas of food shortage and cold, rather than with the cold pragmatic realism, typical of the average farmer of those times.

It is not unrealistic to suggest that the endocarditis, that eventually resulted in his premature death, stemmed from the social and working conditions pertaining during the time he worked on these various farms.

Primitive implements drawn by animals ensured long exhausting days in the fields. Poorly clothed against the elements, with meagre, vitamin-deficient meals – and equally poor, cold and damp conditions within the dwelling place – almost certainly led to the colic and rheumatic fever that was ever-present from an early age.

As is the case with all working farmers, life becomes entwined, regulated and even dominated by the seasons, the prevailing weather and their repetitive traditional tasks demanded of all those who by design work on the land.

Burns, although at times clearly exhausted by physical work, never seemed to tire of observing nature in all its changing roles as presented throughout the four seasons.

His love of flowers, trees and the birdsong of spring is real and evident. For example, he also wrote the memorable lines to Mrs Dunlop: 'I never hear the solitary whistle of a curlew on a summer noon, or the wild mixing cadence of a troop of grey (golden) plovers on a summer morning without feeling an elevation of the soul.'

'Autumn, benefactor kind' was the vital harvest period, on which would depend the financial solvency for the year to come or a heralding of more potential hardships to be faced. Not only did yields fluctuate widely, but on occasions total crop failures occured. It is extremely difficult in 1996 to totally comprehend that in the spring of 1796, for example, food was so scarce that hundreds of families in Dumfries were starving, without their basic oatmeal, which led to riots on the streets that required military intervention.

Burns did in fact say that winter was his favourite season, and he referred to it more often than any other period of the year. This may seem a paradox, since the houses remained most uncomfortable; stock required to be inside and fed, fuel and water carried to the house. Without a hard stand and proper drainage, outside the cottages and steadings became a virtual quagmire of slime.

Nonetheless, with fewer daylight hours it would indeed have been a relatively peaceful and restful time, compared with the rigours of spring ploughing and sowing, and the stress and physical pain of autumnal harvesting without mechanical aids.

There seems little doubt that Burns actually cherished the winter for quite another reason: that he utilised the short working days to work at the tasks dearest to his heart – his songs and poetry.

> No help, nor hope, nor view had I; nor person to befriend me, O,
> So I must toil, and sweat, and moil, and labour to sustain me, O.
> To plough and sow, to reap and mow, my father bred me early, O;
> For one, he said, to labour bred, was a match for Fortune fairly, O.

His total of 176 specific references to the seasons comprised Spring (29), Summer (58), Autumn (17) and Winter (72).

Burns mentions every month of the year a total of 222 times – except April and September (see Appendix 7). May was clearly popular being referred to on 27 occasions. In the same appendix I have listed his 349 references to weather and other related natural phenomena.

## *SPRING* (29)

**'A Winter Night'** (poem):
>That in the merry months o *Spring*…

**Address To The Shade of Thomson**
>While virgin *Spring* by Eden's flood
>Unfolds her tender mantle green…

**'A Lass Wi A Tocher'** (song):
>Ilk *spring* they're new deckit wi' bonie white yowes!

**'My Bonnie Bell'** (song):
>The smiling *Spring* (repeated)comes in rejoicing

**'By Allan Stream'** (song):
>The haunt o *Spring*'s the primrose-brae,

**'Craigieburn Wood'** (song – 2nd version):
>But a' the pride o *Spring*'s return

**'On Captain M. Henderson'** (elegy):
>Mourn, *Spring*, thou darling of the year!

**On Mrs. Riddell's Birthday** (impromptu):
>*Spring*, summer, autumn, cannot match me

**'John Barleycorn'** (song):
>But the chearful *Spring* came kindly on,

**'Phillis the Fair'** (song):
>Viewing the breathing *Spring*, forth I did fare.

**'On the Death of Robert Riddell'** (sonnet):
>Thou young-eyed *Spring*, (repeated), gay in thy verdant stole…

**'The Brigs of Ayr'** (poem):
>Sweet female Beauty hand in hand with *Spring*

**'The Bonie Moor-Hen'** (song):
>Her plumage outlustred the pride o the *Spring*,

**Written in Hermitage at Friars Carse**
>Peace, the tenderest flower of *Spring*…

**'Lament For James, Earl of Glencairn'**
>Nae leaf o' mine shall greet the *Spring*...

**'Lament Of Mary Queen of Scots'**
>And the next flowers, that deck the *spring*,
>Bloom on my peaceful grave.

**'The Ploughman's Life'** (song):
>As I was a-wand'ring ae morning in *spring*...

**'Tam Lin'** (ballad):
>As blythe's a bird in *spring*.

**'Craigieburn Wood'** (verses):
>But the pride o' the *spring* on the Craigieburn Wood

**'The Jolly Gauger'** (song):
>Sae blythe the beggar ... like ony bird in *spring*

**'John Barleycorn'** (alternative lines in variants in **Kilmarnock Edition**)
>The *spring* time came with kindly warmth

**'Now Spring Has Clad The Grove In Green'** (song):
>Now *Spring* had clad the grove in green...

**'Philly and Willy'** (song):
>The little swallow's wanton wing,
>Tho' wafting o'er the flowery *spring*...

**'O, Wat Ye Wha's In Yon Town?'** (song):
>And doubly welcome be the *Spring*...

**'O, Were My Love'** (song):
>O, were my love yon lilac fair
>Wi purple blossoms to the *spring*...

**'The Bonie Lad That's Far Awa'** (song):
>And *spring* will cleed the birken shaw...

**'Young Peggy'** (song):
>As blooming *spring* unbends the brow
>Of surly, savage winter.

**'Epistle to William Simpson'**
>But boils up in a *spring*-tide flood?

**Address To The Unco Guid**
>Each *spring*, its various bias:


## *SUMMER* (58)


**Address To Edinburgh**
>Gay as the gilded *summer* sky...

**Address To The Shade of Thomson**
> While *Summer*, with a matron grace,
> Retreats to Dryburgh's cooling shade...

**'Adown Winding Nith** (song):
> The bloom of a fine *summer*'s day!

**'Blythe Was She'** (song):
> Her smile was like a *simmer* morn:

**'My Bonnie Bell'** (song):
> The flowery Spring leads sunny *Summer*...

**'On The Late Miss Burnet of Monboddo'** (elegy):
> In vain ye flaunt in *summer*'s pride, ye groves!

**'Thou Gloomy December'** (song):
> Till the last leaf o' the *summer* is flown...

**'On Mrs Riddell's Birthday'**
> Spring, *Summer*, Autumn, cannot match me...

**'John Barleycorn'** (alternative lines)
> The *summer* came with sultry heat...

**'By Allan Stream'** (song):
> The *Summer* joys the flocks to follow.

**'To Miss Isabella Macleod'** (verses):
> The *summer* sun the swallow:

**'Highland Mary'** (song):
> There *Summer* first unfald her robes,
> And there the longest tarry!

**'On The Seas And Far Away'** (song):
> When in *summer* noon I faint...

**'Bessy and Her Spinnin-Wheel'** (song):
> While laigh decends the *summer* sun...

**'The Holy Fair'** (verses):
> Upon a *simmer* Sunday morn
> When Nature's face is fair...

**'The Auld Farmer's New-Year Salutation To His Auld Mare, Maggie'**
> For that, or *simmer*...

**'Wandering Willie'**
> Welcome now *Simmer*, and Welcome my Willie...

**'Lassie Wi The Lint-White Locks'** (song):
> And when the welcome *simmer* shower

**'To The Weaver's Gin You Go'** (song):
        As *simmer* days were lang;

**'O, Were I On Parnassus Hill'** (verses):
        Then come, sweet Muse, inspire my lay!
        For a' the lee lang *simmer*'s day...

**'I'm O'er Young To Marry Yet'** (song):
        I'll aulder be by *simmer*, Sir...

**'The Country Lass'** (song):
        In *simmer*, when the hay was mawn...

**'Logan Braes'** (song):
        Like Logan to the *simmer* sun.

**'William Creech'** (lament):
        May sprout like *simmer* puddock-stools...

**'For James, Earl of Glencairn'** (lament):
        Nae *simmer* sun exalt my bloom...

**'To J. Lapraik'** (Second Epistle):
        Now comes the sax-and-twentieth *simmer*...

**'The Birks Of Aberfeldie'**Stanzas:
        Now *simmer* blinks on flow'ry braes,

**'To Mr McAdam'** (verses):
        O mony flow'ry *simmers*...

**'Ay Waukin, O'** (song):
        *Simmer*'s a pleasant time:

**'Halloween'** (verses):
        The *simmer* had been cauld and wat...

**'Lady Mary Ann'** (song):
        The *simmer* is gane when the leaves they were green...

**'On Captain M. Henderson'** (elegy):
        Thou, *Simmer*, while each corny spear
        Shoots up its head...

**'O, Were I On Parnassus Hill'**
        For a' the lee-lang *simmer*'s day

**'To Daundon Me'** (ballad):
        The *simmer* lilies bloom in snaw,

**'John Barleycorn'** (song):
        The sultry suns of *Summer* came...

**'The Ploughman's Life'** (alternative)
        As I was s wand'ring ae *midsummer* e'enin...

**'Of Mary Queen of Scots'** (lament):
>O! soon, to me, may *summer* suns
>Nae mair light up the morn!

**'Lassie wi' the Lintwhite Locks'** (song):
>And when the welcome *simmer* shower…

**'O, Let Me In This Ae Night'** (song):
>The bird that charm'd his *summer* day…

**'O, That's The Lassie O My Heart'** (song):
>(Sweet) As dews o' *summer* weeping,
>In tears the rose-buds steeping!

**'On a Bank of Flowers'** (song):
>On a bank of flowers in a *summer*'s day,
>For *summer* lightly drest…

**'On The Birth of A Posthumous Child'**
>Fair on the *summer* morn;

**'The Brigs of Ayr'** (poem):
>And *Summer*, with his fervid-beaming eye;

**'The Day Returns'** (song):
>Ne'er *summer*-sun was half sae sweet.

**'The Lazy Mist'** (song):
>And all the gay foppery of *Summer* is flown;

**'The Twa Dogs'** (A Tale):
>Thro Winter's cauld, or *Simmer*'s heat;

**'The Twa Herds'** (poem):
>These five and twenty *simmers* past…

**'The Winter It Is Past'** (song):
>The winter it is past, and the *simmer* comes at last…

**'Their Groves o Sweet Myrtle'** (song):
>Where bright-beaming *summers* exalt the perfume!

**'Thine am I, My Faithful Fair'** (song):
>Love the cloudless *summer*'s sun,

**'Epistle To W. Simpson'**
>Whether the *summer* kindly warms,
>Wi' life an light…

**'Wandering Willie'** (song):
>Welcome now *Simmer*, and welcome my Willie
>The simmer to Nature, my Willie to me!

**'Fair Eliza'** (song):

Not the little sporting fairy,
All beneath the *simmer* moon...

**'Below Picture'** (verses):
Bright as a cloudless *summer* sun...

**'Where Are The Joys'** (song):
Is it that *Summer*'s forsaken our vallies...

**'The Gallant Weaver'** (song):
While corn grows green in *summer* showers...

**'The Humble Petition of Bruar Water'** (verses):
In flaming *summer*-pride...

**'The Brigs of Ayr'** (poem):
The bees, rejoicing o'er their *summer* toils...

## *AUTUMN* (17)

**Address To The Shade of Thomson** (with one alternative)
While *Autumn*, benefactor kind...

**'My Bonie Bell'** (song):
The yellow *autumn* presses near,

**'By Allan Stream'** (song):
How cheery, thro' her short'ning day,
Is *autumn* in her weeds o' yellow!

**'On Captain M.Henderson'** (elegy):
Thou *Autumn*, wi' thy yellow hair,
In grief thy sallow mantle tear!

**'John Barleycorn'** (song):
The sober *Autumn* enter'd mild,

Alternative lines to above in **Kilmarnock Edition**
The *Autumn* came with freshning breeze...

**'On Mrs Riddell's Birthday'** (verses):
Spring, Summer, *Autumn* cannot match me'.

**'Of Mary Queen of Scots'** (lament):
Nae mair, to me, the *autumn* winds
Wave o'er the yellow corn!

**'My Nanie's Awa'** (song):
Come *Autumn*, sae pensive in yellow and grey...

**'Now Westlin Winds'** (song):
Bring *Autumn*'s pleasant weather;
Not *Autumn* to the farmer...

**'O Were My Love'** (song):
> By *Autumn* wild and Winter rude!

**'The Brigs of Ayr'** (poem):
> Led yellow *Autumn* wreath'd with nodding corn;

**'The Gloomy Night Is Garthering Fast'** (song):
> The *Autumn* mourns her rip'ning corn

**'The Humble Petition of Bruar Water'** (verses):
> The robin pensive *Autumn* cheer

**'The Lazy Mist'** (song):
> As *autumn* to winter resigns the pale year!

**'The Lass o Ballochmyle'** (song):
> And sweet is night in *autumn* mild,


## *WINTER* (72)


**'A Winter Night'** (poem):
> Or silly sheep wha bide this brattle
> O *winter* war...

**'Address To The Deil'**
> Ae dreary, windy, *winter* night...

**'Address To The Shade of Thomson'**
> While maniac *Winter* rages o'er
> The hills whence classic Yarrow flows...

**'And Maun I Still On Menie Doat'** (song):
> Come *Winter*, with thine angry howl...

**'My Bonie Bell'** (song):
> An surly *winter* grimly flies...

> Then in his turn comes gloomy *Winter*...

**'The Winter Of Life'** (song):
> On *winter* blasts awa...

**'On Captain Mathew Henderson'** (elegy):
> Thou *Winter*, hurling thro the air
> The roaring blast...

**'Thou Gloomy December'** (song):
> Wild as the *winter* now tearing the forest...

**'On The Seas And Far Away'** (song):
> When *Winter* rules with boundless power...

**'Lassie Wi The Lint-White Locks'**
>And when the howling *wintry* blast…

**'Forlorn My Love, No Comfort Near'**
>Around me scowls a *wintry* sky…

**'I'm O'er Young to Marry Yet'** (song):
>The nights are lang in *winter*, Sir…

**On Mrs. Riddell's Birthday** (impromptu):
>Old *Winter*, with his frosty beard…

**'Of Mary Queen of Scots'** (lament):
>And in the narrow house o' death,
>Let *winter* round me rave;

**'Man Was Made To Mourn'** (song):
>I've seen yon weary *winter*-sun…

**'Montgomerie's Peggy'** (song):
>Twice forty times return;
>And *winter* nights were dark and rainy,

**'My Nanie's Awa'** (song):
>The dark, dreary *Winter*, and wild-driving snaw…

**'O, Let Me In This Ae Night'** (song):
>Thou hear'st the *winter* wind and weet:

**'Logan Braes'** (song):
>Like drumlie *winter*, dark and drear…

**'O Wat Ye Wha's in Yon Town'** (song):
>Tho' raging *winter* rent the air,

**'O Were My Love'** (song):
>By autumn wild, and *Winter* rude!

**'The Bonnie Lad That's Far Awa'** (song):
>It's no the frosty *winter* wind…

**'Robin Shure In Hairst'** (song):
>Robin promis'd me A' my *winter* vittle:

**'Scotch Drink'** (poem):
>An' hardly, in a *winter* season,
>E'er spier her (my Muse's) price…

**'For The Sake O Somebody'** (song):
>I could wake a *winter* night
>For the sake of Somebody.

**'The Braes of Ballochmyle'**
>How in your *wintry* beds, ye flowers,
>Again ye'll flourish fresh and fair;

**'On Death of R. Riddell'** (sonnet):
> More welcome were to me grim *Winter*'s wildest roar!

**'On Hearing A Thrush Sing In His Morning Walk'** (sonnet):
> See aged *Winter* 'mid his surly reign…

**'Castle Gordon'** (verses):
> Never bound by *Winter*'s chains…

**'Tam Samson's Elegy'**
> When *Winter* muffles up his cloak…

**'The Author's Earnest Cry and Prayer'** (verses):
> Picking her pouch as bare as *winter*…

**'The Brigs of Ayr'** (poem):
> Potatoe-bings are snuggèd up frae skaith
> O coming *Winter*'s biting, frosty breath;

**'The Day Returns'** (song):
> Tho *winter* wild in tempest toil'd,

**'The Gloomy Night Is Gathering Fast'** (song):
> The Autumn mourns her rip'ning corn
> By early *Winter*'s ravage torn;

**'The Jolly Beggars'** (a Cantata):
> What tho', with hoary locks, I must stand the *winter* shocks,

**'The Lazy Mist'** (song):
> As Autumn to *Winter* resigns the pale year!

**'The Twa Dogs'** (a tale):
> Tho *Winter*'s cauld, or Simmer's heat;

**'The Winter It Is Past'** (song):
> The *winter* it is past, and the simmer comes at last…

**'The Young Highland Rover'** (song):
> Like *winter* on me seizes…

**'Third Epistle to J. Lapraik'**
> I mean your ingle-side to guard
> Ae *winter* night.

**'To a Mouse'** (poem):
> An weary *winter* comin' fast…

**'The Winter of Life'** (verses):
> Sinks in Time's *wintry* rage.

**'My Nanie, O'**
> The *wintry* sun the day has clos'd,
> And I'll awa to Nanie, O.

**'Lament for W Creech'**:
> To thole the *winter*'s sleety dribble, An' cranreuch cauld!
> Streekit out to bleach in *winter* snaw;

**'Epistle to W Simpson'**
> Ev'n *winter* bleak has charms to me...

**'Up In The Morning Early'** (song):
> Sae loud and shill's I hear the blast,
> I'm sure it's *winter* fairly...

> When a' the hills are cover'd wi' snaw,
> I'm sure it's *winter* fairly...

> And lang's the night frae e'en to morn,
> I'm sure its *winter* fairly.

**'Wandering Willie'** (song):
> Loud tho the *Winter* blew cauld at our parting...

**'Where Are The Joys'** (song):
> And grim, surly *Winter* is near?

**'Tho Women's Minds'** (song):
> Tho' women's minds like *winter* winds

**'Young Peggy'** (song):
> As blooming Spring unbends the brow
> Of surly, savage *Winter*.

**'To The Guidwife of Wauchope House'**
> Wi' merry dance on *winter* days...

**'The Vision'** (poem):
> The sun had clos'd the *winter* day...

**'Winter: A Dirge'** (poem):
> The *wintry* west extends his blast...

> The joyless *winter*-day, Let others fear...

**'Lovely Davies'** (song):
> When *winter*-bound the wave is...

**'Election Ballad'**
> When all his *wintry* billows pour
> Against the Buchan Bullers.

**'The Brigs of Ayr'** (poem):
> 'Twas when the stacks get on their *winter*-hap...

**'My Girl She's Airy'** (song):
> And oh, for the joys of a long *winter* night!!!

**'On Mrs Riddell's Birthday'** (verses):
>  And *Winter* once rejoiced in glory…

**'The Brigs of Ayr'** (verses):
>  But twa-three *winters* will inform ye better.

**'The Bonnie Lad That's Far Awa'** (song):
>  O, weary *Winter* soon will pass

**'Epistle To William Simpson'**
>  Or *Winter* howls, in gusty storms,
>  The lang, dark night!

**'The Brigs of Ayr'** (poem):
>  Then *Winter*'s time-bleach'd locks did hoary show…

**'The Lass o Ballochmyle'** (song):
>  Thro weary *winter*'s wind and rain
>  With joy, with rapture, I would toil…

**'Where, Braving Angry Winter's Storms'** (song):
>  Where, braving angry *winter*'s storms,

**'The Cotter's Saturday Night'** (poem):
>  November chill blaws loud wi angry sugh;
>  The short'ning *winter*-day is near a close;

**'On The Death of Lord President Dundas'**
>  Ye howling winds, and *wintry* swelling waves…

**'Strathallan's Lament'**
>  Turbid torrents *wintry*-swelling,
>  Roaring by my lonely care!

*Winter*

# BIRDS

Song Thrush (Keith Brockie)

*Go on, sweet bird, and soothe my care,*
*Thy tuneful notes will hush Despair;*
*Thy plaintive warblings void of art*
*Thrill sweetly thro my aching heart.*

*I never hear the loud solitary whistle of the Curlew*
*in a summer noon, or the wild, mixing cadence*
*of a troop of grey plover in an Autumnal-morning,*
*without feeling an elevation of soul.*

121

# Introduction

Birds have long provided 'stock in trade' material and inspiration for writers, artists and especially poets.

Homer and Anacreon were aware of, and wrote on, for example, bird migration; and arguably the greatest history book of all times, *The Bible*, specifically mentions some forty of the four hundred species likely to have featured in the Holy Lands. The fourteenth century Welsh poet, Daffyddap Gwilym and his English contemporary Chaucer, both waxed lyrically on birds. Shakespeare was able to refer to over 60 species, Wordsworth 39, and Sir Walter Scott 46. Other past poets worthy of special consideration in an ornithological context include Tennyson, Thomas Hardy, John Clare and W H Davies.

That Burns was able to specifically list accurately some 39 species, and mention precisely two other family groups, was highly commendable. I have accredited him with at least describing another two species. Added to the non-specific references, he mentions birds in one form or another no fewer than 328 times. Burns as one would expect 'used' birds throughout his works in many different ways, ranging from the obscure and at times bawdy jocularity to sincere pathos; even anxiety for birds suffering from cold in winter and being wounded during shooting forays. He demonstrated direct observation of species with the eye, if not entirely and specifically of a trained naturalist, then certainly of the 'farmer countryman', frequently displaying knowledge of distribution, behavioural and biological facets including on migration, that were most certainly enlightened for the era in which he lived.

Some species were utilised to amplify and ascribe the current superstitious beliefs, others as descriptive of individual people, colour, moods and politics. His most penetratingly effective use of birds is in his large collection of often very sad love songs, where the 'environmental sprites' are at times given human thoughts or portray deep emotions.

On a purely numerical analysis one could be led to believe that Burns had a favourite bird in the Linnet, with some eighteen references. Most naturalists, and certainly ornithologists, do admit to having 'a favourite'. My own very personal view is that, in common with many farm workers – especially ploughmen even today – his favourite would almost certainly have been the Skylark:

> Where are the joys I hae met in the morning,
> That danc'd to the lark's early sang?

(A concise checklist of the birds mentioned in Burns' writings can be found in Appendix 5. For each species the English, scientific, Scots and Scottish Gaelic names are listed, and I have also summarised the present (1995) status of each species, with particular reference to Ayrshire and Dumfries-shire. Following the

English name I have given the total number of records in small brackets.)

In the more detailed species notes below, I discuss more fully the records and have given as support such historical references that are readily available in the literature. Where possible I have attempted to discuss the status of these species, as likely to pertain in the mid-eighteenth century and as a comparison to the comments in the check list.

I have also included three species in square brackets [Greylag Goose *Anser anser*; Sparrowhawk *Accipiter nisus*; Stock Dove *Columba oenas*], the standard ornithological practice where records retain a possible element of doubt; and I have discussed two bird groups referred to by Burns.

With the benefit of hindsight, and aided by the massive advances of ornithological expertise, close examination has forced strict adjudication and subsequent rejection of three species mentioned specifically by Burns *only* in the context that they were intended. These are: *Grey Plover*; *Stock Dove* and *Woodlark*.

It is noteworthy that, in addition to the more precise use of named bird species, which is the main focus of discussion in the species notes below, Burns also used 'birds' in descriptive terms without being specific. For example he used *bird* and *birdie* no fewer than 62 times; *birring* (as in flight) once; *fowl* or *fowler* (6); *nest* and *nestling* (20); *pouts* or *poult* (for chicks) once; *songster* (5); and *warble*, *warbled*, *warbler* and *warbling* on no fewer than 13 occasions; associations of *wing* (25); others 13 (all to describe *birdsong* or *singing*); a total of 146 references.

It should also be noted that his use of the word 'rook' did not only refer to birds, but was used to describe an 'impudent person or cheat'. Similarly, in *Caledonia*: 'A flight of bold eagles' refers to Roman Legions. In the same work 'harpy-raven' refers to invading Danes. His two references to 'vulture', while derived from the bird species, were meant to imply 'vulturine' behaviour in man.

## BITTERN *Botaurus stellaris*

**Local:** Bittour; Buttour; Bog-drum; Miredrum

Burns mentions this now very rare species only once, in his **'Elegy on Captain Matthew Henderson'**:

> Ye *bitterns*, till the quagmire reels,
> Rair for his sake!

Dr Archbald, among his *Curiosities at Dumfries*, written about 1684, includes '*Bittour* making a great sound in the summer's evenings and mornings'.

Although Burns used the word rair (roar), the male bittern – more often heard than seen – has indeed a most distinctive song known as 'booming'. Early breeding records were obtained from near Mauchline Ayrshire in 1782; the better known breeding places were near Lochmaben and in the Lochar Moss, Dumfriesshire. Although formerly not uncommon, and given protection as a hawking quarry, it decreased as a breeding species as its habitat, mainly tall reed beds (phragmites), were systematically drained to improve land for agriculture.

## HERON *Ardea cinerea*

**Local:** Long-necky Hern; Long Necky; Jenny Hern; Jinny Cranes; Heronsheugh; Craigie; Crane

The first reference to the Heron was in the song **'Now Westlin Winds'** composed in the summer of 1775.

> The Woodcock haunts the lonely dells,
> The soaring *hern* the fountains:

Burns was obviously familiar with the heron and mentions it again in his outstanding natural history list contained in the **'Elegy on Captain Matthew Henderson'**:

> Mourn, sooty coots, and speckled teals;
> Ye fisher *herons*, watching eels;

It is doubly interesting that he recorded the heron as 'watching eels'. Eels frequent the Rivers Ayr and Nith, and their tributaries in large numbers and remain the main food item of these birds. When writing to Robert Graham Esq., of Fintry, whom Burns met during his Highland tour of 1784, the poet included the lines: 'The grave, sage *hern* thus easy picks his frog…'

Similarly, the mention of an important prey item, the frog, indicates that Burns was either personally observant or at least knowledgeable in some of the habits of the heron.

## MUTE SWAN *Cygnus olor*

**Local:** Tame swan

Burns first mentions the mute swan in the song **'And Maun I Still on Menie Doat'**. There appears some dispute about when it was written, but Kinsley has attributed it to the period when Burns was in Edinburgh.

> The stately *swan* majestic swims,
> And ev'ry thing is blest but I.

Writing about one Ann Masterton, daughter of Burns' friend and composer, in undated verses called **'Beware o Bonnie Ann'**, he compared her pale complexion to the white plumage of the swan.

Her een sae bright, like stars by night,
Her skin is like the *swan*.

He again versified with the swan's beautiful shape in the human connotation with the song sent to Johnson from Mauchline in 1788, **'Mally's Meek, Mally's Sweet'**

Her yellow hair, beyond compare,
Comes tumbling down her *swan*-like neck...

The reference, 'Will find that his *Swans* are but geese' is not in the context of a natural history record but was a political point contained in his Dumfries Epigrams.

A version of **'John Anderson, My Jo'** in *MMC* included the line 'I'm breastit like a *swan*...'

Three species of swan may be present in Scotland during winter. It is, in my view, safe to assume that Burns was referring to the one resident species – the Mute Swan – especially where he refers to its 'majestic swimming'.

There are no acceptable records from Ayrshire of either Whooper Swan *Cygnus cygnus* nor Bewick's Swan *Cygnus columbianus*, during the period that Burns lived there. 'Swans' are mentioned as coming to the Lochar Moss, Dumfriesshire in 1792 and probably they were Whooper. Unless obtained by shooting, it appears that field ornithology had not progressed sufficiently to allow accurate identification. Bewick's Swan was not in fact specifically described in Scotland until 1827-28.


**[GREYLAG GOOSE** *Anser anser*]

**Local:** Laggard; Laggie; Wild Coose; Grey Goose

Greylag Geese as a species are common in a feral state, and are regarded as the principal ancestors of most forms of domestic or farmyard geese. Greylags were probably still breeding in the wild in Dumfriesshire during Burns' lifetime. In 1684, the following statement was made concerning Loch Urr near Moniaive: 'In this loch there is an old ruinous castle, with planting of sauch or willow-trees for the most part about it, where many wild geese and other waterfowls breed' (Young, J.G. *in litt*). During the same period they were also breeding further west in Galloway, and in 1710 were said to 'haunt Loch Leven' while elsewhere in Scotland they were said to be in 'thousands'. Both Statistical Accounts mention them as winter visitors to Ayrshire, but especially to Dumfriesshire.

In Dumfriesshire, 'grey geese' have from time immemorial roosted on the sands of the Nith estuary and, even at the beginning of the twentieth century, the records on specific species identification were far from reliable. Geese, especially  young ones, were notoriously difficult to identify then, considering not only the standard of science in those days but also the general lack of useful books on identification.

While Burns was living in Dumfries, and travelling regularly on excise duty, it would have been difficult to avoid seeing and hearing 'grey geese'. Being evocative birds, it is surprising that they are not mentioned more frequently and elegantly in the Poet's works.

It remains a moot point, whether or not the resident breeding Greylag were the remnants of a native Scottish breeding population, as in South Uist, or whether they were the subject of deliberate introduction and escapes; or indeed were founded by wild migratory Icelandic stock, some of which, perhaps through injury for example, remained eventually to nest. Whatever their origin, they were indeed present, the eggs were collected and hatched out under domestic fowl and provided a feature of eighteenth century farmyards. They were also much sought after as a security measure; geese act and serve very well in the role of 'guard dogs'. Not only are they alert and will give warning of approaching strangers but they are also quite capable of mounting a physical attack.

Burns' comment in the **'Address of Beelzebub'**: 'Frightin awa your ducks and *geese*' certainly refer to the keeping of domestic fowl and poultry round the farm. His letter to George Thomson with the rather bawdy verses of the **'Cumnock Psalms'** refers to: 'I spied a *grey goose* and a gled', but this was meant in a sexual connotation rather than any natural history context. In his **'A Dream'**:

> Or faith! I fear, that, wi the *geese*,
> I shortly boost to pasture
> I' the craft some day.

In **'Brose and Butter'** 'A *goose* is hollow within' may not be strictly relevant.

Writing to the Rev. George Husband Baird in 1791, Burns referred to 'the wild-*goose* heights'. Similarly, when in correspondence with James Johnson in 1788 he mentioned 'a wild-*goose* chase'. These are figures of speech but the use of the term 'wild' is certainly worthy of note.

## TEAL *Anas crecca*

**Local:** Jay-Teal

The only reference to this small dabbling duck – which was a common breeding species with its numbers augmented during autumn migrations and with a large wintering population in the Inner Solway especially on Lochar Moss – is to be found in his **'Elegy on Captain Matthew Henderson'**, 'Mourn, sooty coots, and speckled *teals*…'

## MALLARD *Anas platyrhynchos*

**Local:** Mireduck; Moss-Duck; Grey Duck; Wild Duck; Deuck; Deuk;
Flapper (a general term applied to all species of wildfowl when in a flightless state);

The only two specific mentions – of a species that is generally accepted to have been the most common of all the ducks likely to be present in Ayrshire and Dumfriesshire during Burns' sojourn – was in his writings to Robert Graham Esq., of Fintry, 'And thinks the *mallard* a sad, worthless dog…'; and in a letter of 1788 to Mrs Dunlop, where he wrote 'or *Mallards*, creatures with which I could almost exchange lives at any-time…'

Burns refers to 'ducks' and 'deucks' without any precise specific ident-ification. Although the terms have long been used to generalise, the most common useage was to describe the Mallard or Wild Duck and I have included them as such. For the sake of completeness I might add that in his **'Elegy on Captain Matthew Henderson'** he refers to:-

> Ye *duck* and *drake*, wi' airy wheels
> Circling the lake;

In Upper Nithsdale, at least, the term 'drake' was also synonomous with Mallard, and in his **'Address to the Deil'** he uses the line:-

> Awa ye squatter'd like a *drake*,
> On whistling wings

He also refers to the young 'ducks' in the song **'And Maun I Still on Menie Doat'**: 'Amang the reeds the *ducklings* cry.' His references to 'duck' are in his original **'Address of Beelzebub'**: 'Frightin awa your *ducks* an geese.' This obviously refers to the established practice in Burns' time of keeping both ducks and geese as domestic fowl. Not only did they provide eggs and fresh meat but the geese also served as a form of added security on the farm.

In the song **'The Deuk's Dang O'er My Daddie'**, Burns describes a nagging wife beating her husband with a duck! 'The *deuk*'s dang o'er my daddie, O!'


## RED KITE  *Milvus milvus*

**Local:** Gled; Glead

Burns mentions this species in the well known song **'Killiecrankie'**:

> Or I had fed an Athole *gled*,
> On the braes o Killiecrankie, O!

The historical aspect of this song is vital to my decision to include the Kite as a fully identified species. It was the reworking of an old Jacobite song, about the battle fought on 27 July 1689 between the Highlanders – led by Claverhouse and Dundee – and the Anglo-Dutch troops commanded by Mackay of Scourie. Burns sets the words as being spoken by a soldier in the field. There is ample evidence that the Red Kite – which was then very widely distributed – had the awful reputation of feeding from the bodies of dead soldiers. There are no records to suggest that Buzzard *Buteo buteo* did so, thus we may assume that, when he used the local name 'gled' he was in this case referring to Red Kite.

In this case, with an acceptable record from outwith the area in which Burns lived, it is irrelevant that the historical records of Red Kite from lowland Scotland during that era seem less reliable.

The reference to the gled in his letter to George Thomson of September 1794, **'Cumnock Psalms'** is not of natural history significance, but appears to have a definite sexual interpretation.


# EAGLE spp

|  |  |
|---|---|
| Sea Eagle | *Haliaeetus albicilla* |
| Golden Eagle | *Aquila chrysaetos* |

**Local:** Erne; Sea Eagle; Yirn; Yearn; White-Tailed Eagle

The poet made several references to 'eagles', some obviously in the human connotation; for example in his **'Address to Edinburgh'**: 'There learning, with his *eagle* eyes'. The reference to 'A flight of bold *eagles* from Adria's strand' in the song **'Caledonia'**, is in fact referring to Roman legions (soldiers) whose symbol was the eagle.

A fragment, thought to have been written by Burns, has no ornithological connotation; in fact it relates to the defeat of the Austrians by Dumourier at Jemappes, 1792:

> The black-headed *eagle*,
> As keen as a beagle,
> He hunted o'er height and owre howe;
> But fell in a trap,
> On the braes o Gemappe,
> E'en let him come out as he dow.

His reference to eagle in the alternative lines of **'Election Ballad for Westerha''** is a figure of political speech but the poem to Deborah Davies, whom Burns met at Friars Carse, Dumfriesshire: **'Lovely Davies'** – contains a more acceptable reference to the species:

> The *eagle*'s gaze alone surveys
> The sun's meridian splendors.

In 1784, when he was touring Clackmannanshire, Burns visited Sir William Murray and wrote a poem **'On Scaring some Water-Fowl In Loch Turit'**:

> The *eagle*, from the cliffy brow,
> Marking you his prey below,
> In his breast no pity dwells,
> Strong necessity compels:

and in the renowned **'Elegy on Captain Matthew Henderson'**, Burns wrote evocatively 'Ye cliffs, the haunts of sailing *yearns*'; while in Friar's Carse

House near Dumfries, he penned:

> Dangers, *eagle*-pinioned, bold,
> Soar round each cliffy hold;

There is now a problem in assigning his accounts to a particular species. During Burns' lifetime both Sea Eagle and Golden Eagle were breeding widely in Scotland, including Ayrshire and Dumfriesshire. Significantly, Sea Eagle was not, as the name might infer, restricted to coastal cliffs but was just as likely to be present in inland haunts.

The Sea Eagle had become extinct in Ayrshire as a breeding species by 1871, the last known breeding site being on Ailsa Craig. It is likely that Sea Eagles were still breeding successfully at Loch Skene near Moffat, Dumfriesshire in 1792 and into the nineteenth century.

Golden Eagles were certainly still breeding in Ayrshire in the mid-eighteenth century. Indeed, it was stated by Symson in 1684, that 'Eagles, both grey and black, bred in Galloway'. In addition from Minnigaff, Kirkcudbright in 1684 it is recorded that 'the eagles are in plenty, both the large gray and the black' inferring that both Golden and Sea Eagle were involved.

The presumption must be that both eagle species were present during the latter part of the eighteenth century in south-west Scotland. Thereafter, both species declined and became extinct as breeding species, largely due to intense persecution by shepherds, game preservers and egg collectors.

It is not known where or how Burns gained his experience of eagles. He did not specifically mention them in his diary of the 'Highland Tour', where the same problem of identification would have existed. He may, of course, have gained insight from the limited literature of those days. My own view is that eagles would almost certainly have been breeding at a higher density during this period than is the case at present. Carrion feeding on/or the predation of lambs and goats by eagles although usually greatly exaggerated (the black loss), would be one of the major topics of conversation wherever farmers and shepherds met at fairs, markets, gatherings or in hostelries.


## [SPARROWHAWK *Accipiter nisus*]

**Local:** Blue hawk; Woodhawk

There is little of historical significance regarding this hawk in southern Scotland during Burns' era. That they were present in Scotland is not in doubt, having been recorded first in 1235 at Melrose and recorded by Sibbald in 1684 and Pennant in 1789.

A true woodland hawk, even where numerous it remains less conspicuous than the other small raptors, hence it has been consistently under-recorded until relatively recently. The most likely scenario is that, being present at least from an early date, the hawks would have utilised the new woodlands of the early eighteenth century as they became semi-mature, then like all raptorial birds, towards the end of the century, they too undoubtably suffered massive persecution in the interests of game preservation.

More than any other 'hawk' the sparrowhawk was regarded quite correctly as a killer of other birds as its main prey. Being bold, it was frequently seen at the 'doocot' and to take poultry (poults) from the open field or farmyard.

Burns did not mention it specifically, but considering his quotations of 'hawks' killing birds – without mention of the very distinctive attributes and features of the other two smaller raptors, Kestrel *Falco tinnunculus* and Merlin *Falco columbarius*, likely to be contesting the available space and prey – there is, I believe, every justification of my including it here as a possible bird of his time.

In his **'On Sensibility'** Burns talks about the Woodlark *Lullula arborea* (ie Tree Pipit *Anthus trivialis*) as a prey item of a raptor, presumably in open woodland habitat.

> Hear the woodlark charm the forest,
> Telling o'er his little joys;
> But alas! a prey the surest
> To each pirate of the skies!

While it does not absolutely exclude Kestrel or Merlin it certainly is indicative of Sparrowhawk. Similarly in the song **'Bonnie Jean'**:

> But *hawks* will rob the tender joys,
> That bless the little lintwhite's nest...

Here he is specifically mentioning 'hawk' rather than owl or falcon. Perhaps the most supportive comment is in the song **'Phillis the Fair'** where he says:

> Down in the shady walk, doves cooing were;
> I mark'd the cruel *hawk* caught in a snare.

The use of 'shady walk' is interesting: it infers a closed woodland canopy that would not be suitable for some other raptors; and again, the use of the descriptive 'hawk' but especially the final words 'cruel hawk caught in a snare'.

Game preservers, dove and pigeon keepers, among others, have long attempted to control sparrowhawks by trapping, and running snares have been used since mediaeval times up to the present day to take the Sparrowhawk specifically. These hawks, more than any other species, regularly use elevated 'plucking posts' – where they take the prey item after capture and literally pluck it clean – before eating it themselves, presenting it to their mate, or feeding young. Obviously, this causes a 'litter' of very obvious feathers. This has long been exploited as a place to site snares. These were usually made from strands of horse hair formed into a running noose with a slip knot, and it was not unusual for ten to twenty being placed where the hawk might entangle its talons and thus be captured.

Burns continues in similar vein in the song **'O, Let Me In This Ae Night'**:

The bird that charm'd his summer day,
And now the cruel fowler's prey...

This could of course equally refer to other aspects of bird fowling – seabirds for example – but it does however mention 'summer day' which excludes some forms of seasonal hunting. It is worthy of note, and it is on record, that the same 'nets' that were used to catch seabirds and wildfowl in season, were also deployed to catch Sparrowhawks, which habitually hunt on a regular route round wood edges, down rides, and in clearings, and are sufficiently predictable (unlike other raptors), to be taken in nets.

Finally, in the song **'How Cruel are the Parents'**:

The ravening *hawk* pursuing,
The trembling dove thus flies:

While not allied totally to specific Sparrowhawk behaviour, it at least supports the birds inclusion here – albeit in brackets.


## BUZZARD *Buteo buteo*

**Local:** Buzzard-Hawk; Bizzard Gled; Puttock; Glead; Gled

Burns referred to this species in his **'Heron Election: Ballad Forth The Trogger'** in 1796: 'Here is Satan's picture, like a *bizzard gled.*'

There has been a great deal of ornithological confusion, with old records referring to Red Kite and what was then known as the Common Buzzard. We can first of all eliminate from the present discussion the other two Buzzard species that occur in Scotland, Honey Buzzard *Pernis apivorus* and Rough-Legged Buzzard *Buteo lagopus*. Both were exceedingly scarce migrants and/or winter visitors and unlikely to feature in literature during Burns' lifetime. There were in fact no Ayrshire records of Honey Buzzard till one was trapped at Muirkirk in 1863; and in Dumfriesshire the first record was of one shot at Drumlandrig in 1833. Similarly, the standard historical work on Ayrshire did not mention Rough-Legged Buzzard at all; the first record for Dumfriesshire was not recorded until the Duke of Buccleuch's Head Gamekeeper shot one in 1840.

The Common Buzzard was first mentioned in 1457 within an Act of James II: among 'foulys of reif', 'to be destroyed in order to protect wild fowl such as Partridges and Plover'. Although the population apparently fluctuated it appears that the Buzzard was generally distributed in wooded areas during Burns' era and it is perfectly reasonable to accept this solitary reference to it.


## PEREGRINE FALCON *Falco peregrinus*

**Local:** Blue Hawk; Hunting Hawk; Game Hawk; Goshawk; Gos; Pigeon Hawk; Passage Hawk

Raven (lower) with Peregrine (upper)
*(Donald Watson)*

Surprisingly, I can only find a single reference to what undoubtedly is one of our most well known, bold and spectacular raptors.

In **'The Brigs of Ayr'**, written in 1786, Burns wrote: 'Swift as the *gos* drives on the wheeling hare'.

Historically, the peregrine falcon was widespread in Ayrshire, breeding on both inland and coastal cliffs, including a noted historical site on Ailsa Craig. The birds were severely persecuted by game-keepers and egg collectors to the extent that, by the early twentieth century, only some five or six pairs could be found. The position in Dumfriesshire was similar, except that all the sites were in-land, there being no seacliffs.

I have, of course, closely examined and subsequently rejected the possibility of the bird referred to being a Goshawk *Accipiter gentilis*. Suffice it to say, there is a great deal of confusion in the old records between the two species, especially when they share a local misnomer and both being used by falconers.

There is acceptable evidence of Goshawk being in Eskdale, Dumfriesshire in 1235 and that they occurred elsewhere in Scotland in 1578 and were subsequently described as 'fowl of reif'. In 1684, Goshawk was included in the bird lists by Sibbald. Notwithstanding these records, the main and much respected authors of the standard works in both counties did not find any of the more recent records acceptable and very few Goshawks were kept for falconry during this time in comparison with Peregrine Falcons. I am quite convinced that this single record pertained to a specially trained bird.

Further evidence can in fact be gleaned from the Burns' quotation itself, 'Swift as the *gos* drives on the wheeling hare'.

The hunting mode of the Goshawk could not normally be described as sustaining a swift 'jinking' flight. It is basically a broad-winged hawk that spends much of its hunting time waiting on suitable prey to come within gliding range. It is most unlikely to regularly attempt to take a hare in 'open' countryside, although specifically trained hawks become very adept at it.

Equally, it could be argued that Peregrine Falcons seldom take adult hares, although leverets are frequent items. Their mode of hunting is more often characterised by the dramatic pursuit or stoop at other bird species in flight.

Considering the local use of names at that time, especially the *very* widespread and *common* use of 'gos' for Peregrine in Dumfriesshire, the large numbers of Peregrines relative to the scarcity of Goshawks (except those few being kept by falconers), and the fact that Peregrines were also used in falconry and flown then at ground game: these facts sustain my view that, in this case,

Burns inferred Peregrine Falcon rather than Goshawk in his reference.

It may perhaps be noted that the male is the Tiercel, and the female the Falcon, of falconers; and it must be remembered that the species has been erroneously, and therefore confusingly, termed the Goshawk.

Sir Hugh S Gladstone. *The Birds of Dumfriesshire*, 1910

## RED GROUSE *Lagopus lagopus*

**Local:** Grouse; Gorcock; Moorfowl; Moor-cock; Moorhen; Muircock; Muirhen;
  Red-Game

The *Statistical Account of Scotland, 1791-1799*, gives the firm impression that red grouse were plentiful and widely distributed in both Ayrshire and Dumfries. Populations have always been reported as 'fluctuating' due to various factors, such as disease, weather, infestation of tick species and, especially, either a lack of, or over burning of heather – a vital plant which provides cover for nesting, food, and shelter during inclement weather conditions.

Raptorial birds were frequently and quite wrongly blamed for low numbers, and the result was carnage during an era of unparalleled persecution of birds of prey in the so called 'interests' of game preservation. Considering that pheasants were not significantly 'involved' at that time, this wholesale destruction of birds of prey must have largely been carried out in the interests of grouse species and to a lesser extent, partridges.

Although no data are available, heather was obviously more widely distributed during the eighteenth century than the present day. Some estimates suggest that in Scotland we have now lost almost 60% of our heather habitat to agricultural improvement and forestry. Hence, red grouse would be a familiar bird even to town or village dwellers of the mid-eighteenth century. Altitude was no barrier and a large healthy population lived on Lochar Moss, Dumfries, at sea level. In addition, the birds frequented the stubble fields in autumn following harvest to glean grain and, on occasion, to feed from both stooks and stacks.

Burns was quite clearly familiar with grouse, and records them in **'The Elegy on Captain Matthew Henderson'**: 'Ye *grouse* that crap the heather bud'; and while in Kenmore Inn, he wrote 'Th' abodes of coveyed *grouse* and timid sheep.'

In the song **'Yon Wild Mossy Mountains'** written in 1787, we are provided with further notes on the bird: 'Where the *grouse* lead their coveys thro the heather to feed.'

Probably, he further alludes to grouse in **'The Brigs of Ayr'**, 'The wounded *coveys*, reeling, scatter wide' and in the song **'The Gloomy Night is Gath'ring Fast'**, he is more specific with the inclusion of the descriptive 'moor':

The hunter now has left the moor,
The scatt'red *coveys* meet secure;

The collective term of 'covey' was also used extensively to describe a group of partridges which were then very common and often hunted, especially in Ayrshire.

Burns frequently uses other names for grouse; for example in **'Tam Samson's Elegy'** he uses two: 'Ye cootie *moorcocks*, crousely craw' and 'Some spiteful *moorfowl* bigs her nest, to hatch and breed'; and in the song **'The Bonie Moor-Hen'** devoted entirely to the grouse, verses one and four are particularly apt and descriptive – though there are of course sexual undertones:

> The heather was blooming, the meadows were maun,
> Our lads gaed a-hunting ae day at the dawn,
> O'er moors and o'er mosses and monie a glen:
> At length they discovered a bonie *moor-hen*.

> They hunted the valley, they hunted the hill,
> The best of our lads wi the best o their skill;
> But still as the fairest she sat in their sight
> Then whirr! she was over, a mile at a flight.

Shooting grouse for sport was further mentioned in **'The Twa Dogs'**, when Burns had Luath speak: 'Or shooting of a hare or *moor-cock*'. The classic comment by Burns on the shooting aspect is found in the song **'Now Westlin Winds'**:

> Now westlin winds and slaught'ring guns
> Bring Autumn's pleasant weather;
> The *moorcock* springs on whirring wings
> Amang the blooming heather:

and in a song **'My Lord A-Hunting He is Gane'**

> Out o'er you muir, out o'er you moss,
> Whare *gor-cocks* thro the heather pass,

## GREY PARTRIDGE *Perdix perdix*

**Local:** Paitrick; Paitritch

The grey partridge, formerly called the 'common' partridge, is an old inhabitant of Scotland and first received legal protection in 1427. They are mentioned in Sibbald's list of 1684 and were regarded as 'common' in Carrick in 1696. The Old Statistical Accounts records them as 'occurring' in all parts of the country.

One can assume that the farmland habitat during Burns' time in Ayrshire and Dumfriesshire would be ideal for partridge. The adults roost in and feed over farmland on weed seeds, sedges and rushes, but they also require tall ground vegetation and hedges to nest under. Chicks initially require a good insect diet to survive and all those factors would be in abundance prior to the later use of herbicides and fungicides. Predation by crows and foxes, which is regarded as important today, would be relatively insignificant in such uncontaminated conditions providing quality habitat.

With small fields close to habitation, Burns would be very familiar with partridges, especially when the coveys fed in the autumn stubbles and on the stooks. At that time it was normal practice to have organised partridge shooting in the harvest field.

In the song **'Now Westlin Winds'** he mentions the species thus:

> The *paitrick* lo'es the fruitful fells,
> The plover lo'es the mountains;

and in **'Brose and Butter'**, 'The *paetrick* lo'es the stibble.' The song **'On a Bank of Flowers'** contains:

> As flies the *partridge* from the brake
> On fear-inspirèd wings…

**'The Elegy on Captain Matthew Henderson'** includes 'And mourn, ye whirring *paitrick* brood;' and in **'Epistle to J Lapraik'** 'An *paitricks* scraichin loud at e'en,' demonstrates more than a passing knowledge. **'Tam Samson's Elegy'**, produced as a mock epitaph to a keen game shooter, contains:

> Rejoice, ye birring *paitricks* a';
> Ye cootie moorcocks, crousely craw;
> Ye maukins, cock your fud fu braw,
> Withouten dread;
>
> Your mortal fae is now awa:
> Tam Samson's dead!

and in his **'Epistle to John Rankine'**, Burns clearly refers to the species again:

> I gaed a rovin wi the gun,
> An brought a *paitrick* to the grun'-
> A bonie hen…

though this was used as an analogy to describe an adulterous activity.

Finally the song **'Bessy and her Spinin-Wheel'** quotes, 'The *paitrick* whirring o'er the ley.' Two other quotes referring to birds in a 'covey', which could have equally referred to either Red Grouse or Partridge, are not detailed here.

## CORNCRAKE  *Crex crex*

**Local:** Land Rail; Crake; Craik

In the Old Statistical Accounts, the corncrake was recorded from 'Dumfries to Caithness'. The earliest Ayrshire records (written in 1869) report it as being 'abundant everywhere', including on Ailsa Craig. Writing on Dumfriesshire in about

1831, Sir W Jardine considered it extremely common in the Annan area 'its note being heard in almost every alternate field'.

Although subject to apparent fluctuations that may have reflected the standard of reporting rather than biological fact, there is no doubt that the corncrake was a common and widely distributed bird during the lifetime of Burns.

It is, however, now extinct as a regular breeding species in both Ayrshire and Dumfriesshire. The long-term and gradual demise was caused by changes in agricultural practices, principally in mechanical mowing but also due to the destruction of the tall herb communities which this very secretive bird required for successful nestling.

Surprisingly for a bird seldom seen but extremely vocal, Burns only mentioned it on two occasions. In the **'Elegy to Captain Matthew Henderson'**:

> Mourn, clam'ring *craik*'s, at close o day,
> 'Mang fields o flow'ring clover gay!
> And when you wing your annual way
> Frae our cauld shore...

Not only do these lines describe the typical habitat of the hayfield, but also the biological facts that they did indeed have a rather mournful call, which continued to be emitted in the evening and at times throughout the night, to the extent that frequently people were unable to sleep due to its loud incessant calling. In addition it further underlines Burns' knowledge on certain ornithological aspects. In this case he was obviously aware that 'craiks' migrated annually to warmer climes.

The species and its main habitat are again referred to in the song **'Bessy and her Spinnin-Wheel'**: 'The *craik* amang the claver hay.'


## COOT *Fulica atra*

**Local:** Bald Coot

Historical records are exceedingly vague and throw little reliable light on the status of the species during the eighteenth century. The earliest records available show they were present on Mochrum Loch in Ayrshire and on the Lochmaben Lochs in Dumfriesshire at the beginning of the nineteenth century. There is one old record to the effect that (in 1792), 'they frequent the lochs at Inch, Wigtown'.

It is thus credible, historically, that Burns did at least mention the species, firstly in the song **'And Maun I Still on Menie Doat'**

> The wanton *coot* the water skimms,
> Amang the reeds the ducklings cry...

and then in his **'Elegy on Captain Matthew Henderson'**: 'Mourn, sooty *coots*, and speckled teals.'

## GOLDEN PLOVER *Pluvialis apricaria*

**Local:** Pliver; Grey Plover; Green Plover

There is almost total confusion in the old literature concerning the Golden Plover. Many references and protection acts dating from 1427 onwards refer to 'pluivers' but it remains uncertain what species were meant. Colonel Thornton in 1799 described Golden Plover as a 'very common bird in Scotland'. There are no significant comments in the standard works on southern Scotland until the New Statistical Accounts of Scotland mentioned the Golden Plover as 'a local bird', 'being in those days, as now [1910] miscalled the Grey, or Green Plover'.

Burns never mentioned Golden Plover as such; simply another example of a local misnomer being perpetuated. Where Burns referred to Grey Plover, it was in fact Golden Plover that was intended.

Without doubt, Grey Plover *Pluvialis squatarola*, did occur in both Ayrshire and Dumfriesshire – usually irregularly, in small numbers, only during migration, and then invariably confined to a narrow coastal area. Identification was normally only ascertained by shooting specimens and it is most unlikely that Burns ever came in contact with the species. It is worthy of mention in support of this discussion that in late autumn and winter the general plumage of Golden Plover is duller (greyer) than the full breeding dress of spring and summer.

In **'Elegy to Captain Matthew Henderson'** Burns refers to 'Ye whistling *plover*'. The use of the descriptive 'whistling' is also significant. It first of all eliminates the Lapwing or Green Plover; and Tucker (1948), an authority on the subject, describes the call of the Golden Plover as 'a musical liquid whistle', in comparison with that of the Grey Plover which he describes as 'often rather silent, not unlike Golden Plover's but higher-pitched, not so mellow and liquid and typically trisyllabic.'

In the song **'Now Westlin Winds'**, Burns further states 'The *plover* lo'es the mountains'. Again this is indicative – Golden Plovers are more likely to be found at higher altitudes than Lapwing; whilst Grey Plover not at all, except under very unusual circumstances when migrating.

In **'The Brigs of Ayr'**, Burns refers again to the whistling voice and the hill habitat preference: 'Or deep-ton'd *plovers* grey, wild whistling o'er the hill'. On 1 January 1789, Burns wrote to his friend Mrs Frances Anna Dunlop of Dunlop:

> I never hear the loud, solitary whistle of the Curlew in a Summer noon, or the wild, mixing cadence of a troop of *grey-plover* in an Autumnal-morning, without feeling an elevation of soul.

In his **'Cantata - The Jolly Beggars' (Recitativo 6th)** we find 'To speet him like a *pliver*' (a speet is a cooking skewer). The comment, while more likely to refer to Golden Plover, may also have been to a Lapwing.

## LAPWING  *Vanellus vanellus*

**Local:** Green Plover; Pewit; Peesweep; Tee-wheet; De'il's Plover; Crested Lapwing; Peesie

The local name 'De'il's Plover' had an added significance in southern Scotland. It refers to the alleged betrayal of the persecuted Covenanters, whose movements on the hillside were in constant danger of being revealed by the clamorous attention of this bird.

> He minds what Scotland greets for yet,
> When helpless Hill Folk, hard beset,
> Could naewhere but in muirlands get
> A nights safe quarters -
> Ye brought the troopers on them het,
> And made them martyrs.     *(Anon)*

Dr Archbald 'notices' this species in his *Curiosities at Dumfries* written about 1684: 'Green plovers returning every spring in abundance and staying all summer.' There are in fact many local references in the Statistical Accounts; for example, it was recorded from Hutton and Corrie in 1794 that it was 'very numerous forty years since.' During this period there was wholesale collection of lapwing eggs and they were shot by fowlers for food. By 1842 they had decreased very significantly to the extent that, uniquely, Dumfries had its own Wild Bird Protection Act by June 1896. There is little useful historical information from Ayrshire covering the Burns' period. Clearly though, during the mid-eighteenth century the Lapwing was common and widespread as a breeding species in southern Scotland, with at times very large congregations at favoured coastal haunts in autumn and early winter.

In the well loved song **'Sweet Afton'**, composed before 5 February 1789, Burns provided his only and classic reference:

> Thou green-crested *Lapwing*, thy screaming forbear -
> I charge you, disturb not my slumbering Fair.

## SNIPE  *Callinago gallinago*

**Local:** Common Snipe; Mire Snipe; Myre Snipe; Heather-bleater; Heather blite; Heather-blitter

In 1684, Dr Archbald wrote of Myre Snipes and said, 'in pleasant summer evenings they soar high in the air with a quivering voice and are excellent meat.' There are a great many records from all over the country during the eighteenth century and obviously – during that period before significant land drainage and improvement schemes – there would be a surfeit of undrained bogs, mires and static water that would provide optimum conditions for snipe. The species can thus be regarded as having been a common breeding species, augmented in autumn by immigrants.

In the song **'My Hoggie'**, Burns refers to the snipe thus:

> But the houlet cry'd frae the castle wa',
> The *blitter* frae the boggie,
> The tod reply'd upon the hill:
> I trembled for my hoggie.

## WOODCOCK  *Scolopax rusticola*

**Local**: Wood Snipe; Cock

The earliest mention of the Woodcock in Scotland is in a charter of 1334 appointing John de la Forest, a bailiff of 'Wodecok Heyr' (Woodcockair, Annan, Dumfries – 'heyr' is the equivalent to 'aire' an old form of 'aerie', a bird's nest). Although recorded frequently, especially on the east coast as a migrant, breeding information in the mid-eighteenth century is very sparse. There were no breeding records in Ayrshire up to 1869 nor in Dumfriesshire till 1848.

It is thus all the more remarkable that Burns mentioned the species – but he did do so, in the song **'Now Westlin Winds'**, composed in the summer of 1775, while studying near Kirkoswald, Ayrshire:

> The paitrick lo'es the fruitful fells,
> The plover lo'es the mountains;
> The *woodcock* haunts the lonely dells,
> The soaring hern the fountains:

## CURLEW *Numenius arquata*

**Local:** Whap; Whaup

In both the Old and New Statistical Accounts, the curlew is regarded as a common bird, breeding inland on the higher land, then resorting to the shore in winter. It was regarded as 'very abundant' in Ayrshire by 1869. Similarly, to give but one example of Dumfriesshire it was said to be 'plentiful at Wanlockhead.'

Burns mentions the species in his **'Reply to An Announcement by John Rankine'**. This is thought to be Burns' reply, on learning that Elizabeth Paton was pregnant by him -

> But now a rumour's like to rise -
> A *whaup*'s i the nest!

and in his **'Elegy to Captain Matthew Henderson'** 'Ye *curlews*, calling thro a clud.'

His famous letter to Mrs Dunlop of 1789, included, 'I never hear the loud solitary whistle of the *Curlew...*'

## SEABIRD(S)

No seabird species are specifically mentioned by Burns. He does however refer to 'Sea-fowl' a term that persists to this day especially in the countries that continue to allow legal seasons during which certain 'Sea-fowl' may be harvested. This practice still continues in parts of Scandinavia, Iceland, The Faeroe Islands and indeed in Scotland, where on Sula Sgeir the men of Noss still harvest young gannets or gugas. In both versions of the song **'Behold the Hour The Boat Arrive'**, the same line is included -

> Along the solitary shore,
> Where flitting *sea-fowl* round me cry...

'Fowling' was a general term to describe the shooting and catching of birds (that equally applied to *Wild-fowl*, the Ducks, Geese and Swans and to *Muir-fowl*, usually referring to Red Grouse).

That the poet was at least familiar with the group is beyond doubt. Writing to his uncle Samuel Brown from Masgiel (Mossgiel, Ayrshire), dated 4 May 1789 (for 1788) he wrote:

I am impatient to hear if the Ailsa *fowling* be Comenced for this Season yet, as I want three or four stones of feathers, and hope you will bespeak them for me.

'Ailsa' is of course Ailsa Craig, a conical granite island and prominent landmark, some two miles in circumference and situated ten miles west of Girvan, Ayrshire. Burns also referred to the island in the second version of the song **'Duncan Gray'** 'Meg was deaf as Ailsa Craig.'

That Ailsa Craig was a notable seabird colony has been documented since at least 1526. 'Fowling' – the collection of birds' eggs and carcasses for their meat and feathers – has probably occurred there since time immemorial, certainly since 1696. In 1772 the then owner, the Earl of Cassilus (Marquess of Ailsa), was paid £33 per annum for rent 'out of the profits of 'his' birds.' The passing of The Seabird Act of 1869 subsequently gave legal protection to the Ailsa birds, and the practice of fowling had ended by 1880.

Three species mainly were collected during the fowling era – Gannet; *Sula bassana*; Guillemot, *Uria aalge*; and Puffin *Fratercula arctica*. A few Razorbill *Alca torda* were also collected where they bred alongside Guillemots – 'These were sold locally, for consumption among the lower classes, to those who could not afford mutton or beef.' It was thought that some 400-500 gannets were taken annually but that the number of guillemots and puffins could have been in the order of 18,000 killed per season and these were sold, 'cleaned and ready for the pot' at one or two pence each. Feathers sold at sixteen shillings per stone. It has been calculated that it would have required about 100 Gannets or 384 guillemot/puffin carcases to make up one stone in weight of feathers (6.350 kg.).

Local tradition insists that Burns visited Ailsa Craig in 1775 with Douglas Graham of Shanter Farm, whose boat was named *The Tam*, and that later – when Graham became the model for **'Tam O'Shanter'** – it was from the name of the boat that the title was derived.

Personally, I doubt very much that Burns ever visited Ailsa. If he did so, it is most likely that he would have planned a visit during the summer months. Outwith these months, not only would the journey, in presumably a small boat be hazardous, but Burns and Graham would be very busy on their respective farms. In addition, small boats were usually hauled out on shore during the inclement period and fishing did not resume until spring. More importantly, if Burns had indeed visited Ailsa other than in winter or even sailed round it, he could not have failed to have been immediately and totally impressed by its scale and grandeur and the constant hive of activity – the sights, sounds and smell of a veritable 'seabird city' comprising a possible population of some 60,000 pairs of breeding birds of at least nine different species. The large population of puffins was usually greatly exaggerated, but later they decreased dramatically – almost certainly due to predation by rats, and possibly the demise of the small fish species that formed the bulk of their food supply, and their movement to other areas of sea outwith the birds' 'economic' flying range.

An island visit would surely have made an indelible impression on Burns' sensitive mind and attitudes, which almost certainly would have been reflected in many more quotations within his various writings than we have available to us.

## [STOCK DOVE  *Columba oenas*]

**Local:** Rock-Dove; Blue Dove

It is very difficult to document with any accuracy the early history of the Stock Dove in Scotland. There was, not unexpectedly, confusion by the early writers between Stock Dove; Rock Dove *C. livia*; and Wood Pigeon *C. palumbus*. Discussing the topic, Alexander and Lack (1944) point out that, at the beginning of the nineteenth century, the Stock Dove was confined to southern and eastern England. It was not until the end of the century that it colonised northern England, south and east Scotland. It was first recorded breeding in Scotland in 1866 near Cullane, in 1874 at Dalkeith; and in Kirkcudbright by 1876. It was not recorded breeding in Dumfriesshire until 1883; and Stock Doves were not recorded breeding in Ayrshire until C Rose of Kilmarnock said in 1907, '…has now established itself as a nesting species in several parts of the country.'

Burns refers to the Stock Dove in the song **'Sweet Afton'**, composed before 5 February 1789 in the text sent to Mrs Dunlop: 'Thou *stock dove* whose echo resounds thro the glen'.

The identification and use of the species name some 70 years before it was recorded breeding in Scotland is not scientifically acceptable. Either it was a case of mis-identification with the Wood Pigeon, which I personally find difficult to accept, or wrong information from a local source, which is entirely possible. The term 'stock' was also often used to infer or describe species that were common, usual or in general as in 'stock fish' for example.

The explanation I prefer is that, knowing of the existence elsewhere in Britain of a bird called the Stock Dove, Burns indulged in a piece of harmless poetic licence. Stock Dove certainly sits easier in the metre or rhythm of the song.

The ultimate conclusion must be that Stock Doves as a specific species did not exist in Glen Afton in 1789. Indeed, they were not even recorded as breeding in full surveys of Glen Afton in 1954, 1968 and in 1972 (Young, J G and Holden, T: unpublished reports to Nature Conservancy Council).

## WOOD PIGEON  *Columba palumbus*

**Local:** Ring-Dove; Cushat; Cushie; Custie Doo; Cusha-Doo; Doo; Blue Doo; Dow

Gray (1871), wrote of the wood-pigeon as 'cooing in the enchanted groves at Langholm' in 1794, and writing of it in 1842 Sir William Jardine described it as abundant in the south of Scotland by which time it was already regarded as an agricultural pest. The species continued to increase during the late eighteenth and early nineteenth centuries, as improved agricultural crops and forestry provided food and nesting areas. It is mentioned in the song **'How Cruel are the Parents'** 'The trembling *dove* thus flies'; and in **'Phillis the Fair'**: 'Down in the shady walk, *doves* cooing were.'

In the song **'The Battle of Sherramuir'**, he uses the archaic spelling:

> Wi Highland wrath and frae the sheath
> Drew blades o death, till, out of breath,
> They fled like frightened *dows*, man!

and **'The Kiss'** contains '*Dove*-like fondness, chaste concession'.

Burns was more specific when he used the name 'cushat; firstly in his **'Elegy on Captain Matthew Henderson'**: 'Mourn, ilka grove the *cushat* kens!'; and in the song **'Now Westlin Winds'**:

> Thro' lofty groves the *Cushat* roves,
> the path of man to shun it...

In **'One Night as I did Wander'**: 'A *cushat* crooded o'er me'; and in the song **'Bessy And Her Spinnin-Wheel'**: 'On lofty aiks the *cushats* wail'.

When writing his **'Epistle to William Simpson'**:

> While thro' the braes the *cushat* croods
> With wailfu' cry!

## CUCKOO  *Cuculus canorus*

**Local:** Gowk

The Cuckoo is frequently mentioned by the old writers – Sibbald in 1684 and by Martin in 1697 for example – and it is referred to in both Statistical Accounts. Although most records concentrate in documenting its arrival dates in spring, there is no doubt that, during Burns' lifetime, it was a common summer visitor in both Ayrshire and Dumfriesshire.

'Gowk' has a dual meaning, and in his **'The Brigs of Ayr'** and **'To W Creech'**, Burns said: 'Conceited *gowk*! puffd up wi windy pride!' and 'gawkies, tawpies, *gowks* and fools'. In these contexts, gowk refers to a dolt or fool, and I have excluded most of his other references in this context. However, in his letter to Robert Muir of 20 March, 1786, Burns was specific:

> I hope, sometimes before we hear the *Gowk*, to have the pleasure of seeing you at Kilmarnock...

He did mention the species specifically, albeit with the present spelling, in **'A Dream'**:

> 'God save the King' 's a *cuckoo* sang
> Thats unco easy said ay:

and in the song **'Lassie Wi The Lint-White Locks'**:

143

> The primrose bank, the wimpling burn,
> The *cuckoo* on the milk-white thorn,

**'Ballads on Mr Heron's Election',** 1795, includes:

> And even a Lord may be a *gowk*,
> Wi ribban, star, and a' that?

and thus leaves us in absolutely no doubt of the poet's familiarity with the bird and all its connotations.

## BARN OWL *Tyto alba*

**Local:** Screech Owl; White Owl

At one time undoubtably common in Scotland, it became quite scarce. Later it increased but its recovery has never assumed the supposed proportions of former times.

Sibbald mentions the bird in his list of 1684 and Pennant in 1789. In the first *Statistical Account* it was only included from Kirkmichael in Kirkcud-brightshire and from Luss in Dumbartonshire. By the time the second Statistical Account was produced it had clearly re-established itself as a breeding species in most parishes of Southern Scotland, only to decrease again by the mid-nineteenth century, when Gladstone, writing of Dumfriesshire commented, 'it reached such a low ebb as to be, in some places, almost if not quite extinct.'

The birds usually fly quietly and 'softly' invariably at night except in winter, and do emit a loud, rather eerie screech or scream, while at the nest site they may also 'hiss'. These behavioural aspects – allied to their habit of also nesting in barns, old buildings, including of course, ruined churches as well as in hollow trees – have ensured their place in mythology, Scottish folklore and superstition, often associated with illness or death.

Writing to William Dunbar, from Ellisland on 17 January, 1791, Burns includes 'May the blood-hounds of misfortune never track his steps, nor the *screech-owl* of sorrow alarm his dwelling!'

## OWL sp. *Tyto; Strix; Asio*

**Local:** Hoolet (all species); Screech Owl and White Owl (barn owl); Brown Owl and Wood Owl (tawny owl); Luggie and Horned owl (long-eared owl)

Burns refers to 'owl' species, which could theoretically be either Barn Owl *T. alba*; Tawny Owl *S. aluco*; Long-Eared Owl *A. otus* or Short-Eared Owl *A. flammeus*.

At the time when Burns was writing, the records indicate that Barn Owl was 'reasonable plentiful' in Dumfriesshire and Ayrshire; Tawny Owl was almost certainly the most common species; Long-Eared Owl was similarly regarded as 'quite common' in wooded areas; whereas Short-Eared Owl remained very local and scarce.

In his **'Second Epistle to J Lapraik'** Burns says:

> Or in some day-detesting *owl*
> May shun the light.

and in the song **'My Hoggie'**: 'But the *houlet* cry'd frae the castle wa';' while the **'Elegy on Captain Matthew Henderson'** produces:

> Ye *houlets*, frae your ivy bower
> In some auld tree, or eldritch tower...

The famous epic **'Tam O Shanter'** contained the immortal lines:

> Kirk-Alloway was drawing nigh,
> Whare ghaists and *houlets* nightly cry.

and in an early version of **'The Vision'** he said, 'Where th' *howlet* mourns in her ivy bower.' From **'Ballads on Mr. Heron's Election'** (Ballad Third) 1795 we glean:

> Sae in the tower o Cardoness,
> A *howlet* sits at noon.

and **'On the Late Captain Grose's Peregrinations Thro Scotland'** Burns pens, 'By some auld, *houlet*-haunted biggin.' His **'In Defence of a Lady'** or **'The Keekin Glass'** contains 'How daur ye ca' me *howlet*-face'. In a letter to Agnes McLehose (Clarinda) he includes: 'as grave and as stupid as an *owl* – but like that *owl*, still faithfull to my own song...'

Considering the available quotations, it seems unlikely that Short-Eared Owl – the rarest at that time and a predominately day-flying owl – was intended. There are no other habitat or behavioural clues of any significance. Thus further speculation regarding specific species identification is unwarranted. I have, of course, looked very closely at the poem **'To the Owl'**, which is listed as dubious. My own view is that I cannot accept it as the work of Burns.

## SKYLARK *Alanda arvensis*

**Local:** Laverock; Lark

Skylark
*(Donald Watson)*

Surprisingly, for such a distinctive bird, especially when it soars and sings, the historical comments in the standard works are rather poor. The old records from outwith south-west Scotland (1684) and the Statistical Accounts clearly indicate that the Skylark was a common breeding bird during Burns' time, gathering into large flocks in winter when they were probably augmented by immigrants.

There is absolutely no doubt that the poet was familiar with the Skylark, which he called variously Laverock, Lav'rock and Lavrock. My own view is that, in common with many ploughmen even today, the Skylark was Burns' favourite bird. In the song **'Behold, My Love, How Green The Groves'** there is a classic reference:

> The *lav'rock* shuns the palace gay,
> And o'er the cottage sings:

and in his **'Lament of Mary of Scots'**, on the approach of spring:

> Now *laverocks* wake the merry morn,
> Aloft on dewy wing;

The revered Ayrshire song **'The Braes O Ballochmyle'** gives us:

> The Catrine woods were yellow seen,
> The flowers decay'd on Catrine lea,
> Nae *lav'rock* sang on hillock green…

and in **'The Holy Fair'**:

> The *lav'rocks* they were chanting
> Fu sweet that day.

while in his **'The Humble Petition of Bruar Water'**:

> The sober *laverock*, warbling wild,
> Shall to the skies aspire;

The song **'Brose and Butter'** at least mentions the bird if not in an ornithological context:

> The *laverock* lo'es the grass,
> The paetrick lo'es the stubble:

and in his classic poem **'To a Mountain Daisy'** Burns pens:

> Alas! it's no thy neebor sweet,
> The bonie *lark* companion meet…

The **'The Brigs of Ayr'** contains: 'The soaring *lark*, the perching red-breast shrill,' while the song **'And Maun I still on Menie Doat'** gives us the very descriptive:

> And when the *lark*, 'tween light and dark,
> Blythe waukens by the daisy's side,
> And mounts and sings on flittering wings…

In his **'Epistle to Robert Graham Esq., of Fintry'**:

> So, to heaven's gates the *lark*'s shrill song ascends,
> But grovelling on the earth the carol ends.

The song called **'Where Are The Joys'** contains:

> Where are the joys I hae met in the morning,
> That danc'd to the *lark*'s early sang?

and the song **'Sleep'st Thou'** has:

> The *laverock* to the sky
> Ascends, wi sangs o joy.

The well loved song, **'My Nanie's Awa'** has a further indication of the lark's association with the farm worker:

> Thou *lav'rock* that springs frae the dews of the lawn
> The shepherd to warn o the grey-breaking dawn...

and **'Now Spring Has Clad The Grove in Green'** produces:

> The waken'd *lav'rock* warbling springs,
> And climbs the early sky,
> Winnowing blythe his dewy wings
> In morning's rosy eye:

In **'Halloween'** he was in jocular mood with 'Near *lav'rock*-height she jumpet'. The song **'Our Gudewife's Sae Modest'** contains: 'A *laverock*'s leg, or a tittling's wing'. Also, from *MMC* a song entitled **'She Gripet At The Girtest O 't'**, has the line: 'But lang before the *laverock* sang.'

From the same source, writing in 1794 to George Thomson, Burns included the revision of an Irish song which he called **'Una's Lock'**. The revised first verse contains:

> The dew the meads adorning,
> The *larks* melodious singing;

In his version of an old ballad, **'The Ploughmans Life'** underlines the ploughman's association with a bird that must have been his constant companion:

> The *lav'rock* in the morning she'll rise frae her nest,
> And mount i' the air wi the dew on her breast,
> And wi the merry ploughman she'll whistle and sing,
> And at night she'll return to her nest back again.

In **'Ode to Spring',** the mention of 'And the *lark* that soar'd aboon, Sir,' was of a sexual connotation, as was his reference in his letter of 1787 to James Smith, 'like a mounting *lark* in an April morning.'

Finally in **'Delia'**, submitted by Burns to *The London Star*, 18 May, 1789:

> Sweet the *Lark*'s wild-warbled lay,
> Sweet the tinkling rill to hear.

## SWALLOW *Hirundo rustica*

**Local**: House Swallow; Barn Swallow; Chimney-Swallow

The swallow was included in parish lists from all parts of mainland Scotland in the *Old Statistical Account*, inferring that is was a widespread breeding species in the eighteenth century. Although Swift *A. apus*; House-Martin *Delichon urbica*; and Sand-Martin *Riparia riparia* were also known to be present in South West Scotland during Burns' lifetime – and were often collectively referred to as Swallows – my view is that his references are quite specific to *Hirundo rustica*.

In **'The Auld Farmer's New-Year Morning Salutation to His Auld Mare, Maggie'**:

> When thou was corn't, an I was mellow,
> We took the road ay like a *swallow*:

In the song **'Now Westlin Winds'** he refers to it thus:

> But, Peggy dear, the ev'ning's clear,
> Thick flies the skimming *swallow*;

and in **'Philly and Willy'**: 'The little *swallow*'s wanton wing'. The song **'Bessie and Her Spinnin-Wheel'** contains 'The *swallow* jinkin round my shiel,' and in verses **'To Miss Isabella Macleod'**:

> The crimson blossom charms the bee,
> The summer sun the *swallow*:

## TREE PIPIT *Anthus trivialis*

**Local:** Treelark; Wood-Lark; Woodlark

Burns never mentions the Tree Pipit but it is certain that the Tree Pipit was in fact his 'Woodlark'.

Woodlark and Tree Lark were well known and widely used as the local names or misnomers for Tree Pipit in both Ayrshire and Dumfriesshire. This common confusion continued in Dumfriesshire up to 1962 at least, and in Ayrshire with some local people till 1980.

Burns waxed lyrically on his Woodlark; he devoted a song to it **'To The Woodlark'** supposedly written at the request of one Mr McMurdo of Drumlanrig near Thornhill, Dumfriesshire in 1795. In addition, he mentions the species in the song **'Here is the Glen'** in 1794:

> So called the *woodlark* in the grove
> His little cheerful mate to cheer:

and again in the 1790 poem **'On Sensibility'**, 'Hear the *woodlark* charm the forest'.

To compound the matter further, Burns selected the 'woodlark' to be depicted when he composed his own heraldic device. This he devised himself, and the Woodlark *Lullula arborea* was quite accurately illustrated and is certainly recognisable as such.

Writing to Alexander Cunninham on 3 March 1794, on the subject Burns said:

> I am a bit of a Herald; and shall give you, *Secundum artem*, my ARMS: On a field, azure, a holly-bush, seeded, proper, in base; a Shepherd's pipe and crook, Salteir-wise, also proper, in chief. On a wreath of the colours, a *woodlark* perching on a sprig of bay-tree.

Although records of Woodlark are included in the Statistical Account of the County of Ayrshire 1837 and by Gray in *Birds of the West of Scotland 1871*; and while the latter was convinced that it did occur in Scotland, all of these records are now rejected. The first acceptable record of a Woodlark on mainland Scotland was from Fife, on 7 April 1924.

There is no evidence, either, that Burns ever visited other areas in southern Britain where he might have become familiar with the species. On the contrary, his main works mentioning the species all occurred between 1790 and 1795 while he lived at Ellisland near Dumfries. All early evidence of the species' possible occurrence in Ayrshire has been rejected. More important was the opinion of the respected Dumfriesshire historian Sir H S Gladstone of Capenoch near Keir, who stated in 1910:

> The most common name in this country for the Tree-Pipit is the 'Wood Lark' and this fact accounts for the numerous reports of the occurrence locally of a species which has hitherto only occurred in Scotland at Fair Island' (Shetland, a renowned stopping off place for rare migrants)

*and*

> There is no satisfactory evidence as to the occurrence of this species in the country, and I have no doubt that the older records of the 'Woodlark' refer to the Tree Pipit.

Thus in hindsight, we can now be certain that Burns was not guilty of misidentification of a species, only in following a local misnomer, which is perfectly understandable considering that both species were not described scientifically in Britain until 1787, and there was no locally-available literature that he could have consulted.

The fact that his coat of arms (now officially registered by The International Burns Federation) depicted accurately a 'Woodlark' is almost certainly due to the artist or illustrator that was commissioned to draw the bird. Burns asked for a 'Woodlark' and got it!

### To the Woodlark

O, stay, sweet warbling wood-lark, stay,
Nor quit for me the trembling spray!
A hapless lover counts thy lay,
Thy soothing, fond complaining.
Again, again that tender part,
That I may catch thy melting art!
For surely that wad touch her heart,
Wha kills me wi disdaining.

Say, was thy little mate unkind,
And heard thee as the careless wind?
O, nocht but love and sorrow join'd
Sic notes o woe could wauken!
Thou tells o never-ending care,
O speechless grief and dark despair-
For pity's sake, sweet bird, nae mair,
Or my poor heart is broken!

## WREN *Troglodytes troglodytes*

**Local:** Kitty; Kitty-Wren; Kitty-Raan; Cutty; Cutty-Wren; Jenny-Wren; Chittie (Ayrshire only)

Sibbald includes the Wren in his list of 1684 and both Statistical Accounts mention it from a 'goodly number of parishes in south-west Scotland'. Writing in 1841, Gray said, 'This hardy little bird is everywhere common, inhabiting the most densely wooded glens of the main-land and the barest rocks of distant islands.... it is common on Ailsa Craig.'

Young Wrens in Heather *(Donald Watson)*

Burns is reputed to have written down the words of the song **'The Wren's Nest'** as recited from memory by his wife:

The Robin cam to the *wren's* nest
And keekit in and keekit in,

## ROBIN *Erithacus rubecula*

**Local:** Redbreast

Although mentioned by Sibbald in 1684 the Robin was not mentioned in the

*Old Statistical Account of Scotland* (1791-99) for south-west Scotland. Obviously, since Burns was familiar with it, this is an oversight in the Account.

In **'The Brigs of Ayr'** written in 1786, he says 'the perching *red-breast* shrill,' and in the same work 'Except perhaps the *robin*'s whistling glee, Proud o the height o some bit half-lang tree.'

**'The Humble Petition of Bruar Water'** has the lines:

> The *robin*, pensive Autumn cheer
> In all her locks of yellow.

and in **'Election Ballad'** of 1790 Burns pens:

> So, when the storm the forest rends,
> The *robin* in the hedge descends,
> And, patient chirps securely.

The song **'The Wrens Nest'** has: 'The *Robin* cam to the wrens nest'.

## NIGHTINGALE *Luscinia megarhynchos*

A summer visitor to Britain, breeding mainly in the south-easterly counties of England, and at times north to Yorkshire. There were no acceptable records from either Ayrshire or Dumfriesshire in the eighteenth century. It occurred in Scotland only as a rare displaced migrant, usually on offshore islands on the eastern side of the country.

Burns mentions the species twice when corresponding to one George Thomson, a musician, who had encouraged Burns to collect songs and to improve some existing lyrics. Writing on 7 April 1793, the following extract from his letter is, in a historical and biological context, ornithologically fascinating:

> 'Banks of the Dee' is, you know, literally, Langolee, to slow time. The song is well enough, but has some false imagery in it, for instance... 'And sweetly the *nightingale* sung from the tree'.
> In the first place, the *nightingale* sings in a low bush, but never from a tree; and in the second place, there never was a *nightingale* seen, or heard, on the banks of the Dee, or on the banks of any other river in Scotland.

Both of these statements are absolutely accurate and serve well to underline Burns' wide ornithological knowledge.

Later the same year (29 October) he recommends to Thompson an address by G Turnbull whom he describes as an old friend: 'The *Nightingale*' by G Turnbull will suit as an English Song to the air.'

## BLACKBIRD *Turdus merula*

**Local:** Blackie; Merle

Historical records are vague until the New Statistical Account included the species 'in lists all over Scotland'. Burns was not vague! In his famous song **'Sweet Afton'** of 1789: 'Ye wild whistling *blackbirds* in yon thorny den'.
 **'Epistle to Davie', A Brother Poet** contains:

> In days when daisies deck the ground,
> And *blackbirds* whistle clear,

**'The Fête Champetre'**: 'They heard the *blackbird*'s sang, man' and **'The Humble Petition of Bruar Water'**: 'The *blackbird* strong, the lintwhite clear.'
 In the **'Sketch'** we can find -

> Where *blackbirds* join the shepherd's lays
> At close o day.

His **'Lament of Mary, Queen of Scots'** in 1790 contains:

> The *merle*, in his noontide bow'r,
> Makes woodland echoes ring;

Also in the song **'Ode to Spring'**: 'The *blackbird* next, his tuneful text' was not exactly meant in an ornithological sense.
 His reference to 'take your *blackbird*' in the letter of 1788 to Agnes McLehose, refers to a poem she had written that Burns intended to improve.

## SONG THRUSH *Turdus philomelos*

**Local:** Mavey; Mavis; Thrush

Burns used the term 'Mavis', which is acceptable without doubt as Song Thrush, but more frequently he simply used the collective 'thrush'. Of the other five species of the genus turdus occurring regularly in Scotland, any supposed confusion with Ring Ouzel *T. torquatus* with its distinctive plumage, voice and breeding habitat requirements can be safely ignored.
 Similarly, the migrant and winter visiting Fieldfare *T. pilaris* (although recorded in Dumfriesshire by 1684) and Redwing *T. iliacus* can also be excluded, largely due to not being named till later in the century, but also to the fact that virtually all of the bird records referred to were either spring, summer or breeding birds.
 The remaining Thrush species, the Mistle Thrush *T. viscivorus*, was formerly exceedingly rare in the south of Scotland. In 1791, in an account of the Parish of Kirkmichael, it is included in the list of 'rare birds', and writing in 1832, Sir William Jardine states 'Fifteen years ago they were rarely to be seen'. In addition none of the other early writers mention the species, either by its proper

or local names, 'felty' and 'storm cock'.

We can therefore, in my view, feel totally secure that, when Burns wrote of Mavis or 'thrush' he had in mind only the Song Thrush *T. philomelos*.

In his song, **'And Maun I Still on Menie Doat'**, he uses 'The *mavis* and the lint-white sing'; and the second version of **'Ca' The Yowes To the Knowes'**:

> Hark, the *mavis* e'eving sang
> Sounding Clouden's woods amang...

This latter quotation and the following two, not only show that Burns was indeed referring to the Song Thrush, but also demonstrates that he was aware that, unlike some other species of Thrush, they were likely to sing at twilight.

From the **'Lament of Mary, Queen of Scots'** 'The *mavis* wild wi monie a note,' and in the song **'My Nanie's Awa'**:

> And thou mellow *mavis* that hails the night-fa'
> Give over for pity-my Nanie's awa.

**'The Humble Petition of Bruar Water'** has the line 'The *mavis* mild and mellow'; and in the poem of 1786, **'The Night Was Still'**:

> The *mavis* sang, while dew-drops hang
> Around her on the castle wa':

The very popular song **'The Lass O Ballochmyle'** includes:

> In ev'ry glen the *mavis* sang,
> All Nature list'ning seem'd the while,
> Except where greenwood echocs rang,
> Amang the braes o Ballochmyle.

The use of the term 'thrush' is first exemplified in the song **'Now Westlin Winds'**: 'The hazel bush o'erhangs the *thrush*,'; and the song **'Logan Braes'** has a classic:

> Within yon milk-white hawthorn bush,
> Amang her nestlings sits the *thrush*:

In the song **'The Lass Of Cessnock Banks'**, Burns continues with the theme:

> Her voice is like the ev'ning *thrush*,
> That sings on Cessnock banks unseen,
> While his mate sits nestling in the bush...

and in **'Sae Flaxen Were Her Ringlets'**:

> While falling, recalling,
> The amorous *thrush* concludes his sang!

**'The Brigs O Ayr'** includes 'The chanting linnet, or the mellow *thrush*' and in **'On Hearing A Thrush Sing In His Morning Walk'** :

> Sing on, sweet *thrush*, upon the leafless bough,
> Sing on, sweet bird, I listen to thy strain:

The song **'Ode to Spring'** mentions '*Thrush*' in what was a mock pastoral written as a wager.

### On Hearing A Thrush Sing In His Morning Walk

> Sing on, sweet thrush, upon the leafless bough,
> Sing on, sweet bird, I listen to thy strain:
> See aged Winter, 'mid his surly reign,
> At thy blythe carol, clears his furrowed brow.
> So in lone Poverty's dominion drear
> Sits meek Content with light, unanxious heart,
> Welcomes the rapid moments, bids them part,
> Nor asks if they bring ought to hope or fear.
> I thank thee, Author of this opening day,
> Thou whose bright sun now gilds yon orient skies!
> Riches denied, Thy boon was purer joys:
> What wealth could never give nor take away!
> Yet come, thou child of Poverty and Care,
> The mite high Heav'n bestow'd, that mite with thee I'll share.

## MAGPIE  *Pica pica*

**Local:** Piet; Pie; Pegpie; Pyet

In the Old Statistical Account the Magpie is mentioned 'pretty often' from the lower-lying parts of Scotland. At the beginning of the nineteenth century the Magpie was 'generally distributed throughout Scotland' (Sir A B Duncan *in litt.*) and by 1899 James Laurie, a gamekeeper at Kirkconnel, Nithsdale, was recorded as having 'killed three hundred during the year.'
    Burns refers to it in his **'Epistle to James Tennant of Glenconner'**:

> To cast my een up like a *pyet*
> When by the gun she tumbles o'er...

He was similarly quite specific in his letter of 1788 to Mrs Dunlop, when he included 'I had better been a rook or *Magpie* all at once.' The species is alluded to in the song **'Ken Ye Na Our Lass, - Bess?'** attributed to Burns in *MMC*: 'She's biggit a *magpie*'s nest.'

## ROOK  *Corvus frugilegus*

**Local:** Corn Crow; Crow; Craw

Agricultural damage by the rook was referred to in an Act of Parliament of James I of Scotland in 1424. The species is specifically mentioned once by

Burns, although it was certainly a common breeding resident in both Ayrshire and Dumfriesshire during his time.

The rookery at Eliock, in the parish of Sanquhar, Dumfriesshire for example, is said to have been in existence since at least 1640 and as early as 1765 there is reference to 'great flocks' at Eskdalemuir.

As a further general indication of abundance, on the estate of the Earl of Haddington, East Lothian, 76,655 rooks were killed between 1779 and 1793; and during this same period, organised rook 'shoots' were also a feature in Dumfriesshire.

Writing to Mrs Dunlop from Ellisland on 7 December, 1788, Burns clearly depressed about the future of the farm, states:

I had better been a *rook* or a magpie all at once, and then I would not have been plagued with any ideas superior to breaking of clods and picking up grubs:

My other evidence to fully support the inclusion of the rook is from **'The Cotter's Saturday Night'**, a rich historical poem, composed during the winter of 1785-86. In the second verse he refers to 'The black'ning trains o *craws* to their repose'.

This succinctly describes the behaviour of rooks flying to roost in winter – the birds fly steadily on a direct flight path, with group following group towards the selected, at times traditional, roost site in woodland.

On some occasions, Ravens *C. corax* and Carrion/Hooded Crows *C. corone* also fly to communal roost sites. Neither species would, however, be so numerous as to warrant the description of 'black'ning trains'.


## CARRION/HOODED CROW *Corvus corone*

**Local:** Corbie; Corbie Craw; Hoodie Craw; Hoodie Grey Crow; Grey backed Crow; Sea Crow

Carrion and Hooded Crows were formerly treated as separate species by earlier ornithologists due to their different plumage. They inter-breed freely and successfully and are now consequently regarded as belonging to the same species.

In the older records the 'hoodie' and the 'black craw' are so confused that it is now quite impossible to say to which species comments refer – especially in Dumfriesshire and Galloway, where Carrion Crow was also frequently called the 'corbie', further confusing it with the Raven *C. corax*.

They have certainly been around for a long time. The Act of James II (1457) refers to and directs that 'Crawys should be destroyed and prevented from building in orchards and kirkyards'. These comments could equally also have referred to rooks. During the mid-eighteenth century the 'hoodie', or rather the crow with the greyer plumage, was breeding mainly in the eastern highlands and islands, south to Ayrshire and including Ailsa Craig and the Isle of Man;

whereas the black Carrion Crow was more in evidence in Dumfries and Galloway, the Borders and north to Aberdeenshire on the east coast. Apparently there has always been a zone of hybridisation, which has indeed altered during the present century in favour, it seems, of grey-plumaged crows, due to factors that are not yet fully understood by biologists.

The situation is further complicated by the arrival in late autumn and winter of immigrant grey Crows, especially to the Ayrshire coast, thought largely to be of Scandinavian origin. The local name 'Sea Crow' has been used to describe these migrants, in conjunction with descriptions of nesting on sea cliffs. Apparently, in the mid-eighteenth century, they were more likely to be coastal rather than inland breeders, at least in Ayrshire.

Burns mentions the species in his **'Lament For the Absence of William Creech, Publisher'** referring to Creech's non-payment of fees due to the poet following publication of the Edinburgh Edition of 1787:

> He cheeps like some bewinder'd chicken
> Scar'd frae its minnie and the cleckin,
>      By *hoodie-craw*

In **'The Ronalds of the Bennals'**, he quotes:

> Though I canna ride in well-booted pride,
> And flee o'er the hills like a *craw*, man,
> I can haud up my head wi the best o the breed,
> Though fluttering ever so braw, man.

and in his letter of 1787 to James Smith he includes 'or *craws* prognosticating a storm in a hairst day', which could similarly have equally applied to either rook or hooded crow.

His reference to *hoodie-craw* in the alternative lines for **'Election Ballad for Westerha''** was a figure of speech.

## RAVEN *Corvus corax*

**Local:** Corbie; Hoodie; Craw

There were 'many ravens' in Berwick-upon-Tweed in 1584 and they were considered common as scavengers of human waste on the streets of Edinburgh and Leith in 1597. By the end of the eighteenth century the raven was still considered a reasonably common breeding bird in Scotland, although significant decreases were being widely reported.

The Statistical Accounts of Ayr showed that, prior to 1832, the raven was common in most parishes and similarly in Dumfriesshire, although the records were sparsely distributed. There is little doubt that, despite increased persecution, the species retained a tenuous hold as a breeding resident.

Burns refers to it in **'The Brigs O Ayr'** thus:

> As for your priesthood, I shall say but little,
> *Corbies* and clergy are a shot right kittle:

Writing specifically on the 'raven' in **'The Cotter's Saturday Night'**: 'That he who stills the *raven*'s clam'rous nest'.

The remaining references are in the connotation of describing aspects to the black plumage of the raven.

In the well known song **'John Anderson, My Jo'** for example, 'Your locks were like the *raven*'; and in the **'Fragment'**, or **'Her Flowing Locks'** - 'Her flowing locks, the *ravens*' wing'. 'Come in thy *raven* plumage, Night' is mentioned in the now obscure song **'The Goud'** (renamed **'Yestreen I Had A Pint O Wine'**). The reference to 'Harpy *Raven*' in **'Caledonia'** refers to Danes.


## JACKDAW  *Corvus monedula*

**Local:** Daws, Jackie, Hill Craw, Keea, Keeaw, Kaes

The jackdaw was first recorded in Sibbald's *List of Scottish Birds* in 1684 and The Old Statistical Accounts indicate that the bird was fairly common in the Stirling and Lanark Hills.

There are, however, no substantiated records for either Dumfriesshire or Ayrshire until 1813. No doubt they may well have been under recorded; they were certainly in an expansive phase during the mid-eighteenth century and without doubt were then scarcer and more restricted geographically than they are today. They were known to have exploited the rapidly expanding mid-eighteenth century rabbit population, by utilising their burrows as nest sites, especially on higher open ground; hence the local name of 'hill craw'.

Burns was certainly familiar with at least one aspect of their behaviour when in his **'The Author's Ernest Cry and Prayer'** he penned:

> God bless your Honours, a' your days
> Wi sowps o kail and brats o claes,
> In spite o a' the thievish *kaes*,
> That haunt St. Jamie's!


## HOUSE SPARROW  *Passer domesticus*

**Local:** Speug(ie); Sparry; Sparra; Tittling

Historically a common and widespread breeding species throughout Scotland, especially in association with human habitation and, of course, the growing of cereal crops. It was largely regarded as a pest species. Altitude does seem to provide a barrier to complete distribution and it remains scarcer in some upland areas. During the mid-eighteenth century and until the end of the nineteenth, House Sparrow remained very rare in the Dumfriesshire village of Wanlockhead – well known to Burns.

This may have been partly altitudinal, but more likely to have been the direct result and effect of high levels of lead which escaped into the environment, polluting both the air, land and water (there were no fish in the streams and the local people could not keep caged birds as pets) – a direct consequence of the lead mining processes in the area.

Although the Dunnock *Prenella modularis* was called the Hedge-Sparrow locally, and the Tree Sparrow *Passer montanus* was possibly present – but certainly extremely rare – my view is that it can be safely concluded that Burns was referring to *P. domesticus* in his letter of 1789 to Robert Aiken when he included:

Ignorance, superstition, bigotry, stupidity, male violence, self conceit, envy – all strongly bound in a mossy frame of brazen impudence. Good God, Sir! to such a shield, humor is the peck of a *sparrow*, and satire the pop-gun of a school-boy.

In the song **'Our Gudewife's Sae Modest'** from *MMC* :

Our gudewife's sae modest,
When she is set at meat,
A laverock's leg, or a *tittling*'s wing,
Is mair than she can eat;

## GOLDFINCH *Carduelis carduelis*

**Local:** Goldie; Goldflinch; Gouldspink; Gooldie; Gowdspink; Greypate (of the young)

First mentioned in the Old Statistical Accounts, Goldfinches were described as in 'great abundance' on the Dryfe, Dumfriesshire. The history of the Goldfinch in southern Scotland has long been related to two main factors: the availability of weed seeds (principally thistle and ragwort); and the activities of bird fanciers who caught the birds in large numbers for aviaries.

Obviously, as farming techniques improved, there were fewer weeds available or at least surviving to produce heads of seeds as food. Gray, writing about Dumfriesshire in 1870, says, 'For many winters past I have been surprised at the very large numbers that are sent weekly from Dumfriesshire to Glasgow. Many hundreds must be taken in a season'.

In actual fact the 'many hundreds taken' were the least of it! In those days the practice, which continues to this day, was to use caged call birds to lure the winter 'charms' onto strings or twigs covered with bird lime. Those that were discarded as unfit for breeding or sale were either killed, or cleaned with coal oil or paraffin and released. This latter practice destroyed the natural waterproofing oils in the feathers, and since most catching took place in winter, the birds subsequently died while roosting.

It was not unusual for up to 80% of 'the catch' to be destroyed in one way or another. Thus the total mortality must have been enormous, and gave rise to marked fluctuations and local variations in Goldfinch numbers, depending on the location of and mobility of the bird catchers.

Burns refers to the Goldfinch in his **'The Humble Petition of Bruar Water'**: 'The *gowdspink*, Music's gayest child'. Writing to Maria Riddell on December 1793, while in Dumfries, he also made a very significant comment when referring to his own mood at the time:

> ...my soul flouncing and fluttering round her tenement, like a wild *Finch* caught amid the horrors of winter and newly thrust into a cage.

His letter of 1794 to Alexander Cunningham alluded to his knowledge of bird lime, although as usual couched in human emotions: 'I must conclude that wealth imparts a bird-lime quality to the Possessor'. It remains indicative of its widespread use over a very long period of time and the suffering that the substance must inevitably have caused to thousands of small birds.

## LINNET *Carduelis cannabina*

**Local:** Red Linnet*; Rose-Linnet*; Rose-Lintie*; Brown Linnet; Redpoll;
Whin-Lintie; Lintwhite; Lintie
(*the first three local names refer only to the male in breeding plumage)

The early records are very poor regarding the Linnet considering that its existence in Scotland was first documented by 1684. It is mentioned in the Old Statistical Accounts but without useful detail, other than rather vague adjectives on its status from a few areas. Certainly in Ayrshire it remained 'common' by the middle of the nineteenth century and similarly, writing about Dumfriesshire in 1832, Jardine at least inferred that it was not uncommon in most areas. There can be little doubt that the bird retracted its range in both counties in the face of agricultural advance, and the demise of large areas of broom and gorse, its preferred nesting habitat.

Of all the birds mentioned in the various works of the Bard, the Linnet is referred to most frequently and I have abbreviated the references.

In the songs:

**'And Maun I Still on Menie Doat'**
> The mavis and the *lint-white* sing...

**'Bessy And Her Spinnin-Wheel'**
> The *lintwhites* in the hazel braes...

**'There was a Lass (Bonnie Jean)'**
> But hawks will rob the tender joys,
> That bless the little *lintwhite*'s nest...

**'A Rose-Bud By My Early Walk'**
> Within the bush her covert nest
> A little *linnet* fondly prest...

**'A Mothers Lament'**
>> The mother *linnet* in the brake
>> Bewails her ravish'd young;

**'Now Spring Has Clad the Grove in Green'**
>> Which, save the *linnets* flight, I wot,
>> Nae ruder visit knows…

**'Now Westlin Winds'**
>> The hazel bush o'er hangs the thrush,
>> The spreading thorn the *linnet*.

**'Sleep'st Thou'**
>> In twining hazel bowers,
>> His lay the *linnet* pours…
>>> Alternative 'The *lintwhite* in his bower'

**'The Winter It is Past'**
>> May have charms for the *linnet* or the bee:

**'Their Groves O Sweet Myrtle'**
>> A-list'ning the *linnet*, aft wanders my Jean.

**'The Humble Petition of Bruar Water'**
>> The blackbird strong, the *lintwhite* clear…

**'Epistle To William Simpson'**
>> Where *lintwhites* chant amang the buds…

**'Despondency'-An Ode**
>> Ye tiny elves that guiltless sport,
>> Like *linnets* in the bush…

**'The Brigs of Ayr'**
>> The chanting *linnet*, or the mellow thrush…

Written in Friars Carse House near Dumfries, 'Cheerful peace, with *linnet* song', and in the 1787 letter to William Nicol: 'as blythe's a *lintwhite* on a flowrie thorn'.

And finally, in his **'Ode to Spring'** the song of the Linnet was referred to in a rather bawdy verse: 'The *linnet*'s lay come then in play'.


**YELLOWHAMMER** *Emberiza citrinella*

**Local:** Yoit; Yellow Yite; Yeorlin; Yeldrock

The Yellow Youling, which one may assume to be of this species, is mentioned by Sibbald in 1684. Although not recorded in Southern Scotland in the Old Statistical Accounts, it is included in subsequent lists from most parishes, and thereafter most writers record it as common on mainland Scotland.

Certainly by 1800 it was regarded as a common resident in both Ayrshire and

Dumfriesshire. More often it was associated with lowland arable and pastoral habitats, later gathering into mixed flocks with finches and sparrows during autumn and winter, to exploit stubble and other sources of spilled grain in the vicinity of farms.

The superstition that the yellowhammer has some association with his Satanic majesty still persisted in Dumfriesshire and Southern Ayrshire up to the 1960s, and remained the subject of 'school boy' doggerels. The familiar song is often likened in textbooks to the refrain 'a little bit of bread and no cheeee-se'. In Southern Scotland, however, this usage was widespread, but was often preceded by - 'Diel, diel, diel, he'll take ye'.

In *MMC* Burns included a song entitled **'The Yellow, Yellow Yorlin'** but in this bawdy folksong the 'yellow yorlin' alluded to female genitals.

### *Additional Notes*

The ornithological records contained within the collective writings of Burns are among the earliest reliable local ones available to us. They are thus obviously of significant historical interest, especially to the conservationist when compared to the position pertaining now.

Of the 41 species and two groups he referred to, it is rather sad to record that three species – *Bittern, Sea Eagle* and *Red Kite* – became extinct as breeding species in Scotland relatively soon after Burns' death. A fourth, the *Corncrake*, is very restricted in range, being mainly present only on the Western Islands. Indeed, apart from *Carrion Crow, Jackdaw* and *House Sparrow*, all the remaining species have undergone quite dramatic and significant decreases including retraction of their range. From his lists only *Carrion Crow* has managed to increase during the last two centuries and that, significantly, in spite of continued persecution.

In recent years, the *Sea Eagle* has been successfully re-introduced by the Nature Conservancy Council, largely from Scandinavian stock, and attempts are currently being made to restore the *Red Kite* as a regular breeding species to Scotland. For the others the outlook remains bleak indeed. The *Bittern,* whose last remaining breeding station was within the Lochar Moss area near Dumfries, typically became the victim of drainage and land reclamation, while the *Corncrake* has succumbed on the mainland largely due to changes in agricultural practices, especially the production of silage and the earlier mechanical cutting of grain crops.

Many such detrimental changes as far as wildlife habitats are concerned are patently obvious, such as direct habitat loss through wetlands being drained, hedges uprooted, fences replacing stone walls and generally the land being brought into intensive agricultural production in so called land improvements. The devastation is augmented by the demands of planners for increased house building, often within green belt areas and the inevitable motorway services. Arguably the most damaging aspect remains the continued and intensive use of agricultural fertilisers and herbicides which inevitably destroy or contaminate vital insect and invertebrate food sources with obvious widespread and long term ecological and biological effects.

Direct illegal intervention by man also remains an extremely vexed problem. The catching of small song birds to retain in aviaries for showing continues, with mist nets and powered clap nets being added to the traditional armoury of bird lime – an awful substance which, although banned, is still imported and used illegally in a substituted form.

In addition, in spite of dramatic changes in legislation, egg collecting continues unabated with an estimated 200 collectors active in Britain. Since a large number of the rarer birds attempting to breed in Britain locate in Scotland, we thus receive a disproportionate amount of attention from these uncivilised kleptomaniacs. Even if the eggs do survive to hatch, birds of prey in particular, continue to be removed in significant numbers from nests to bolster the archaic sport of falconry and, in addition, to supplement birds already kept for private breeding programmes and in zoological collections. Ever greater numbers of raptors are annually destroyed by irresponsible gamekeepers in the continued so called interests of 'game preservation'. There exist in many parts of Scotland 'black holes' or 'raptor sumps' – large areas of eminently suitable habitat which are very obviously totally devoid of birds of prey, indicating in a very negative frame, the illegal activities of land management.

The hundreds of incidents notified during the last two decades are but the tip of the iceberg. It is obviously proving incredibly difficult to get gamekeepers, estate factors and owners – who often behind the scenes are responsible for giving direct instructions to their gamekeepers – to understand that such activities are totally counterproductive to the continuance of gamebird shooting; and when uncovered to public knowledge, only succeed in providing verbal ammunition to those determined to apply added pressure to have bird shooting severely curtailed in Britain. By continuing with such policies they also underline their ignorance of predator/prey relationships. They fail to comprehend that the volume of prey items available control raptors – not the reverse!

These policies are often allied to the obscenity of large-scale pheasant and partridge releases of artificially reared birds. They are of limited sporting value and it would greatly alleviate the present hiatus and enhance the credibility of sport shooting if such practices were to cease within Britain and legislation followed the excellent example in Holland where only wild bred birds may be shot. There also remain too many physchological and financial pressures placed on the lowly paid gamekeeper to show or produce game often for badly behaved foreign guns. They must be subjected to greater control and initiation into improved shooting ethics, and we must strive towards legislation to make estate factors and land owners directly responsible for the action of their employees in this field.

As an ornithologist, conservationist and one who also likes to shoot responsibly, I feel that the way forward is to promote gamekeepers towards a more professional standing with a remit as land managers in the countryside. They should be subsidised, trained, certificated and provided with a properly structured condition of service with a commensurate salary scale. Thus elevated to the professional class that their undoubted expertise would justify, and with the ever present deterrent of having certification removed – along with the required licence to use firearms – the illegal persecution of raptors, practiced over centuries would become insignificant.

No employee should be required or instructed to break the law in the execution of their duties; and when caught doing so, the landowner should be held responsible too!

# FISH
## AND OTHER WILDLIFE

Salmon (Keith Brockie)

*O Nature! a' thy shews an forms*
*To feeling, pensive hearts hae charms!*

## Introduction

Outwith the main groups of plants and animals already discussed, throughout his writings Burns regularly referred to other species that are, in my view, certainly worthy of inclusion here in a review of his natural history records.

Principally, they serve to indicate the broad scope of his knowledge, gained mainly within his role as a working farmer; but also in a more general sense, as an intelligent observer of a wide range of other natural history phenomena. In addition, the formal listing of these records that were considered to be sufficiently specific as to warrant acceptance, provides a very good record and indication of the general level of the so called 'scientific knowledge' of the non-academic but practical 'countryman' during this period in history.

A short, precise list is available in Appendix 6. The following brief species notes, while not exhaustive, are sufficient to support the inclusion of the main species giving a modicum of explanatory evidence and to place the references within the poetic licence and natural history context.

I have excluded references to some of the very exotic and non-native species – for example, Silkworm *Bomby x mori* and Tarantula *Lycosa tarantula*.

His reference to 'stockfish' in the **'Elegy On Captain Matthew Henderson'** is a general term applied to any common species of fish that was either cured or salted. Two references to *buckie(s)* in **'To A Gentleman'** and his **'Epistle to John Maxwell, Esq. of Terraughtie'** refer either to young people or in the diminutive, and not to the Scots for a whelk or its shell *buccinidae*.


## HERRING   *Clupea harengus*

This well known fish (the silver darling) was an abundant resident in the colder North Atlantic and widely distributed, during the eighteenth century, round all of our coastline – a vital component of an otherwise limited diet. The 'type' fished then was the Shelf Herring, which shoaled in massive numbers and was thus exploited as a valuable protein source. Sold fresh at the landing harbours, it was also salted down into barrels and smoked to provide kippers. It is very difficult now, to appreciate the immense size of these fish populations prior to modern drift netting aided by sonar devices; but even up to 1848, so great were the numbers stranded on the sand banks near Caerlaverock, in Dumfriesshire for example, that they were carted away by farmers for manure. By 1850, over one hundred boats were still fishing in the inner Solway, primarily for herring. Historically the Ayrshire fishing ports were similarly renowned in Britain for their landings.

Surprisingly, Burns only mentions the species three times. In his **'Death and Doctor Hornbook'** he wrote:

I'll nail the self-conceited sot,
As dead's a *herrin*;

and in the famous epic of **'Tam o' Shanter'**:

Ah, Tam! Ah, Tam! thou'll get thy fairin!
In hell they'll roast thee like a *herrin*!

Writing to David Sillar, from Ellisland on 5 August, 1789, Burns said:

...this comes to advise you that your fifteen barrels of *herrings* were, by the blessing of God, shipped safe...


## ATLANTIC SALMON *Salmo salar*

**Local:** Grey-back

A large and much prized fish – one of 67 lbs (30 kg) is recorded officially from the Nith, although larger fish are known to have been taken illegally at Sanquhar. Significantly reduced in numbers during the past three decades, it is still traditionally fished during its upstream migration to breed. Swimming thus against the currents it often provides spectacular displays while negotiating waterfalls to spawn in shallow tributaries with suitable gravel beds. Salmon rivers known to Burns are listed in Appendix 4.

Burns produced a different version of the well known song **'John Anderson, My Jo'** in *MMC* which includes: 'I'm ba-ckit like a *salmon*'.

In **'The Auld Farmer's New-Year Morning Salutation To His Auld Mare, Maggie'** he says :

Tho now ye dow but hoyte and hobble,
An wintle like a *saumont*-coble...

A coble, a traditional, small, one-masted flat bottomed boat of Celtic origin, was also used to assist salmon netsmen in Scotland.

In **'Tam Samson's Elegy'**, as a mock epitaph to a well known sportsman, Burns penned: 'Now safe the stately *saumont* sail'.

Many salmon were cured by smoking. Burns says, in his letter of 1794 to Peter Hill: 'I sent you a Kippered *Salmon*', and in 1796 to the same person, 'I send your annual Kipper.'

Writing to Robert Graham of Fintry in 1789 inviting him to dine, Burns included: 'I shall promise you a good piece of good old beef, a chicken, or perhaps a Nith *salmon* fresh from the ware'.

The 'grey-backed' salmon, which traditionally run the Nith, Tweed and a few other rivers, was a variety of very large, stocky, deep-bodied salmon with some colour variations not regularly found on other Scottish fish, although once they begin to change from sea silver to breeding colours the range is hugely variable. The 'grey' colour on the back becomes visible through the translucent outer skin, as fat deposits put on at sea dissipate in fresh water, becoming more apparent as the fish appear in the upper reaches.

A late run fish, whose population in the rivers peaked in late September or October, they were not of any sub-specific or named variety, but regarded by some authorities as an example of an isolated population or group which remained sufficiently biologically separate long enough to develop minor genetic differences, in accordance with every river and tributary which has an unique population.

Their virtual disappearance, at least in the Nith by about 1960, is thus more easily explained in that, if it is accepted they were a biologically separate group, they would by definition breed, migrate and develop at sea together as a group.

They would thus be extremely vulnerable: to specific area trawling at sea, estuarine netting, river pollution or systematic poaching – the combined effects of which could inevitably eliminate the total population which would indeed be a disgraceful loss, not only to river or estuarine fishermen, but to our natural heritage.

## BROWN TROUT/SEA TROUT  *Salmo trutta*

**Local:**  Brown Trout - Burn Trout
Sea Trout - Salmon Trout (netsmen)

On returning to fresh water after a summer at sea, these fish are at a 'grilse' stage and are known by several names in different parts of Scotland: *Borders* – Herling, Blue back, Yellow Fin Herling; *Tweed* – Whiting; *Central and North* – Finnock; to give only a few examples. Brown and Sea Trout are of course the same species with a variable life history.

Varieties of *Salmo trutta*, the brown trout, spend all their life in fresh water, typically in fast clear streams but also in lochs. Silvery sea trout occur off the coastline and like salmon migrate to spawn in fresh water. Unlike its larger cousin it feeds during these migrations and does not die after breeding. Trout were present in all of the rivers mentioned by Burns.

In **'The Humble Petition of Bruar Water'**, written in 1787 to The Noble Duke of Atholl:

> The lightly-jumping, glowrin *trouts*,
> That thro my waters play...

and in the song **'Now Spring Has Clad the Grove in Green'** there is a classic verse :

> The *trout* within yon wimpling burn
> Glides swift, a silver dart,
> And, safe beneath the shady thorn,
> Defies the angler's art:
> My life was ance that careless stream
> That wanton *trout* was I,

> But Love wi unrelenting beam
> Has scorch'd my fountains dry.

The song **'Guidwife, Count the Lawin'** or **'Gane is the Day'** contains the line:

> And Pleasure is a wanton *trout*:
> An ye drink it a', ye'll find him out!

Burns regularly visited the Globe Tavern in Dumfries and described it as his 'favourite howff'. He is reputed to have written several lines on the windows, one such piece included:

> My bottle is a holy pool
> That heals the wounds o care and dool;
> And pleasure is a wanton *trout*,
> An ye drink it, ye'll find him out.

Finally **'Tam Samson's Elegy'** produced: 'And *trouts* bedropp'd wi crimson hail'.

## PIKE  *Esox lucius*

**Local:** Ged

A voracious, predatory fish, with exceedingly large and powerful jaws, armed with strong teeth – one of 45 lbs (20.4 kg) was reputed to have been taken in Hightae Loch, Lochmaben, although modern authorities tend to disregard such unauthenticated records as mere 'anglers' tales'. Its banded colouration enables it to lurk unseen among reeds and other vegetation and await its prey, which includes other fish, frogs, water voles and ducklings. It has taken, for example,

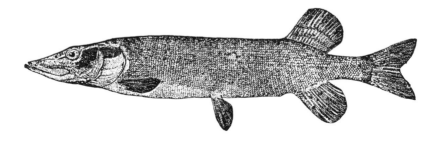

other fish up to 11 lbs (15 kg); full grown Moorhen *Gallinula chloropus* (Derek Skilling *pers.comm.*); and an almost fully grown Greylag Goose *Anser anser* was found complete in the stomach of one taken in Galloway (Young, J G *in litt*). Present in many lochs and rivers in both Ayrshire and Dumfriesshire, its original distribution was not necessarily extended by birds but mainly from original introductions as a fresh food source in winter. The flesh is firm at that time, when other fresh water and river species are inedible. Redistribution within Scotland dated from the era of monastic settlements, when it was discovered that pike could be kept alive in wet sphagnum moss, and they were transported over large distances in pony panniers.

**'Tam Samson's Elegy'** mentions the species:

> And eels, weel-kend for souple tail,
> And *geds* for greed…

In some parts of Ayrshire, the name 'ged' was only applied to the young male or 'jack' pike.

## PERCH *Perca fluviatilis*

Common in lochs, ponds and the slower flowing stretches of rivers, it can be recognised by its separate dorsal spines, olive green banding and quite vivid red pelvic and anal fins. Perch mainly eat invertebrates when young; later they predate other fish. Single females can lay up to 30,000 eggs in strands over water plants, twigs or stones.

In his song **'The Campbells Are Comin'**, the melody and part of the chorus came from a Jacobite song of the 1715 uprising. The other verses by Burns allude to the imprisonment of Mary Queen of Scots in Loch Leven Castle, Kinross, in 1567.

> Upon the Lomonds I lay, I lay,
> I looked down to bonie Lochleven,
> And saw three bonie *perches* play

## MINNOW *Phoxinus phoxinus*

**Local:** Beardie

Common and geographically wide-spread in Scotland, they are absent only from some areas in Galloway, from the Outer Isles, and the Highlands. A small fish species with dark markings, it is common especially in lowland rivers and lakes. They form midwater summer shoals and disperse to deeper water in winter. Their main food are invertebrates and plant material. In turn, they provide a very important food source for larger fish species, birds and other animals. Surprisingly for a small fish, their lifespan can exceed six years.

Burns mentions the species in a letter written to Helen Craik on 9 August, 1790 'watching the frisks of the little *minnows* in the sunny pool'.

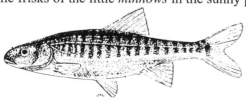

**EEL** *Anguilla anguilla*

An unmistakeable species characterised by a very thin, long, body. Common in all fresh waters in southern Scotland where it spends a large part of its life as an immature or 'yellow eel'. With the onset of sexual maturity they descend, at times overland, to the sea, prior to an amazing migration across the Atlantic to the Sargasso Sea where they spawn. At about the age of three the young (elvers) return and ascend the river systems to grown into 'yellow eels'. Males will remain for seven to fourteeen years in fresh water, females nine to nineteen years, before the cycle is completed.

In his **'Elegy on Captain Mathew Henderson'**, Burns said 'Ye fisher herons, watching *eels*;' and in **'Tam Samson's Elegy'** we find 'And *eels*, weel-kend for souple tail'.

There remains some doubt about the authenticity of an **'Epitaph For Johnston of Elshieshields'**, attributed to Burns:

> Wha's left Lochmaben's bonnie fields
> An a' her lochs and a' her *eels...*

There is less doubt that he penned the words to the song **'Ellibanks'**:

> I'll clasp my arms around your neck,
> As souple as an *eel*, jo;

**COD** *Gadus morhua*

Formerly, large cod were common in the Solway Firth and in the Irish Sea off the Ayrshire coast. Now scarce and overfished, only codling survive and they are caught regularly, although nursery areas persist. Cod also inhabit the continental shelf and deeper coastal waters. It was probably the deep sea fishery, rather than the inshore one that Burns had in mind, when in **'The Twa Dogs'** he referred to:

> But whalpit some place far abroad,
> Whare sailors gang to fish for *cod*.

His further use of 'cod' referred to the Scots word for a pillow.

## *Shellfish*

Shellfish species cannot of course be classified as true fish, having no backbone, but I have included the records here simply as a convenience.

**LIMPET** *Patella vulgata*

The most characteristic of the inter-tidal molluscs with a broad base and conical shape; there are several species but the common limpet is *patella*, frequently found exposed in the upper part of the shore or in pools. Common along the

Ayrshire coastline especially where rocks are exposed, but less so in Dumfriesshire where sand and silts predominate.

In **'The Author's Earnest Cry and Prayer'**:

> Triumphant, crushin't like a mussel,
> Or *lampit* shell

## MUSSEL  *Mytilus edulis*

Mussels are widely distributed on the Ayrshire coast and on both the limited rocky shoreline of the inner Solway and also in the predominately sandy areas of, for example, Powfoot, near Annan. Where they occur, they are frequently the most common animal attached to the surface of inter-tidal rocks.

The only acceptable reference I can find is the one quoted above, 'crushin't like a *mussel*'.

## COCKLE  *Cardium edule*

The cockle is common and widespread on the Ayrshire and Dumfriesshire shores. They spend most of their lives quietly buried in the sand. Where they occur, they can do so in spectacular numbers, up to millions per hectare and are thus a valuable food source, especially for birds of the shore.

Burns provides a single record, in the song **'Tibbie Fowler'**:

> She's got pendles in her lugs,
> *Cockle*-shells wad set her better;

## SHRIMP

Burns' use of the word shrimp is not in the context of a crustacean.

## OYSTER  *Ostrea edulis*

Now scarce in the wild in Scotland, this bivalve was at one time common between the tide zones and in the shallow bottoms of tidal creeks. In the mid-eighteenth century they were thought to have medicinal qualities, and were in addition certainly harvested as an important food item.

Burns mentions the species in a letter to Margaret Chalmers: 'or an *oyster* on some of the desart [sic] shores' and again, when writing to Robert Cleghorn, 'I have left me as little soul as an *oyster*'.

It is also evident that Burns was the recipient of a barrel of oysters sent by Peter Hill from Edinburgh in 1795.

## LOBSTER  *Homarus vulgaris*

One would expect Burns to have been familiar with this marine crustacean. He did mention it in one letter to Maria Riddell, but in a rather derogatory tone and meaning perhaps the red colour of lobster following cooking:

> ...the first object which greeted my view was one of these *lobster*-coated
> PUPPIES, sitting, like another dragon, guarding the Hesparian fruit.

He was however quite specific when writing to George Thompson in 1793, with
a version of **'Green Grow The Rashes'** where, when referring to a person
clearly associated with fishing people, he said, 'And sell'd it for a *labster*, O'.

## CRAB

The reference to 'crab' in the bawdy song Effie McNab does not in my view
refer to the marine crustacean (*see also* Lice).

ജ ജ ജ ജ

## COMMON EARTHWORM *Lumbricus terestris*

**Local:** Reptile

A rather general descriptive term applied to a great many related animals that
have a soft elongated body without auspicious appendages.

Presumably Burns was referring to the commonest worm species, which may
still live at densities of some millions per hectare and grows up to 12 inches (30
cm). Much sought after as bait for anglers; it performs a most vital function to
man, assisting to aereate the soil and thus move nutrient salts to the surface.

Burns mentions worms in his **'Epitaph for Mr. Walter Riddell'**:

> So vile was poor Wat, such a miscreant slave,
> That the *worms* ev'n damn'd him when laid in his grave
> 'In his skull there's a famine' a starved *reptile* cries,
> 'And his heart it is poison!' another replies.

and, **'To Gavin Hamilton, Esq., Mauchline'**, a derogatory term to infer a low
self esteem, 'To meet the 'warld's *worm*'. Similarly, in a stark couplet, collected
by James Grierson:

> Lo *worms* enjoy the seat of bliss
> Where Lords and Lairds afore did kiss.

Burns in his 1781 letter to Alison Begbie said, 'The sordid *earth-worm* may
profess love to a woman's person'. In the poem **'Scotch Drink'**, the use of the
word 'worm' refers to a coil used in the distillation process.

## HORSELEECH *Haemopis sanguisuqa*

Despite its name, the Horseleech, an aquatic animal with suckers at each end,
does not attack horses but feeds on frogs and fish species. Like most blood

suckers, it secretes an anticoagulant; thus leech wounds take a long time to heal. It was used in primitive healing.

Burns mentions, or refers to the behaviour of this 'blood sucking' carnivorous worm in the song **'Scotch Drink'**, obviously as a derogatory term: 'Thae curst *horse-leeches* o' the' Excise'.

### SNAIL sp. *Helicidae*

Possibly Common Snail *Helix aspersa*, which is widespread and common in fields, gardens and on house walls. They hibernate during the winter. During the Burns period they were eaten widely throughout England but not apparently in Scotland. Snails represent a large, varied group of shelled gastropod mollusc, diverse in size and ecologically being either terrestial, fresh water or marine. They are characterised by a spiral shell which they withdraw into when disturbed or threatened.

There are only two references: in **'To Robert Graham Esq., of Fintry'** which is as one would expect, unspecific as to exact species: 'Thou giv'st the ass his hide, the *snail* his shell'.

Similarly, when writing to Mrs Dunlop in 1789, he was in political and humanist mood when he wrote -

> It has suggested itself to me as an improvement on the present Human figure, that a man in proportion to his own conceit of his consequence in the world, could have pushed out the longitude of his common size, as a *snail* pushes out his horns.

### SCORPION sp. *Scorpiones*

Arachnids with large claws and a slender tail tipped with a sting, they are largely nocturnal and mostly of tropical distribution but a few species live in southern Europe. Species occasionally found in British ports are generally harmless to humans. The sting of some tropical species can prove deadly; hence they are at times quoted in the context of 'danger'.

In his **'Passion's Cry'** written during his affair with Clarinda and completed in 1793 he wrote, 'Love grasps his *scorpians*, stifled they expire'; and in his **'To Robert Graham Esq., of Fintry'** he penned what was a scathing comment on William Creech, an Edinburgh publisher, who owed Burns a considerable sum of money for a long time, before finally providing a settlement.

> Vampyre booksellers drain him to the heart,
> And *scorpian* critics cureless venom dart.

In a letter of 1788 to Mrs Dunlop, referring to a press comment of his own, 'mine is the madness of an enraged *Scorpian* shut up in the thumb-phial'.

## SPIDER sp. *Araneae*

A very large group, with many species resident in south-west Scotland. They are all predatory creatures and many of them spin elaborate silken snares (webs) to trap insects for food. It is not possible to assign Burns' comments to specific species but he most certainly referred to the order.

In the rather bawdy song **'Bonie Mary'** he had one line, ''S a *spider* wad bigget a nest on't'; and **'Epistle to Colonel De Peyster'** comments:

> Syne weave, unseen, thy *spider* snare
> O Hell's damn'd waft!

Writing to George Thomson in 1794, Burns said -

> I spun the following stanzas for it; but whether my spinning will deserve to be laid up in store like the precious thread of a Silk-Worm, or brushed to the devil like the vile manufacture of the *Spider*, I leave my dear Sir, to your usual candid criticism.

## MITE *Ixodes ricinus*

**Local:** Tick; Sheep bug

Both Ticks and Mites are of the Class *Arachnida*. The commonest and therefore most likely to feature is the Sheep Tick *I. ricinus*. It lives in grassy areas and feeds on many mammals – the young will attach itself to and take blood from man.

The term 'mite' is also used in the diminutive sense; nonetheless the *arachnida* is specifically referred to and the examples are worthy of record.

In **'On Some Commemorations Of Thomson'** :

> 'To whom hae much, more shall be given,'
> Is every great man's faith;
> But he, the helpless, needful wretch,
> Shall lose the *mite* he hath.

and in an early version of a **'Sonnet, written on his Birthday'** (later called **'On Hearing A Thrush Sing In His Morning Walk'**): 'The *mite* high heaven bestowed, that *mite* with thee I'll share'.

More specifically in **'Death and Dr Hornbook'** -

> 'Or *mite*-horn shavings, filings, scrapings,
> Distill'd *per se*;'

## LOCUST  *Locusta migratoria*

The locust is very rare in Britain and it is almost certain that in quoting this insect Burns was not intending to infer that it was evident. Rather, he was either demonstrating his extended reading on such agricultural pests – the devastation of crops, especially in Africa, were widely reported in the press of that time – or it may well have been that the reference was gleaned from a biblical source.

In **'Verses In Friar's Carse Hermitage'** he wrote -

> Those that would the bloom devour -
> Crush the *locusts*, save the flower.

## LICE  *Pediculus humanus/Pthirus pubis*

**Local:** Louse; Crab(s); Beas'

Wingless parasites of birds and mammals, the order referred to is almost certainly the *Anoplura*. This blood-sucking lice is confined to mammals including of course, humans, and well known as a carrier of Typhus fever. The crab louse is another species, *Pthirus pubis* – restricted in humans mainly to the pubic hair. The word is often used to describe human attributes.

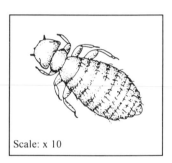

Scale: x 10

In his **'Address to the Deil'** of 1785/86 the poet says:

> Is instant made no worth a *louse*,
> Just at the bit.

and in a **'Reply To A Trimming Epistle Received From a Tailor'** sent by Burns to a tailor:

> What ails ye now, ye *lousie* bitch
> To thresh my back at sic a pitch?

From the same source:

> Gae mind your seam, ye *prick-the-louse*,
> An' jag-the-flae!

**'The Heron Election Ballads'** provides yet another connotation:

> A lord may be a *lousy* loun,
> Wi' ribbon, star and a' that.

The song **'Wha'll Mow Me Now'** has the line 'But deevil damn the *lousy* loun,' and in **'Address To The Deil'**:'Is instant made no worth a *louse*'.

An old song at times attributed to Burns, **'My Eppie McNab'** which he described as having 'more wit than decency' ended with the line: 'And thy ——— was as black as a *crab*, a *crab*', and did not refer to a marine crustacean of the genus Cancer.

Burns wrote a complete eight verse poem **'To A Louse'**, probably written in 1785 on seeing one on a lady's bonnet at church. Although the title is obvious and conclusive, the species is not specifically mentioned in the text, but extracts confirm the Poet's intention:

> Ye ugly, creepin, blastit wonner,
> Detested, shunn'd by saunt an sinner,
> How daur ye set your fit upon her -
>     Sae fine a lady!
> Gae somewhere else and seek your dinner
>     On some poor body.

and his famous conclusion:

> O wad some Power the giftie gie us
> To see oursels as ithers see us!
> It wad frae monic a blunder free us,
>     An foolish notion:
> What airs in dress an gait wad lea'e us,
>     An ev'n devotion!

In the epigram **'The Toadeater'**, of which there are several versions, Burns infers lice with the lines:

> Yet an insects an insect at most,
> Tho it crawl on the curl of a Queen!

One alternative gave the lines:

> No more of your titled acquaintances boast,
> Nor of the gay groups you have seen;
> A *crab louse* is but a *crab louse* at last,
> Tho stack to the arse of a Queen.

and in his **'Address of Beelzebub'** 'Flaffin wi duds, an grey wi *beas*'.'

'Louse' also means, in Scots, to loosen or slacken; for example, from **'The Jolly Beggars'**: 'To *louse* his pack, an wale a song'.

## GRASSHOPPER sp. *Acrididae*

Usually only active in sunshine, there are several species. Burns would almost certainly have been referring to the Common Field Grasshopper *Chorthippus brunneus* when he wrote to Helen Craik in 1790: 'tracing the *grasshopper* to his haunt by his chirping song'.

**BUTTERFLY** sp. *Lepidoptera*

A large group of day-flying and usually colourful insects. Although clearly aware of them as a group, there is no evidence in the quotations to specific species.

There are five references to 'butterflies'. From **'Verses in Friars Carse Hermitage'** written in 1788:

> Pleasures, insects on the wing
> Peace, th' tend'rest flow'r of spring,
> Those that sip the dew alone -
> Make the *butterflies* thy own;

and **'Monody'**: 'on a Lady famed for her caprice', **'The Epitaph'** served only to demonstrate the fraility of the Lady's character -

> Here lies, now a prey to insulting neglect,
> What once was a *butterfly*, gay in life's beam:
> Want only of wisdom denied her respect,
> Want only of goodness denied her esteem.

In a letter to Helen Craik, he also referred to, 'or hunting after the intrigues of wanton '*butterflies*' and in a letter to Jean McMurdo, he was in chauvanistic mood when describing girls as...

> ...*butterflies* of the human kind: remarkable only for and distinguised only by, the idle variety of their gaudy flore; sillily straying from one blossoming weed to another...

Demonstrating a remarkable knowledge of the biology of at least one species of Lepidoptra, Burns said when writing to Colonel William Fullarton in 1791:

> Fortune, must yet, like the *Caterpillar*, labor a whole lifetime before they reach the wished height, there to roost like a stupid Chrysalis.

Writing to a publisher Burns was reputed to have said:

> I see everyday new musical publications advertised, but what are they? Gaudy, hunted by *butterflies* of a day, and then vanish forever.

**MOTH** spp. *Lepidoptra:Heterocera*

A huge family, clearly no specific identification is possible from the single available record in his **'Epistle to James Smith'**:

> There's ither poets, much your betters,
> Far seen in Creek, deep men o letters,
> Hae thought they had ensur'd their debtors,
> A' future ages;

> Now *moths* deform, in shapeless tatters,
> Their unknown pages.

## MAGGOT  *Diptera*

**Local:** Grub; Worm

Collectively given to the hatched larva of many dipterous insect species, housefly and blowfly for example. Eggs are laid in living or decaying flesh of animals, but applies also to eggs laid in or around organic matter in water or injected into bushes or trees.

Referred to in the song **'Whistle o'er The Lave O 't'**:

> Wha I wish were *maggot*'s meat,
> Dish'd up in her winding sheet...

and in his **'Epitaph For William Nicol of The High School Edinburgh'**:

> Ye *maggots*, feed on Nicol's brain,
> For few sic feasts you've gotten;
> And fix your claws in Nicol's heart,
> For deil a bit o't's rotten.

When writing to Agnes McLehose (Clarinda) in 1788 -

> ...and give him the most glorious boon she ever had in her gift, merely for the *maggot*'s sake,

In **'The Book Worms'**, inscribed in a bible for a friend of John Syme:

> Through and through th' inspir'd leaves,
> Ye *maggots*, make your windings;
> But O, respect his lordship's taste,
> And spare the golden bindings!

The 'book worm' is the larva of various beetle species, for example, *Anobium spp.*

## MIDGE  *Ceratopogonidae* species of the genus *Culicoides*

**Local:** Gnat; Mosie

A large group of insects, some of which bite; they swarm in vast numbers, often to the extent of making life virtually intolerable to both animals and humans, and breed in water-logged soil and peat. From the available references it is not prudent to suggest a specific identification.

In his **'Heron Election Ballad: Fourth - The Trogger'** he penned: 'By a thievish *midge* they had been nearly lost'.

'Midge' of course, is also used in the diminutive – a more relevant record is in his **'Death and Dr. Hornbook'**: Sal-alkali o' *Midge-tail* clippings,'; and when writing to James Smith in 1787 he referred to 'like *midges* sporting in the mottie sun.'

**FLY** *Muscidae spp*

| | | |
|---|---|---|
| Probably: | HOUSEFLY | *Musca domestica* |
| Possibly: | SWEAT FLY | *Hydistaea irritans* |

**Local:** Flie; Flae; Flee

The most common and widely distributed fly, although now a decreasing species. Breeds in and around houses and is especially numerous around farms, middens, rubbish dumps – indeed wherever decaying matter is left to rot down. It swarms round cattle and people; sun bathes on walls and fences, eventually entering buildings to hibernate. Burns may have also been more familiar with the Sweat Fly *H. irritans*, which were attracted to working horses.

In the song **'The Country Lass'** we can find his first reference:

> For Johnie o the Buskie-Glen
> I dinna care a single *flie*:

and the song **'Philly and Willy'** in the chorus and the final verse, provides a similar line:

> For a' the joys that gowd can gie,
> I dinna care a single *flie*!
> The lad/lass I love's the lad for me,
> And that's my ain dear Willy/Philly.

The song **'Tibbie Fowler'** contains:

> A *flie* may fell her in the air,
> Before a man be even till her.

The well known song **'Whistle An I'll Come to You, My Lad'** contains the lines:

> At kirk, or at market, whene'er ye meet me,
> Gang by me as tho that ye car'd na a *flie*;

and in his **'Epistle to Colonel De Peyster'**:

> Poor Man, the *flie*, aft bizzes by,
> And aft, as chance he comes thee nigh.

**'The Jolly Beggars - A Cantata'** has:

> But for how lang the *flie* may stang,
> Let inclination law that!

Exactly the same lines were included in **'Tho Women's Minds'**. The song **'Wee Willie Gray'**, a nursery jingle revised by Burns, contains: 'Feathers of a *flie* wad feather up his bonnet'.


FLEA *Siphonaptra:Pulex irritans*

**Local:** Flae; Human Flea


Known from time immemorial to be associated with man and his buildings, the original hosts were probably fox and badger.

In his **'Reply To A Trimming Epistle Received from a Tailor'**, Burns, in sarcastic mood, described him as -

> Gae mind your seam, ye prick-the-louse,
> And jag-the-*flae*!

Burns referred to 'human fleas' in the old ballad **'The Taylor'**:

> The Taylor rase and sheuk his duds,
> The *flaes* they flew awa in cluds...

He is also attributed with a different version **'The Tailor He Came Here To Sew'** (Herd D. 1769) in which: 'He filled the house a' fou o' *fleas*'; and the bawdy song from *MMC* **'Ye'se Get A Hole To Hide It In'** included a final line: 'To keep it frae the *flaes*'.

From a similarly disputed source in the rewritten song **'Ellibanks'**:

> My wame if fistles ay like *flaes*,
> As I come o'er the knowe, man:


CLEG *Haematopota pluvialis*

**Local:** Gad-Flies; Horse Fly


A common and widely distributed fly, especially in damp wooded areas and very troublesome to both man and horses, it is especially active during thundery weather.

Burns mentions the species in a verse-epistle written **'To Alexander Findlater'**:

> And wi his kittle, forket *clegs*,
> Claw weel their dockies!

and again in his **'Epistle To Major Logan'**:

But as the *clegs* o feeling stang,
Are wise or fool.

## GALL WASP/CANKER WORM *Cynipidae*

A small ant-like insect which induces gall formation in plants especially oak trees. Locally abundant during outbreaks, the 'canker worm' is a caterpillar (Lepidoptera) which destroys buds and leaves. The term has been in English usage since 1530.

Although some doubt remains regarding authenticity, this species is mentioned in the 'verses' on the destruction of the woods near Drumlanrig, Thornhill, Dumfriesshire.

Was it the bitter eastern blast,
That scatters blight in early spring?
Or was't the wil' fire scorch'd their boughs,
Or *canker-worm* wi secret sting?

And on my dry and halesome banks
Nae *canker-worms* get leave to dwell:
Man! cruel man! the genius sigh'd -
As through the cliffs he sank him down -
'The worm that gnaw'd my bonie trees,
That reptile wears a ducal crown'.

Writing to Mrs Dunlop in 1788, replying to her comments on his work, Burns said, 'They are not the blasting depredations of a *canker*toothed caterpillar'.

## ANT sp. *Hymenoptera:Formicidae*

With a family of some 40 known species in Britain all of whom are social, we can but note that the poet mentioned their existence.

When writing in 1788 to Mrs Dunlop he included:

…as the lordly Bull does on the little, dirty *Ant-hill*, whose puny inhabitants he crushes in the carelessness of his ramble…

## WASP sp. *Vespidae*

A large family with some hundreds of species found worldwide. There are six social species in Britain, obviously no specific identification can be assumed even considering his use of the term 'cell'.

In his **'To Robert Graham, Esq., of Fintry'** the reference is quite specific: 'Th' envenom'd *wasp*, victorious, guards his cell'.

**BEE** sp. *Hymenoptera*

Honey bee     *Apis mellifera*
Bumble bee    *Bombus sp.*

A large group, with ample evidence of widespread distribution in south-west Scotland during Burns' lifetime.

Although managed in hives, notably at monastic settlements, by the eighteenth century there is no evidence that it had become a common practice among the farmers known to Burns. He leaves us in no doubt about bees and honey in **'The Brigs of Ayr'**:

The *bees*, rejoicing o'er their summer toils –
Unnumber'd bud's an flowers' delicious spoils,
Sealed up with frugal care in massive waxen piles -
Are doom'd by Man, that tyrant o'er the weak...

In the verses **'To Miss Isabella Macleod'** he wrote 'The crimson blossum charmes the *bee*'; and in a contribution to the *London Star* in 1789, entitled 'Delia' he penned:

The flower-enamour'd busy *Bee*
The rosy banquet loves to sip;

The famous tale of **'Tam O Shanter'**, contains the immortal lines:

As *bees* flee hame wi lades o treasure,
The minutes wing'd their way wi pleasure:

and

As *bees* bizz out wi angry fyke,
When plundering herds assail their byke;

In **'Fair Eliza'** we can find the quotation:

Not the *bee* upon the blossom
In the pride o sinny noon...

and in the song **'Philly and Willy'**:

The *bee* that thro the sunny hour
Sips nectar in the op'ning flower...

Another song, written as a compliment to the famous Scottish fiddler, Niel Gow, which he called **'Amang The Trees'** commences with the lines:

Amang the trees, where humming *bees*
At buds and flowers were hinging, O...

and in the song **'Logan Braes'**: 'The *bees* hum round the breathing flowers.'
**'My Tocher's The Jewel'**, a song typical of the 'Peasantry in the West', includes 'It's a' for the hiney he'll cherish the *bee*!'

A traditional ballad **'The Gallant Weaver'** 'While *bees* delight in opening flowers,' and the song **'Where Are The Joys?'** contains:

No, no the *bees* humming round the gay roses
Proclaim it the pride o the year.

The political ballad abridged by Burns, **'The German Lairdie'**, contains: 'The Revolution principles Has put their heads in *bees*, Sir…' (meaning confusion); the ballad **'The Winter It Is Past'** is more specific, with:

The rose upon the brier, by the waters running clear
May have charms for the linnet or the *bee*:


**BEETLE** Cockchafer: *Melolontha melolontha*

**Local:** Bum-clock; May-Bug

A common and widespread beetle, which inhabits crops, gardens and woods, it often swarms around trees during evening flights and often crashes against any lighted window. Burns refers to it in **'The Twa Dogs'** -

By this, the sun was out o sight,
An darker gloaming brought the night;
The *bum-clock* humm'd wi lazy drone;

Two other references to insects are non-specific. Written at Friars Carse, near Dumfries: 'Pleasures, *insects* on the wing'; and from **'Delia an Ode'**:

But, Delia, on thy balmy lips
Let me, no vagrant *insect*, rove!


**ADDER** *Vipera berus*

**Local:** Viper; Ither; Ether

The earliest local records from Ayrshire and Dumfriesshire suggest that the adder was quite numerous in many areas – Muirkirk, Lochar Moss and Upper Nithsdale being specifically mentioned in the mid-eighteenth century.

In his **'Dumfries Epigrams'** he comments on an Irish politician, one Mr Burke, whom Burns clearly did not regard at all highly:

Oft I have wonder'd that on Irish ground
No *poisonous Reptile* ever has been found:
Revealed the secret stands of great Nature's work:
She preserved her poison to create a Burke!

While not mentioning adder or viper specifically here, quite clearly not only was it intended, as the only poisonous British snake, but the quotation also clearly shows that Burns was aware that its distribution did not extend to Ireland.

In the old ballad **'Tam Lin'** collected by Burns we find a direct reference:

They'll turn me in your arms, lady,
Into an ask and *adder*…

The term 'ask' was used to describe several species in the mid-eighteenth century – lizard, newt(s), and grass snake (not resident in Scotland), and in **'The Fête Champetre'**:

> When Politics came there, to mix
> and make his *ether*-stane, man...

An early version of the song **'Duncan Gray'** contained the descriptive line: 'But like an *ither* puff'd an' blew'.


## TOAD *Bufo bufo*

**Local:** Frog; Puddock; Puddick

A common and widely-distributed amphibian in both Ayrshire and Dumfriesshire in the mid-eighteenth century, it featured in folklore and superstition.

In his verses **'To Robert Graham, Esq., of Fintry'** he refers to it thus: '*Toads* with their poison, doctors with their drug'; and in his **'Heron Election : Ballad Forth'**:

> Here is Satan's picture, like a bizzard gled
> Pouncing poor Redcastle, sprawlin like a *taed*.

Writing to W Nicol in 1793, Burns refers to the species:

> ...I look to thee, as a *toad* through iron-barred or a pestiferous dungeon to the cloudless glory of a summer sun!


## FROG *Rana temporaria*

**Local:** Toad

Common and widely distributed in south west Scotland during the mid-eighteenth century. 'Found in all suitable localities' infers wet areas but includes even the highest hills.

In his 1787 letter to Margaret Chalmers, he gave a very descriptive quotation:

> ...with as much hilarity in my gait and countenance, as a May *frog* leaping across the newly harrowed ridge, enjoying the fragrance of the refreshed earth after the long-expected shower!

In his verses **'To Robert Graham Esq., of Fintry'**: 'The grave, sage hern thus easy picks his *frog*.'

# AGUE

Formerly endemic in flat areas, ditches, bogs and small lochs; a tiny animal parasite of the blood transmitted by the bite of infected mosquitoes. Burns refers to it in his classic **'Address to the Toothache'**: 'When fevers burn, or *aque* freezes'.

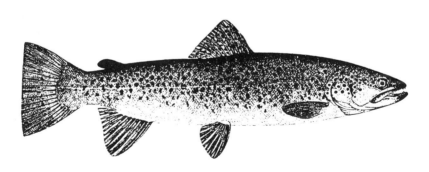

*Trout*

# BURNS AND NATURE CONSERVATION

*'Mark the winds, and mark the skies,*
*Ocean's ebb and ocean's flow.*
*Sun and Moon but set to rise,*
*Round and round the seasons go.*

*Why then ask of silly man*
*To oppose great Nature's plan?*
*We'll be constant, while we can -*
*You can be no more, you know!'*

## The People's Poet

Some six years after the death of Robert Burns in 1796, the first of the commemorative suppers – which are now held traditionally each year on his birthday, 25 January – commenced in Greenock, although the Burns' 'season' now extends until March.

From such humble beginnings, Burns is now celebrated and revered all over the world. There are for example over 200 memorials to him in different parts of the globe, and he is now translated into some 42 languages - Portuguese, Finnish and Gaelic being the latest.

Would-be intellectuals have often attempted unsuccessfully to suppress the Burns cult which so effectively and comprehensively dominates the rest of Scottish historical poetical literature. Burns remains celebrated and popular even 200 years after his death, quite simply sustained by public opinion; not only in Scotland or to where expatriate Scots have been literally forced to emigrate – in Canada, Australia or New Zealand – but also now in such diverse locations as Alaska, Argentina, Bangladesh, Botswana, South Pole Base, Russia and China. Suffice to say, he is honoured wherever his tender, moving, humanitarian philosophies find fertile ground among intelligent people. No other European poet or writer in modern times has enjoyed such prolonged international acclaim and popular support.

Nonetheless, it remains unusual to attend a properly structured Burns' Supper anywhere, without at least one of the principal speakers referring to either his love of, or inspiration by, 'nature', and with some 2,880 references to it who can deny that! Nature, in turn, is invariably either rarely defined or, more commonly, inaccurately quoted, the *raison d'être* of course for this review. Burns-loving naturalists do remain rather scarce on the ground.

185

Burns was described and eventually adopted officially as Scotland's National Bard. He has also been variously titled as 'The People's Poet' or 'The Ploughman Poet'. He himself obliquely suggested another very appropriate title – that of Poet of Nature – to which he ascribed admirably in his **'Epistle to William Simpson'** in which he quite deliberately surrenders the fierce, competitive, city-based ground of the then current literature sources to others. In obvious preference to what he interpreted as nature:

> O Nature! a' thy shews an forms
> To feeling, pensive hearts hae charms!
> Whether the summer kindly warms,
>   Wi life an light;
> Or winter howls, in gusty storms,
>   The lang, dark night!
>
> The Muse, nae poet ever fand her,
> Till by himsel he learn'd to wander,
> Adown some trottin burn's meander,
>   An no think lang:
> O sweet to stray, an pensive ponder
>   A heart-felt sang!
>
> The warly race may drudge an drive,
> Hog-shouther, jundie, stretch, an strive,
> Let me fair Nature's face descrive,
>   And I, wi pleasure,
> Shall let the busy, grumbling hive
>   Bum owre their treasure.

Extract from *Epistle To William Simpson*

He thus demonstrated his astute philosophical knowledge and genuine love of all things natural, that springs only to the born and bred countryman, and gained of a deep sincere respect, an enquiring mind and most importantly – and often missing in present day would-be conservationists – humility! These are aspects that no amount of training can instill for 'the cit'.

Burns' writings encompassed the whole scene – the broad canvas of landscape in season, the plants, trees and animals that lived independently within it – what we now call ecological systems. He especially did not exclude the people living and working in the countryside as part of nature, but rather he recognised, and indeed emphasised, the interdependence of both from a practical and humanitarian point of view. He and his family, principally as farmers, were very much part of the struggle to simply survive in the harsh, demanding, unrelenting but nonetheless beautiful, interesting and artistically inspiring rural environment of the mid-eighteenth century.

Burns was, as most of us are today, privileged to work, live in, or at least visit, what, in my view, can only be described as the *magnificence* of Scotland's landscape, whether one's personal needs are simply to enjoy the scenery, study, conserve or sport with the associated wildlife, or socialise with and serve the people.

## Access

Scotland's landscape, although significantly modified during the past two centuries – notably by agriculture, forestry and industrial revolution – has now reached a crisis point where much conservation and communicative interpretive work requires to be done. Scotland remains truly unique, but people must continue to maintain viable settlements in the most remote areas and live off the produce that sustainable exploitation can provide.

Although undoubtedly a large, sensitive and at times extremely controversial issue, the demands for greater access to the open countryside by the eighty per cent of the population who are now urban-based is real enough and totally understandable.

To them, the open spaces providing a wilderness experience is a necessary release from the stress and pressures of town life. In turn, they must appreciate that the land they tend to regard as a play or recreation area is indeed someone else's workplace, vital to the ecomomy of Scotland – and they too demand very careful consideration.

It is now surely obvious to all, that a policy of totally unplanned and unrestricted access, without responsible stewardship, can only lead to the rapid demise of this precious resource.

The main problem remains rather simple: on an island with a fixed area of land, the demands of an increasing, mobile, human population for multi-land use simply cannot now be ignored, and solutions to accommodate the inevitable increase and demand for countryside access must be put in hand sooner rather than later. In Scotland, fortunately, we seem to have a limited degree of time to resolve our town and countryside planning – at least when compared with some of the rather frantic developments experienced in the more affluent south.

At a basic level of philosophy such problems are indeed only for solving. In this case the apparently conflicting demands can indeed be compatible given a vehicle for discussion and the sincere goodwill of the various countryside users to sit down at the proverbial table.

Clearly the vehicle must now be the new Scottish Natural Heritage agency, financed from the Scottish Office at St Andrew's House and launched on 1 April, 1992. The new, enthusiastic and capable directorship deserves support. They simply must be assisted by the people of Scotland to succeed; it is not just landscape, plants and animals which are at risk now. Indeed it is the total rich diverse natural sphere, affecting the very fabric of society; the countryside scenario, the essence of which can either restore or stimulate the mind to provide the artistic and the sensitive with the essential and valuable 'quality of life' that has made Scotland the envy of the world.

## History

I had originally planned to prepare a potted history of nature conservation in Scotland but, on reflection, other authors have done so in greater detail than I would care to inflict on readers, but more importantly, my personal philosophy is that in a dynamic nature conservation programme, historical reviews can only be useful if we can resolve to learn from the inevitable mistakes that were made. Conservation of the natural heritage in Scotland can only be forward looking – while conscious of the need to look critically at ourselves, and hopefully be distanced from what is the current use of hyperbole, gobbledygook, the crippling and soul destroying administration, and departmental so-called procedures that have alienated the bulk of the population to date.

The late Sir James Fisher, who was arguably the doyen of latter day authors on the history of nature conservation and ornithology in Britain, included Burns in his list of some 30 notable 'birdwatchers' active in Britain during the eighteenth century, a list which included such notable figures as George Montagu, William Blake, Mary Lamb, James Hogg, Sir Walter Scott and Thomas Moore.

Sir James was obviously and specifically dealing with birds; had he encompassed the full range of Burns' records, I have no doubt that he too would have agreed with my supposition and described the Bard as Ornithologist-Naturalist and Conservationist.

It is fair enough to compare the natural history lists of Burns with those of his contemporaries but totally futile by present day standards. The upsurge of interest in 'The Natural World' has been fuelled by concern for the environment, aided by publicity and massive public exposure to generally excellent documentary and biologically explicit educational films on television.

These have all followed on from the first of the BBC *Look* programmes, hosted by the late Sir Peter Scott, which demonstrated the potential power of television as a communicating medium taking the conservation message into the living rooms of large numbers of people.

Since that era, interest in the environment has accelerated at an amazing pace. Pre- and immediately post-Second World War naturalists, armed with butterfly net, vasculum and lens, or those who dared to 'look' at birds with no intention of shooting them, other than with a camera, were formerly, quite literally, regarded as cranks.

Suddenly they found themselves accepted, and their numbers inevitably multiplied; but new-found popularity, unfortunately, mainly attracted the so-called middle classes, to the virtual exclusion of rural and urban-based working people.

The veritable flood of well presented and widely distributed films to an ever-increasing audience; the availability of good cheap books, the new interest in, for example, extra-mural classes; and an added emphasis on biological and conservation training in colleges and schools, brought a new awareness, and had the effect of drawing in thousands of devotees. This in turn, and relatively quickly, brought rising standards in fieldcraft and species identification. The ornithologist – previously judged by his egg collection – and the botanist, by his herbarium, had become not only respectable but 'in' people. Societies representing the various natural history groups flourished and the official stamp of conservation approval was at last given by the Government of the day, establishing the Nature Conservancy in 1949. These indeed were exciting times, largely influenced by Max Nicholson, and under the skilled Chairmanship of a

Dumfriesshire Burns' enthusiast, the late Sir Arthur Bryce Duncan – a well known, popular and respected farmer, keen game shot and allround naturalist, but above all, a country gentleman ever ready to share his time and expertise with anyone who showed an interest. 'The fine beginnings' were unfortunately not to last. To date, nature conservation in Scotland has been characterised by weak science, direction, political naivety and the subsequent recruitment or promotion of low calibre middle managers into vital planning structures.

As a result it has for some decades remained financially under-resourced, and has failed to relate 'to the people'; indeed, until recently it failed also to motivate a dedicated pool of skilled staff, who see their environmental work as a vocation, the main reward for which is satisfaction with a job well done, and progress gained from 'unrecorded hours devoted to what they see as the 'cause', and certainly not for significant financial gain in comparison with other fields of public service.

## *Towards A New Beginning*

One can now only encourage the policy of recruitment of dynamic, well known, firm, able, practical managers with a proven background of sound scientific integrity and an ability and willingness to communicate to all. Allied, one can at least hope, indeed pray, with an acknowledgement that the people at the sharp end (on the ground as it were), should preferably be recruited from native Scots, who would naturally not only be the best people for the job anyway but would communicate more efficiently with the people living, working and spending their leisure time on the land.

There are already too many disastrous examples of the proverbial 'Liverpudlian sailors', attempting the impossible by trying to naturalise in Scotland and pose as conservationists.

To be progressive, surely the key words in nature and countryside conservation in Scotland must now be COMMUNICATION with the people, leading to CONSULTATION, and CO-OPERATION thus avoiding CONFRONTATION. In other words – FOR THE PEOPLE, BY THE PEOPLE!

Respected countryside managers or communicators simply cannot be produced on the conveyor belt of ecological courses at some obscure English college, turning out Land Agent clones with matching plum accents. They can only emerge from thorough training in the 'university of life', the textbook of the real world.

Progression must also commence from a base of honesty, and an acknowledgement that, during the last three decades the Government agencies involved with countryside management have, following the retirement of John Berry and the late Joe Eggeling –, and with the notable exceptions of the late Countryside Commission for Scotland and the Forestry Commission – have failed rather sadly in their attempts to communicate successfully with landowners when involved in either major or sensitive environmental issues, and, more especially, with the urban populations.

Full of their own importance, they have failed to take the proverbial step backwards to review the overall scene. An appreciation of Burns' philosophy could well have prevented most of the resultant hiatus and alienation.

> O wad some Power the giftie gie us
> To see oursels as ithers see us!
> It wad frae monie a blunder free us,
>     An foolish notion:
> What airs in dress an gait wad lea'e us,
>     An ev'n devotion!

From To A Louse

It is indeed fortunate that during a relatively undistinguished era the scientific credibility of conservationists was at least maintained by a very few high profile scientists. People like Hugh Boyd of the then Wildfowl Trust, latterly Director of the Canadian Wildlife Service – typically forced to express his unique talents abroad; the late Geoffrey Harrison, who served wildfowling so well; Dick Potts at the Game Conservancy; and Mike Harris at the Institute of Terrestrial Ecology were of that group.

The outstanding duo of Derek Radcliffe and Norman Moore at the former Nature Conservancy Council; latterly the late Sir William Wilkinson; and the late Ian Prestt, who gave bird protection an acceptable platform from which to, optimistically, launch into the twenty-first century, must also be mentioned.

## Scotland's Natural Heritage

We thus prepare to enter a new and exciting century, with the merger of Countryside Commission for Scotland and Nature Conservancy Council for Scotland. Chaired by Magnus Magnusson and with a much respected first Chief Executive in Roger Crofts, to form Scottish Natural Heritage; it was intended to be a marriage of scientific and species protection expertise, with communication skills and interpretive knowledge. Alas, this strong leadership has, too, allegedly been burdened by a poor appreciation of the need to build and manage on a sound scientific base. The demise of Professor George Dunnet was particularly sad. Allegedly, there now apparently pertains an almost total lack of understanding of nature conservation requirements and species management by their regional lieutenants.

With the millstone of southern bureaucratical domination removed from the scene it was hoped that the nature conservation image in Scotland could at last be removed from the perceived notion of bearded scientists clad in oiled coats, green wellies, clipboards round their neck, and all accompanied by a seemingly endless correspondence, or in a panoply of inevitable meetings, cloaked usually with an air of superiority. The use of condescending language meant to 'educate the locals' and all with a sickening moral cloak of condescension – 'the rank is but the guinea's stamp, the man's the gowd for all that'.

Emphasis has now changed direction especially in the minds of the general public. While conservation of landscape, plants, animals, birds and fish remains important they are now literally bombarded with totally justified concern about the whole future of the environment.

These problems are on a scale that, during the eighteenth-century, Britain could not possibly have ever been even dreamt about. The issues that are now gripping public attention are the holes in the ozone layer; air, oceanic, and soil contamination; the massive over-use of pesticides and chemicals to boost agricultural production; the so-called acid rain effect; and the horrific slaughter of intelligent sea mammals. Most worrying is the obvious destruction of the world's rainforests and the subsequent effects that that is having on our weather patterns. These are but examples of the threats that are now at the very 'centre of life' as we know it. It is not an exaggeration to state that we have now entered the most destructive era the natural world has ever had to contend with.

> Think ye, that sic as you and I,
> Wha drudge and drive thro wet and dry,
>  Wi never ceasing toil;
> Think ye, are we less blest than they,
> Wha scarcely tent us in their way,
>  As hardly worth their while?
> Alas! how oft in haughty mood,
>  God's creatures they oppress!
> Or else, neglecting a' that's guid,
>  They riot in excess!
> Baith careless and fearless
>  Of either Heaven or Hell;
> Esteeming and deeming
>  It a' an idle tale!

### Burns as a Conservationist

To follow from Sir James Fisher's remarks, Burns was not only one of our first bird watchers or ornithologists – the titles are now synonomous – but also our first notable all-round naturalist and conservationist.

His natural history knowledge was undoubtably wide and ranged over many species and aspects. He refers to several exposed rock and soil types and apparently appreciated and was impressed by the vastness of geological and evolutionary scale. When he versified the 90th Psalm, he included the lines:

> '...Before the mountains heav'd their head' and 'Those mighty periods of years which seem to us so vast...'

His awareness of natural phenomena went far beyond the relatively common thunder, lightning and aurora borealis contained in his classic **'Tam O' Shanter':**

> Or like the borealis race,
> That flit ere you can point their place;
>
> The lightnings flash from pole to pole,
> Near and more near the thunders roll:

Previous analysts have inferred that his use of the words 'race' and 'flit' were in this casè suggestive of referring possibly to one of the group of glowing firefly insects. I have considered this and reject the supposition entirely. 'Borealis' is from the fifteenth century Latin *boreas* (of, or relating to, the north). None of the fireflies *Luciola lusitanica* have a geographical range extending to such latitudes. In the same vein, he demonstrates his geographical reading by referring to volcanos in Iceland and the ice fields of Greenland. His list of, and concern for trees, was admirable. He probably remonstrated with the Duke of Queensberry on his destruction of the woods near Drumlanrig and appealed successfully to the then Duke of Atholl to plant up both sides of the river near the Falls of Bruar. His concern for trees was probably instilled by the influence of a most remarkable and underestimated man - his father William Burnes – who had advocated and carried out much planting to assist cultivation of the poor Ayrshire soils at that time, long before it became either fashionable or acknowledged that there was an agricultural benefit to so do. The romantic in Burns is more evident in his treatment of the flowers, which he referred to on over four hundred occasions, with examples available to convey every mood.

> Adown winding Nith I did wander,
> To mark the sweet flowers as they spring…

> …But here, alas! for me nae mair
> Shall birdie charm, or floweret smile;
> Fareweel the bonnie banks of Ayr!
> Fareweell fareweell! sweet Ballochmyle!

That he cared deeply and passionately for them is beyond any reasonable dispute.

> Or when the deep green mantled earth
> Warm cherish'd ev'ry flow'ret's birth…

His views on mammals are exemplified by his reference to the small humble mouse and by his comments to Mrs Dunlop on the wounded hare.

On 21 April, 1789, Burns wrote to Mrs Dunlop: 'Two mornings ago as I was at a very early hour, sowing in the fields, I heard a shot, and presently a poor little hare limped by me, apparently very much hurt. You will easily guess, this set my humanity in tears and my indignation in arms. The following was the result'.

## The Wounded Hare

Inhuman man! curse on thy barb'rous art,
And blasted by thy murder-aiming eye;
May never pity soothe thee with a sigh,
Nor never pleasure glad thy cruel heart!

Go live, poor wanderer of the wood and field,
The bitter little of life that remains!
No more the thickening brakes and verdant plains
To thee shall home, or food, or pastime yield.

Seek, mangled wretch, some place of wonted rest,
No more of rest, but now of dying bed!
The sheltering rushes whistling o'er thy head,
The cold earth with thy bloody bosom prest.

Oft as by winding Nith I, musing, wait
The sober eve, or hail the cheerful dawn,
I'll miss thee sporting o'er the dewy lawn,
And curse the ruffian's aim, and mourn thy hapless fate.

Local tradition has it that Burns later remonstrated with the shooter in question and threatened to 'throw him into the river Nith' but this cannot now be substantiated.

His references to bird welfare are also one the main planks in my claim that he was indeed a caring conservationist. Clearly concerned for their plight during winter, he penned:

Ilk happing bird,-wee, helpless thing!-
That in the merry months o spring,
Delighted me to hear thee sing,
What comes o thee?
Where wilt thou cow'r thy chittering wing,
An close thy e'e?!

In addition, he was even concerned – as all good ornithologists should be – that he disturbed waterfowl during a visit to Loch Turit in Clackmannanshire, as an extract from verses he wrote immediately following the incident proves:

Why, ye tenants of the lake,
For me your wat'ry haunt forsake?
Tell me, fellow-creatures, why
At my presence thus you fly?
Why disturb your social joys,
Parent, filial, kindred ties? -
Common friend to you and me,
Nature's gifts to all are free:
Peaceful keep your dimpling wave,
Busy feed, or wanton lave;
Or, beneath the sheltering rock,
Bide the surging billow's shock.
Conscious, blushing for our race,
Soon, too soon, your fears I trace.

Man, your proud, usurping foe,
Would be lord of all below:
Plumes himself in freedom's pride,
Tyrant stern to all beside.'
'Or, of Man's superior might
Dare invade your native right,
On the lofty ether borne,
Man with all his powers you scorn;
Swiftly seek, on clanging wings,
Other lakes, and other springs;
And the foe you cannot brave,
Scorn at least to be his slave.'

## Field Sports

Burns was obviously very much aware of the so called sporting scene and many of his friends were involved in it, as he made very clear in his **'Tam Samson's Elegy'**. The subject of the poem was one Thomas Samson of Kilmarnock who Burns described as 'a zealous sportsman, and a good fellow'.

Rejoice, ye birring paitricks a';
Ye cootie moorcocks, crousely craw;
Ye maukins, cock your fud fu braw,
Withouten dread;
Your mortal fae is now awa:
Tam Samson's dead!

Although Burns presented a dedication to the Caledonian Hunt, it was in recognition of their support in subscribing financially towards publication of an Edinburgh edition of his poems.

There is no real evidence available to us to indicate that he supported hunting or shooting *per se*, nor that he ever enjoyed or glorified in a day in 'the field' actively involved in such pursuits. He did own guns, including a brace of pistols that he carried during his excise duties, but I am unaware of any occasion when he discharged rifle, musket or shotgun deliberately to shoot animals for either food or fun.

Clearly, however, hunting – with horse and hounds; shooting driven game and over pointers; wildfowling; falconry; hare coursing and fishing – were well developed and organised country sports during his lifetime.

One could assume that the field sportsman of today might even tingle yet with some excitement at the numbers and variety of wild game that probably would have been available then in such diverse natural habitats.

As a farmer Burns latterly was primarily dependent on sheep to provide a cash income, and as such was aware of the necessity to control fox predation on lambs. In the song **'My Hoggie'** he wrote -

The tod reply'd upon the hill
I trembled for my hoggie.

Another agricultural aspect that was vital to economic survival was the fact that the improved fields remained close to the heather clad moors, with heather growing to sea level near Dumfries.

The slow growing and ripening corn was eventually cut by hand, bundled into sheaves and then propped together in stooks in the fields and left to complete ripening and to dry.

Depending obviously on the vagaries of the weather, this meant that in some seasons the stooks would be left out till the end of October or even November and there are records of stooks being taken in 'before the winter snows'.

The significant point is that, during all this prolonged 'harvest' period, the potential produce remained vulnerable to being eaten by birds. Young boys were retained to ward off crows with noise and sling shot, while the grouse and partridges which also invaded the small fields were shot at in a combination of crop protection and sport.

Nonetheless, in spite of such economic necessity, Burns remained anti-shooting.

> The death o devils smoor'd wi brimstone reek:
> The thundering guns are heard on ev'ry side,
> The wounded coveys, reeling, scatter wide;
> The feather'd field-mates, bound by Nature's tie,
> Sires, mothers, children, in one carnage lie:
> (What warm, poetic heart but inly bleeds,
> And execrates man's savage, ruthless deeds!)
> Nae mair the flower in field or meadow springs;
> Nae mair the grove with airy concert rings,
> Except perhaps the robin's whistling glee,
> Proud o the height o some bit half-lang tree;
> The hoary morns precede the sunny days,
> Mild, calm, serene, widespreads the noontide blaze
> While thick the gossamour waves wanton in the rays.

Extract from: *'The Brigs of Ayr'*

Burns gives several examples of his disdain for premature unnecessary killing. In **'The Twa Dogs'**, for example, he is critical of people who take it casually.

> Or speaking lightly o their limmer,
> Or shooting of a hare or moorcock...

and in his **'Epistle to James Tennant of Glenconner'**, he also indicated that he was concerned with life and death as an issue, not whether the species involved was a 'so called' pest species or not -

> To cast my e'en up like a *pyet*
> When by the gun she tumbles o'er,
> Flutt'ring an gasping in her gore.

His early composition **'Now Westlin Winds'** really does say it all, and one can rest the case for Robert Burns, Poet of Nature, Naturalist and Nature Conservationist.

## *Now Westlin Winds*

Now westlin winds and slaught'ring guns
    Bring Autumn's pleasant weather;
The moorcock springs on whirring wings
    Amang the blooming heather:
Now waving grain, wide o'er the plain,
    Delights the weary farmer;
And the moon shines bright, as I rove by night,
    To muse upon my charmer.

The paitrick lo'es the fruitfu fells,
    The plover lo'es the mountains;
The woodcock haunts the lonely dells,
    The soaring hern the fountains:
Thro lofty groves the cushat roves,
    The path o man to shun it;
The hazel bush o'erhangs the thrush,
    The spreading thorn the linnet.

Thus ev'ry kind their pleasure find,
    The savage and the tender;
Some social join, and leagues combine,
    Some solitary wander:
Avaunt, away, the cruel sway!
    Tyrannic man's dominion!
The sportsman's joy, the murd'ring cry,
    The flutt'ring, gory *pinion*!

But, Peggy dear, the ev'ning's clear,
    Thick flies the skimming swallow;
The sky is blue, the fields in view,
    All fading-green and yellow:
Come let us stray our gladsome way,
    And view the charms of Nature;
The rustling corn, the fruited thorn,
    And ilka happy creature.

We'll gently walk, and sweetly talk,
    While the silent moon shines clearly;
I'll clasp thy waist, and, fondly prest,
    Swear how I lo'e thee dearly:
Not vernal show'rs to budding flow'rs,
    Not Autumn to the farmer,
So dear can be as thou to me,
    My fair, my lovely charmer!

# Appendix 1

## Systematic List of Flowers

| | | | Scots | Gaelic |
|---|---|---|---|---|
| **Wallflower** | (1) | Cheiranthus cheiri | waafleur | lus leth-an-t-samhraidh |
| **Bog Myrtle/Sweet Gale** | (4) | Myrica gale | gall | roid |
| **Common Dog Violet** | (6) | Viola riviniana | | sail/dail- chuach |
| **Bluebell** | (1) | Endymion non-sciptus | bleawort | fuath-mhuc |
| **Harebell** | (2) | Campanula rotundifolia | blawort | currac-cubhaige |
| **Ladies Smock** | (1) | Cardamine pratensis | pink | Biolain-Ghriagain |
| **Spear Thistle** | (4) | Cirsium vulgare | thrissle | cluaran |
| **Bracken** | (2) | Pteridium aquilinum | breckan | raineach |
| **Clover** | (3) | Trifolium repens<br>Trifolium pratense | hauket clavur<br>reid clavur | seamrag-bhàn<br>seamrag-chapaill |
| **Foxglove** | (2) | Digitalis purpurea | thummles | lus nam ban sìdh |
| **Snowdrop** | (2) | Galanthus nivalis | snawdrap | gealag-làir |
| **Stinging Nettle** | (1) | Urtica dioica | jaggie nettle | deanntag/ feanntag |
| **Broad Leaved Dock** | (1) | Rumex obtusifolius | docken | copag leathann |
| **Primrose** | (12) | Primula vulgaris | fauline | sòbhrag/mùisean-s(e)òbhraeh |
| **Common Poppy** | (1) | Papaver rhoeas | chasbol | crom lus |
| **Cowslip** | (5) | Primula veris | | mùisean/ bainne bò buidhe/ buidheachan bò blioch |
| **Common Ragwort** | (5) | Senecio jacobaea | stinkin billy | buaghallan |
| **Heather** | (25) | Calluna vulgaris | ling | fraoch |
| **Wild Thyme** | (2) | Thymus drucei | thyme | Lus mhic rìgh Bhreatainn |
| **Rue** | (2) | Ruta graveolens | rue | Rù-Ghàraidh |
| **Daisy** | (13) | Bellis perennis | gowan | neòinean |
| **Lesser Burdock** | (1) | Arctium minus | | mecan-dogha/seircea suirich/ leadan liosda |
| **Dog Rose** | (63) | Rosa canina | hip | ròs-nan-con |
| **Flax** | (8) | Linum usitatissimum | lint | lìon |
| **Lily** | (27) | Lilium spp | | lili |
| **Vine** | (2) | Vitus vinifea | | finonan/ crann-fiona |
| **Fig** | (1) | Ficus caria | | fiogais; crann-fige |
| **Hemp** | (7) | Cannabis satirva | tow/touw | còrcach/cainb |
| **Hop** | (2) | Humulus lupulus | | lus an leanna |
| **Common Reed** | (2) | Phragmites australis | seg | cuilc/lachan |
| **Sedge sp.** | (1) | Carex sp. | seg | seileasdair/ seisg |
| **Soft Rush** | (8) | Juncus effusus | thresh/rashes | luchair-bhog |

**Appendix 1 (cont)**

| | | | | |
|---|---|---|---|---|
| **Grass sp.** | (15) | Gramineae sp. | gress | fuer |
| **Common Bent/Brown Top** | (3) | Agrostis tenuis | | muran |
| **Rye Grass** | (1) | Secale cereale | | feur seagail seagal |
| **Toadstool sp.** | (1) | | puddock stuil | balg-losgainn |
| **Seaweed sp** | (3) | Fucas sp. | wrack | feamainn |

236 specific records of 37 species.

# Appendix 2

## SYSTEMATIC LIST OF TREES AND SHRUBS

| | | | Scots | Gaelic |
|---|---|---|---|---|
| **Poplar** | (1) | Populus sp. | | critheann |
| **Aspen** | (1) | P. tremula | trummle ais | critheann a chritheann |
| **Silver Birch** | (17) | Betula pendula/ b. pubenscens | birk | beith (-chlrasach) |
| **Hazel** | (14) | Corylus avellana | cowden | calltainn |
| **Beech** | (1) | Fagus sylvatica | | faidhbhile |
| **Oak** | (15) | Quercus spp | aik | darach |
| **Wych or Scots Elm** | (1) | Ulmus glabra | | leamhan |
| **Wild Cherry** | (3) | Prunus avium | gean | geanais; sirist |
| **Common Hawthorn** | (39) | Crataegus monogyna | haw | sgitheach |
| **Holly** | (4) | Ilex aquifolium | | cuileann |
| **Ash** | (2) | Fraxinus excelsior | ais | uinnseann |
| **Bay tree** | (2) | Laurus nobilis | | craobh-labhrais |
| **Honeysuckle** | (14) | Lonicera periclymenum | hinniesickle | iadh-shlat |
| **Ivy** | (4) | Hedera helix | eivie | eidheann |
| **Gorse** | (2) | Ulex europaeus | whin | conasg |
| **Bramble** | (1) | Rubus fruticosus | blackberry | smeur (berry); dris (bush) |
| **Willow** | (4) | Salix spp. | sauchie | seileach |
| **Lilac** | (1) | Syringa vulgaris | | craobh liath-chòrcra |
| **Broom** | (12) | Cytisus scoparius | | bealaidh |
| **Blackthorn** | (4) | Prunus spinosa | | àirne |
| **Elder** | (1) | Sambucus nigra | bour | droman |
| **Crab Apple** | (1) | Malus sylvestris | soor aiple | ubhal-fhiadhain |
| **Apple** | (6) | M. domesticus | aiple tree | craobh-ubhail |
| **Rowan** | (1) | Sorbus aucuparia | mountain ash | caorann |
| **Scots Pine** | (2) | Pinus sylvestris | fir | giuthas |
| **Yew** | (1) | Taxus baccata | | iubhar |

154 specific records of 26 species.

# Appendix 3

## Systematic List of Mammals

|  |  |  | Scots | Gaelic |
|---|---|---|---|---|
| Hedgehog | (3) | Erinaceus europaeus | hurcheon | gràinneag |
| Mole | (4) | Talpa europaea | moudie | famh |
| Bat spp | (3) | Chiroptera/ D.rotundus | bawkie/flitter mous | ialtag |
| Rabbit | (1) | Oryctolagus cuniculus | kinner/kinnin/mout | coineanach |
| Brown Hare | (19) | Lepus capensis | pousie/maukin | maigheach |
| House Mouse | (6) | Mus musculus | hous mous | luch-taighe |
| Beaver | (1) | Castor fiber |  | beathadach |
| Ship Rat | (4) | Rattus rattus | ratton | radan-dubh |
| Fox | (9) | Vulpes vulpes | tod | sionnach/ madadh- ruadh |
| Weasel | (1) | Mustela nivalis | whittreck | neas |
| Stoat | (1) | Mustela erminea | foumart | neas |
| Badger | (3) | Meles meles | brock | broc |
| Polecat | (3) | Mustela putorius | whumart | taghan |
| Wildcat | (1) | Felis silvestris | wulk | cat-fiadhaich |
| Elk | (1) | Alces alces |  | lon |
| Fallow Deer | (1) | Dama dama |  | fiadh-breac |
| Red Deer | (5) | Cervus elephus | hairt | fiadh/damh (stag) |
| Roe Deer | (2) | Capreolus capreolus |  | erba boc-earba (roebuck) maoiseach (doe) |
| Wolf | (2) | Canis lupus |  | madadh-allaidh |

70 specific records of 19 species.

# Appendix 4

## RIVERS, LOCHS AND HILLS

*RIVERS*

a)  Major Scottish Rivers (34):

| | | | |
|---|---|---|---|
| Afton | Coil | Gala | Sark |
| Allan | Dee | Garpal | Scaur |
| *Ayr | Devon | Girvan | *Stincher |
| Bruar | Doon | Greenock | *Spey |
| Cairn | Earn | Irvine | *Tay |
| Cart | Eden | Jed | *Tweed |
| Cessnock | Ettrick | Logan | Yarrow |
| *Cluden | Fail | Lugar | |
| Clyde | *Forth | *Nith | |

*\* Salmon Rivers known to Burns.*

b)  Other major rivers (26) mentioned by Burns in his writings but not ascribed to prose, song or special comment include:

Almond; Badenoch; Branwater; Carron; Coquet; Findhorn; Garie; Illisssus; Indus; Kilravok, May; North Esk; Rannoch; Roole; St Lawrence; Seine; Teith; Teviot; Tyne; Thames; Tiber; Tilt; Tummel; Leader; Lyon; *and* Niagara.

*LOCHS* (6)

Great Lakes (Canada); Loch Tay; Loch Leven; Loch Loang; Loch Turit; Loch Lomond.

*HILLS* (26)

His use of the term 'braes' is synonymous in the Scots with 'hill'. Burns also often refers to hillocks, usually within the catchment areas of rivers.

Ayr; Afton; Ballenden; Ben Ledie; Ben Lomond; Bonshaw; Coil; Corsincon; Cowden Knowes; Cragie; Criffel; Cumnock; Cupar; Doon; Ednam Hill; Edinburgh; Kellyburn; Killicrankie; Logan; Lomonds; Lowther; Lugar; Nith; Ochiltree; Ochils; Yarrow.

## Appendix 5

## SYSTEMATIC LIST OF BIRDS

This list includes all the bird species found in the writings of Burns which can be identi-fied, named and attributed as his personal work or to his knowledge. It also lists two bird groups 'Seabirds' and 'Owls' mentioned by Burns, with only one individual species within the latter group being named – the poem **'To The Owl'** (Cromek, Reliques, 1808) not being accepted.

   In addition, I have included in square brackets three species not mentioned in Burns' writing but which in my view can be inferred. I have given my own reasons for such an inclusion in the individual species discussion notes. They must, of course, always remain speculative and never be regarded as certain. Three species are rejected as such, although two are revised, and renamed. Only Stock Dove should in my view be removed from the context in which it was referred and is thus also bracketed.

   Common or local names used in Ayrshire and Dumfriesshire during the Burns' era and up to 1950 are also given in the discussion notes. I have here, in addition to current scientific nomenclature, where appropriate, also given the Scots and the Scottish Gaelic names where they exist, largely following *Nicolaisen, Gray, Madder Rennie* and *Gorman*. A brief description of the current (1995) status of the birds in Ayrshire and Dumfriesshire follows a more general comment on their current status in Scotland largely following Madders and Welstead.

* * *

| **English** *Scientific* | **Scots** | **Gaelic** |
|---|---|---|

***Bittern*** *Botaurus stellaris* ***(1)***          Bittoun          corra ghràin
Uncommon visitor, mostly recorded in Winter. Rare winter visitor to Ayrshire and Dumfries.

***Grey Heron*** *Ardea cinerea* ***(3)***          Hern          Corra-ghritheach
Resident and widespread in Scotland, absent only from Shetland as breeding species. Decreased markedly in Ayrshire and Dumfries, continues to breed and widely distributed in small numbers.

***Mute Swan*** *Cygnus olor* ***(4)***                              eala-bhàn
Resident. Widespread but not generally abundant in lowlands. Absent from Shetland and some western islands. Decreased during last decade in Ayrshire and Dumfries. Continues to breed in moderate numbers, with concentrations of non breeding birds at harbours and at the Caul in Dumfries town although decreasing there of late.

***[Greylag Goose]*** *Anser anser* ***(4)***          Guse          gèadh-g(h)las
Resident breeder in Outer Hebrides. Winter visitor and passage migrant in abundant numbers. Feral stock continues to breed in Ayrshire, Dumfries, and Galloway. Large numbers visit, either as passage migrants in both spring and autumn and as winter visitors.

**Teal** *Anas crecca (1)*                    lach-bheag
Widespread breeding species. Wintering and passage migrant with a generally
scattered distribution. Scarce breeding resident in both Ayrshire and Dumfries,
with numbers augmented in autumn and winter.

**Mallard** *Anas platyrhynchos (5)*       Deuk       Lach(-bhreac/Mhoire/
                                                       riabhach/vaine) tunnag-fhiadhaich
Widespread breeding species. Large numbers involved as passage migrants and
to winter. Remains a common breeding duck on the lochs and rivers of both
Ayrshire and Dumfriesshire. With large numbers wintering in the inner Solway
and in the Irish Sea.

**Red Kite** *Milvus milvus (1)*          Gled         clamhan-gòbhlach
Scarce vagrant, formerly bred and in process of re-introduction. Rare visitor to
both Ayrshire and Dumfriesshire.

**Eagle sp.** *(4)*
    Golden Eagle *Aquila chrysaetos*    [a]  Gowden Earn     iolaire-bhuidhe
    Sea Eagle *Haliaeetus albicilla*    [b]  Earn            iolaire-mhara
a) Resident especially in Highlands and Hebrides. Remains scarce in southwest
Scotland. Occasional records of individuals as they disperse.
b) Recently re-introduced to west coast and now a very scarce breeding species.

*[Sparrow Hawk] Accipiter nisus (5)*    Speug gled        speireag
Widespread resident except in Shetland or Outer Hebrides. Also passage
migrant and winter visitor. Population in Dumfries and Galloway increased
markedly during last two decades in spite of continued persecution in the
interest of game, now declining.

**Buzzard** *Buteo buteo (1)*          Gled          clamhan
Widespread resident breeding species especially in the west. Absent only from
Shetland. Increasing markedly throughout Scotland where ???traps have
displaced the use of poison. Breeds widely especially in Nith Valley,
Dumfriesshire when unmolested.

**Peregrine** *Falco peregrinus (1)*      Gos        seabhag(-ghorm)
Widespread breeding species in Scotland, except on eastern coasts. Total
recovery in South West Scotland since 1945 except on some coastal sites in
western Solway. Persecuted especially on grouse moors.

**Red Grouse** *Lagopus lagopus (10)*    Throthie bogle    cearc-fhraoich (f)
                                          Cock             coileach-fraoich (m)
Resident in moorland habitat. Liable to marked fluctuations due to weather at
hatching, infestation by parasites, disease, and the quality of the heather.
Responds to good moor management.

**Grey Partridge** *Perdixperdix (8)*     Pairtrich       cearc thomin (f)
                                                          coileach-tomain (m)
Widespread breeding resident especially in lowland agricultural habitat. Absent
only from the islands. Marked decrease in most areas usually associated with

chemical spraying of agricultural weeds and subsequent scarcity of saw fly larva essential for chick survival.

**Corncrake**  *Crex crex* **(2)**              Craik              trèun-ri-trèun
                                                                     traon/rac-an-abrbair

Local migratory breeding species, mainly to Hebrides and Orkney. Now extinct as breeder in Ayrshire and Dumfriesshire.

**Coot**  *Fulica atra* **(2)**              bell-kite              bel-poot/lach a'bhàir

Widespread resident breeding species except in Highlands and on most Islands where scarce or absent.

**Golden Plover**  *Pluvialis apricaria* **(4)**   Pliver         feadag (-bhuidhe)

Widespread breeding species in uplands. Also features as passage migrant and winter visitor.

**Lapwing**  *Vanellus vanellus* **(1)**          Teuchat              curracag

Widespread breeding species and passage migrant/winter visitor. Decreased alarmingly in Dumfriesshire and Ayrshire during the last decade as a breeding bird.

**Snipe**  *Gallinago gallinago* **(1)**          Blitter/hoars gowk    naosg

Widespread breeding species, passage migrant and winter visitor. Decreasing in South West Scotland especially as breeding species due almost certainly to drainage of wet areas.

**Woodcock**  *Scolopax rusticola* **(1)**    Cock         coileach-coille

Widespread breeding species except in North Scotland and in the Western Isles. Remains sparsely distributed in south west counties as breeding bird. Occasionally large autumnal influxes are apparent especially in Southern Ayrshire.

**Curlew**  *Numenius arquata* **(3)**        Whaup/waup        guilbneach

Widespread breeding species, passage migrant and winter visitor. In spite of cessation of shooting as quarry species has continued to decline in southern Scotland at least as a breeding bird.

**'Seabird' sp (1)**

**[Stock Dove]**  *Columba nasoe* **(1)**                       calman-gorm

Resident breeding species especially in south and east of Scotland.

**Wood Pigeon**  *Columba palumbus* **(9)**   Cushet/Cushie    calman-coille-fiadhaich

Widespread resident breeding species, passage migrant and winter visitor. Often in pest proportions. Recent decreases in Fife and Tayside due to indiscriminate shooting.

**Cuckoo**  *Cuculas canorus* **(3)**        Gowk              cuach/cuthag

Widespread migratory breeding species and passage migrant, not scarce in South west Scotland.

**Barn Owl** *Tyto alba* *(1)*          Screech owl          comhachag bhàn
                                                              sgreuchag-oidhche
Breeding resident in the South and East of Scotland. Absent from much of
Highlands; Islands.

**'Owl' sp** *Stringidae/Tytonidae* *(10)*          Houlet          comhachag/
                                                                    cailleach-oidhche
No other specific identification of species possible. (For status in Scotland, see
Thom, V. M. 1986.)

**Skylark** *Alauda arvensis* *(22)*          Laverock          uiseag
Widespread breeding species, passage migrant and winter visitor. Has decreased
alarmingly during last two decades in both Dumfriesshire and Ayrshire.

**Swallow** *Hirundo rustica* *(5)*                          gòbhlan-gaoithe
Migratory breeding species and passage visitor. Has decreased markedly
especially in Dumfriesshire during the last decade.

**Tree Pipit** *Authus trivialis* *(4)*          Teetan/          uiseag/riabhag-
                                                 Wekeen           choille
Migratory breeding species, except in Northern Scotland and Western Islands.
Scarce breeding summer visitor to south west Scotland.

**Wren** *Troglodytes troglodytes* *(1)*          Thoumie          dreadhan-donn
Widespread breeding species.

**Robin** *Erithacus rubecula* *(5)*          raibert; reid breist          brù-dhrearg
Widespread breeding species except to Shetland. Also passage migrant and
winter visitor. Remains a common bird both in Dumfriesshire and Ayrshire.

**Nightingale** *Luscinia megar hynchos* *(4)*          Rosignell          spideag
Remains a scarce vagrant to Scotland, most frequently recorded in spring. No
recent records in Southwest Scotland.

**Blackbird** *Turdus merula* *(8)*          merl          lon-dubh
Widespread breeding species in gardens, hedges and woodlands. Augmented
during migration periods and by winter visitors.

**Song Thrush** *Turdus philomeols* *(14)*          Mavis          smeorach
Widespread but decreasing breeding species, though large numbers now breed
in the Galloway spruce forests; scarce only in Shetland. Also occurs as a
passage migrant and winter visitor.

**Magpie** *Pica pica* *(3)*          Pyet          poighaid
Resident breeding species except for northern islands and most of Highlands.
Increasing in both Ayrshire and Dumfriesshire in spite of 'control' in the
interests of game.

**Rook** *Curvus frugilegus* *(2)*          Craw          ròca(i)s
Resident breeding species, especially in agricultural areas. Winter roosts remain

widespread and large in southern Scotland. Total numbers tend to fluctuate but relatively stable in the long term.

**Carrion/Hooded Crow** *Corvus corone (3)*     Corbie          feannag/starrag
Widespread breeding species, in spite of intense efforts to reduce numbers in the interests of game and sheep husbandry. Hooded Crow predominate in North and West. Carrion Crow in South and East. Hybrids overlap. Increasing in Dumfries and Ayr including in proximity to urban sprawl.

**Raven** *Corvus corax (5)*               Croupie          fitheach
Resident breeding species in uplands with marked decline during last decade in southern Scotland but continues as breeding resident, with evidence of a recovery.

**Jackdaw** *Corvus monedula  (1)*        Jackie Daw       cathag
Widespread breeding species; scarce in northwest highlands. Northern and Western Islands. Also passage migrant and winter visitor.

**House Sparrow** *Passer domesticus (2)*    Speug          gealbhonn
Common, widespread resident, but decreasing.

**Goldfinch** *Carduelis carduelis (1)*     Gowdspink        deargan-fraoich/
                                                             lasair-choille
Widespread breeding species, except in the north of Scotland and in the Western Isles. Much reduced in Ayr and Dumfries, continues to breed in marginal and rough ground where weed seeds allowed to flourish.

**Linnet**   *Carduelis cannabina (19)*    Lintie           breacan-beithe
Widespread breeding species, especially in South East Scotland although significantly reduced as breeding species in Ayr and Dumfries during last 30 years, remains a reasonably common bird. Perceptibly augmented in late autumn and winter, when large flocks can still be found, for example, near Kirkconnel, New Cummock, and on the Solway shores.

**Yellowhammer**  *Emberiza citrinella (1)*   Yoit         biudheag(-luachrach)
                                                           buidhean/na coille
Widespread breeding species except in Shetland; scarce in Orkney and all Western Islands. Common resident in lowland Scotland, flocks in Autumn but remains mainly sedantry.

220 records which include 39 full species;  Two groups (seabirds and owls) 3 species retained in brackets as lacking formal proof.


Three misnomers corrected: *Golden Plover* for *Grey Plover*;
*Tree Pipit* for *Woodlark*; *Stock Dove* for *Wood Pigeon*.

# Appendix 6

## SYSTEMATIC LIST OF FISH AND OTHER WILDLIFE

| | | | Scots | Gaelic |
|---|---|---|---|---|
| **Herring** | (3) | Clupea harengus | spirlin/ scattan | sgadan |
| **Atlantic Salmon** | (5) | Salmo salar | saumon | bradan |
| **Brown Trout** | (6) | Salmon trutta | burnie | breac |
| **Pike** | (1) | Esox lucius | gled | geadas |
| **Perch** | (1) | Perca fluviatilis | | muc-locha |
| **Minnow** | (1) | Phoxinus phioxinus | minnoch/ meenock | doirbeag |
| **Eel** | (4) | Anguilla anguilla | | easgann |
| **Cod** | (1) | Gadus morhua | keelin | trosg |
| **Limpet** | (1) | Patella vulgata | lampit | bàirneach |
| **Mussel** | (1) | Mytilus edulis | clabbiedou | feusgan |
| **Lobster** | (2) | Homarus vulgaris | lapstur | goimach |
| **Cockle** | (1) | Cardium edule | | coilleag/srùban |
| **Oyster** | (2) | Ostrea edulis | aistur | eisir |
| **Common Earthworm** | (5) | Lumbricus terrestris | yirdie | cnuimh-thalmhainn/ daolag/ baoiteag |
| **Horse Leech** | (1) | Haemopis sanquisuga | souker | deal'-each |
| **Snail** | (2) | Helicidae sp. | | seilcheag |
| **Scorpion** | (3) | Scorpionida | | nathair-nimhe/ sqairp |
| **Spiders** | (3) | Araneae sp | attercap | damhan-allaidh |
| **Mites** | (3) | Ixodes ricinus | | fineag |
| **Locust** | (1) | Locusta migratoria | | lòcast |
| **Lice** | (9) | Pediculus humanus/ Pthirus pubis | povie/poulie boo/ crabs/ cart | mial/mail iognach |
| **Grasshopper** | (1) | Acrididae | gres lowpur | fionnan-fèoir |
| **Butterfly sp.** | (5) | Lepidoptera | flitterby | dealan-dè |
| **Moth sp.** | (1) | Lepidoptera/ Heterocera | | lèoman |
| **Maggot (Grub)** | (4) | Dipterous sp | mauch | cnuimh |
| **Midge** | (3) | Culicoides | midgie | meanbh-chuileag |
| **Fly sp.** | (7) | Musidae sp. | flee/flae | cuileag |
| **Flea** | (5) | Pulex irritans | flee/flae | deargad/ deargann |
| **Cleg** | (2) | Haemotopota pluvialis | | creithleag |
| **Gall Wasp (Canker worm)** | (3) | Cynipidae | | cnuimh-lobhta |
| **Ant sp.** | (1) | Hymenoptera/ Formicidae | emmerteen | seangan |

Appendix 6 (cont):

| | | | | |
|---|---|---|---|---|
| **Wasp** | (1) | Vespidae sp | wasp | speach |
| **Bee sp.** | (10) | Hymenotera Apis mellifera/ Bombus sp. | bumble/ bumart/ beach | seillean/ beach |
| **Beetle (Cockchafer)** | (1) | Melolontha melolontha/ Anobium sp. | clock/ hummin/ bumclock | daolag/ghormdagag |
| **Adder** | (4) | Vipera berus | nether/neddyr | nethair |
| **Toad** | (3) | Bufo bufo | pudduck | muile- mhàg |
| **Frog** | (2) | Rana temporaria | puddock | losgann |

109 specific records of 37 species, plus 2 other unnamed 'insects' and ague.

# Appendix 7

## (A): *Numerical Summary of Wildlife Records*

| | Species | Specific | (%) | General | (%) | Total(s) |
|---|---|---|---|---|---|---|
| **Flowers** | 37 | 240 | (54) | 206 | (46) | 446 |
| **Trees** | 26 | 154 | (34) | 303 | (66) | 457 |
| **Mammals** | 19 | 70 | (76) | 22 | (24) | 92 |
| **Birds** | 41 | 220 | (60) | 146 | (40) | 366 |
| **Fish & Others** | 37 | 109 | (97) | 3 | (3) | 112 |
| **TOTALS** | **160** | **792** | | **680** | | **1473** |

*As a corrected percentage of the total wildlife records:-*

Flowers (30); Trees (31); Mammals (6); Birds (25); Fishes and Others (8)

Specific Wildlife Records 54%; General Records 46%

## (B): *Numerical Summary of Landscape Features* *

| **Aquatic** | | **Highland** | | **Lowland** | |
|---|---|---|---|---|---|
| Rivers | 164 | Mountains | 27 | Howe | 18 |
| Waters | 38 | Hills | 152 | Bankings | 52 |
| Burns | 80 | Moorland | 33 | Plain | 33 |
| Waterfalls | 9 | Glens | 45 | Fields | 33 |
| Lochs | 11 | Cliffs | 20 | Meadow | 37 |
| Pools | 7 | Valley | 32 | Soil | 4 |
| Bogs | 25 | Ridge | 15 | | |
| **TOTALS** | **334** | | **324** | | **177** |
| | *(40%)* | | *(39%)* | | *(21%)* |

**Total Records: 835**

*Excluding seascape, forestry and other minor features.

## (C): *Numerical Summary of Seasonal Records*

| Month | | | Season | | Total | (%) |
|---|---|---|---|---|---|---|
| March | 2 ) | | | | | |
| April | - ) | 30 | Spring | 27 | 57 | (25.1) |
| May | 28) | | | | | |
| | | | | | | |
| June | 8 ) | | | | | |
| July | 1 ) | 10 | Summer | 57 | 67 | (30.1) |
| August | 1 ) | | | | | |
| | | | | | | |
| September | - ) | | | | | |
| October | 2 ) | 7 | Autumn | 17 | 24 | (10.7) |
| November | 5 ) | | | | | |
| | | | | | | |
| December | 5 ) | | | | | |
| January | 2 ) | 8 | Winter | 69 | 77 | (34.1) |
| February | 1 ) | | | | | |
| | | | | | | |
| **TOTAL(S)** | | **55** | | | **170** | **223** |

## (D): *Numerical Summary of Natural Elements*

| | | | | |
|---|---|---|---|---|
| Rain | 16 | | Tempest | 20 |
| Rainbow | 2 | | Storm | 43 |
| Snow | 38 | | Gale | 9 |
| Sleet | 5 | | Wind | 75 |
| Hail | 3 | | Breeze | 17 |
| Frost | 32 | | Zephyr | 3 |
| Thaw | 3 | | Calm | 5 |
| Mist | 7 | | Thunder | 7 |
| Fog | 5 | | Lightning | 3 |
| Dew | 55 | | Auora | 2 |
| | **166** | | | **184** |

**TOTAL    350**

## (E): TOTAL RECORDS: *WILDLIFE, LANDSCAPE, SEASONS* and *NATURAL PHENOMENA*

| | | |
|---|---|---|
| **Wildlife** | 1472 | 51% |
| **Landscape** | 835 | 29% |
| **Season** | 223 | 8% |
| **Elements** | 350 | 12% |
| | **2880** | 100% |

# Appendix 8

## DERIVATION OF PLACE NAMES

| | |
|---|---|
| **Alloway** | Possibly an anglicisation of the Gaelic *al a'mhaigh* – rock of the plan. |
| **Ayr** | *Inbhir Air* – mouth of the river. The town takes its name from the river, which was named earlier. |
| **Ballochmyle** | *Bealach* 'pass', and *maol* ' bare' – to give Bare Pass. |
| **Carrick** | Carraig from *Gaidplig*, Gaelic for rock. |
| **Doon** | Possibly derived from the name of a Celtic God, connected with river worship |
| **Dumfries** | *Dun* 'hill fort'; plus *phrea's* 'a copse with shrubs' – In the Gaelic *Dun phris*. An alternative is 'fort of the Frisians' (from North Holland). |
| **Friars Carse** | Carse from the Welsh *cors* 'a pool marsh or fenland'. |
| **Kilmarnock** | Church of my Ernoc (*m'Ernoc/mo Ernoc*) – my little Ernan (Uncle of St. Columba)? |
| **Kirkoswald** | 'Church of Oswald'; from Scandinavian Kirk with Oswald, King of Northumberland. |
| **Mauchline** | From Gaelic *magh* 'a plain'; plus linn 'a pool' – plain with the pool. |
| **Mossgiel** | Old norse 'gil' – a narrow glen. |
| **Nithsdale** | Before 1256 called Strath-nith. |
| **Irvine** | In Gaelic *Irbhinn*, river of green water. |
| **Sanquhar** | Gaelic *Sean*, 'old' and *cathair* 'an old fort'. |

For complete details of place names, see *The Ayrshire Book of Burns Lore* by A.M. Boyle and *Burns-Lore of Dumfries and Galloway* by J.A. Mackay.

# GLOSSARY

| | | | |
|---|---|---|---|
| agley | off, not on expected course. | burr-thistle | spear thistle |
| aik | oak | byke, bike | bee hive, multitude |
| Ailsa | Ailsa Craig, Girvan | cairn | loose pile of stones |
| aits | oats | caper | play, carry on |
| ape | to imitate | carl-hemp | male stalk of hemp |
| ask | a lizzard *sp.* | carp | to complain |
| bag | a bag, container | chant | to sing |
| baggie | the stomach | chittering | trembling with cold |
| bank | raised earth, us. grassed over | claver | clover |
| bass | low pitched | claw | scratch, a claw |
| baukie-bird | bat sp. | cleckin | a brood |
| baudrans | cat | clockin-time | incubating, hatching time |
| bawk | strip of untilled land | clud | cloud |
| bay | mare, female horse | clutch | catch |
| bear | a bear; barley; to carry | cod | a fish *sp*, pillow |
| bea's | lice sp. | cootie | feather covered legs |
| beast | animal, us. a horse, or cattle | corbie | a raven, crow *sp.* |
| beating | driving | corn | oats |
| beaver | a hat | covert | small wood |
| bedeck | to cover | covey | broods of grouse or partridge |
| beet | add fuel to fire | crag (craig) | rock outcrop |
| bent | grass *sp.* | craik | a corncrake |
| biel | shelter | craw | a crow, the crow of a cock |
| big | to build | crood | to coo, as a dove |
| bike, byke | a swarm, hive | cukoo | cuckoo |
| billow | wave at sea | cushat | a wood pigeon |
| birk | birch tree | daimen-icker | an occasional ear of corn |
| bit | small, little | dam | urine; female |
| bizz | to buzz | daw | to dawn |
| bizzard | buzzard *sp.* | dell | small wooded hollow |
| blae | blue | den | small wooded valley |
| blitter | a snipe *sp.* | deuck,deuk | duck *sp.* |
| boar | descriptive term for Vikings | dow | dove *sp.* |
| boggie | a bog | dub | small pool, puddle, mud |
| bole | recess | eerie | frightened |
| bobby | foolish person | elder | older, church office bearer |
| boortries | elder shrubs | fallow | untilled land; deer *sp.* |
| boreas | north wind | | a person |
| bower | shady leafy shelter | fell | high (*usu.* rocky land) |
| brae | slope of hill | fen | low lying flat, wet land, |
| brakes | bracken, area of dense | | marshy |
| | undergrowth, thicket | feg | a fig |
| breer | briar, as in rose *sp.* | flae | flea *sp.* |
| brent | high and straight | flie | fly *sp.* |
| briny | tears | foggage | course grass |
| brock | badger | foumart | a polecat |
| brush | fight, skirmish | flounder | to stumble |
| buckie | a buck, male | flush | filled up |
| bum-clock | humming beetle *sp.* | fyke | restless, fidget |
| burdie | a bird, woman | ged | pike (a fish *sp.*) |
| burn | small stream | gentoo | native of India |

| | | | |
|---|---|---|---|
| gled | hawk, kite *sp.* | mead | meadow |
| goos | goose *sp.* | meere | mare, female horse |
| gor cock | red grouse | merle | a blackbird |
| gos | peregrine falcon | mire | boggy area, marsh, mud |
| gowan | daisy *sp* | modewark | a mole |
| gowspink | goldfinch | monkey | mischevious person |
| gowk | cuckoo | moorcock | red grouse male |
| grape | grope | muir-hen | red grouse female |
| grouss, grous | red grouse | mousie | mouse *sp.* |
| gully | large knife | muir | moor |
| hag(g) | a scar, often on peat | muscle | mussel *sp.* |
| hairst | harvest | mute | silent |
| hail | shotgun pellets; frozen hail | nip | frosted |
| hark | to listen | nit | nut *sp.* |
| hart | deer *sp.* us. male deer at least 5 years old | patrick | partridge |
| | | park | a field |
| haugh | low lying fields beside river | pearl | tears |
| heath | heather moorlands | pike, pyke | to pick, pluck |
| hern | a heron | pliver | plover *sp.* |
| herrin | herring (fish *sp.*) | poosie | hare *sp.* |
| heugh | ravine, coal pit | pouther, powther | gun powder |
| hide | last | | |
| hiney, hinney | honey | puddock stool | toadstool, mushroom *sp.* |
| hip | pelvis | | |
| hoar | hoar frost | powt, howt | poult, young gamebird *sp.* |
| hallow | empty, depression | pyet | a magpie |
| hoodie | hooded/carrion crow | pyke | a pike |
| houlet, howlet | an owl *sp.* | quail | to shrink back, fear, cower |
| hurchin | a hedgehog | ragweed | ragwort |
| jade | chance | rail | speachify |
| kae | a jackdaw | rair | to roar, shout |
| knot | a knot, join | rape | a rope |
| knowe | hillock | rase | a rose *sp* |
| kye | cattle | rash | a rush *sp* |
| lade | load | ratton | a rat *sp.* |
| laimpet | limpet *sp.* | rede | to advise |
| lair | grave; bed | rigg | a ridge of land |
| lallan | lowland | rill | stream, gulley |
| lan' | land | rook | impudent fellow, cheat. |
| lane | alone | rye | grass *sp.* |
| lang | long | sallow | yellow coloured |
| laverock | lark *sp.* | saugh | willow *sp.* |
| lea, lay, ley | land under grass | saumont | salmon *sp* |
| lea-rig | ridge under grass | scar | a cliff |
| limpet | to limp | seal | to seal |
| linn | a waterfall, cascade | shank | to go to foot |
| lint | flax | shaw | a wooded dell, wild natural woodland |
| lintwhite | a linnet | | |
| loon | a fellow | sheugh | a ditch |
| lough | a loch, lake | shrimp | small |
| marle | fine grained rock | snaw-drop | snowdrop |
| mast | a mast | sole | only |
| maukin | a hare *sp.* | spruce | neat, smart |
| mavis | songthrush | staggie | stag, male deer *sp.* |

| | | | |
|---|---|---|---|
| **stank** | pool stagnent water | **troop** | a group of |
| **stibble** | stubble | **tyke** | a dog *sp.* |
| **strath** | level land between hills, through which a river flows | **v'ilet** | violet *sp.* |
| | | **wab** | web |
| **swift** | quickly | **wa-flower** | wallflower |
| **swirlie** | bent, knotted, gnarled | **warbler** | a singer, often applied unspecifically to bird *sp.* |
| **taed** | a toad *sp.* | | |
| **tangle** | seaweed *sp.* | **weaver** | a person who weaves |
| **thrisstle** | thistle *sp.* | **whaup** | a curlew |
| **thrummart** | polccat | **whidden** | a quick motion, nimble |
| **timmer** | timber | **willcat** | wild cat *sp.* |
| **tim'rous** | timid | **willie** | a willow *sp.* |
| **tod** | a fox | **woodbine** | honeysuckle |
| **towmond** | a year, a 'twelve month' period | **worm** | a worm *sp.* spiral condenser used in spirit distillation |
| **tow** | string, flax fibre | **wrack** | seaweed *sp.* |
| **tread** | a step | | wreckage, flotsam |
| **trip** | journey | **yearn** | an eagle *sp.* |

# ENVIRONMENTAL TERMS LISTED BY HABITAT

**Water** *(40)*     a clear, colourless, tasteless, odourless liquid that is essential for all plant and and animal life and constitutes in impure form, rain, oceans, rivers and lochs.

**Ocean** *(15)*     a very large area of sea, one of the five oceans of the world, a body of salt water covering approximately 70 per cent of the earth's surface.

**Sea** *(47)*     the mass of salt water on the earth's surface as differentiated from the land, one of the smaller areas of ocean.

**Waters**     any body or area of water such as, the sea; lochs,rivers, streams.

**Watershed**     dividing line between two adjacent river systems, such as a ridge.

**Catchment**     the area of land, bordered by watersheds draining into a river or loch.

**River** *(164)*     flow of fresh water, larger than a stream, flowing on a definite course, usually into the sea, being fed by tributary streams.

**Burn; Stream; Brook** *(74)*   a natural freshwater flow of water, smaller than a river.

**Waterfall; Cascade; Linn** *(9)*   fall of water, where there is a vertical or almost vertical step in the levels of the river or burn bed or base.

**Rivulet; Rill** *(7)*     small stream, channel or gulley.

**Spring; Fountain** *(12)*   a natural outflow of ground water forming the source of a burn.

**Torrent** *(12)*     a fast voluminous or violent flow of water.

**Spate** *(2)*     a fast flow or sudden rush of water, usually following heavy downpour in a well drained catchment area.

**Flood** *(24)*     the state of a river or tributary burn that is at an abnormally high level. Also the inundation of land that is normally dry.

**Flash**     a sudden rush of water, down an existing watercourse.

**Loch; Lake** *(11)*     an expanse of water, entirely surrounded by land and unconnected to the sea, except by rivers or burns that may issue from it.

**Sea Loch**     a long bay or arm of the sea in Scotland.

**Lochan**     a small inland loch in Scotland.

**Pool** *(7)*     small body of either still water, or the deep part of a river, where the water runs slowly.

## *SEMI AQUATIC*

**Flush**     wet ground, often on hillside, where water flows or perculates but not within a definite channel.

**Stank** *(1)*     small area of standing, usually stagnant water.

**Sheugh** *(4)*     a shallow drainage ditch.

**Bog; Moss** *(16)*     wet spongy land usually poorly drained, highly acid and rich in plant residue.

**Marsh; Mire** *(8)*   a community of plants, on wet but not peaty soils.

**Fen** *(1)*   a community on alkaline, neutral or slightly acid peat.

**Dubs** *(7)*   very small isolated muddy pool or puddle.


*TERRESTRIAL*

**Mountain** *(27)*   higher and steeper than a hill, often with a rocky summit. Usually with an altitude of at least 3000 feet (914 metres).

**Hill; Brae** *(139)*   rounded elevation, less high and craggy than a mountain. Brae is also used to describe the slope or incline of a hill.

**Moor; Muir; Heath** *(29)*   upland plant communities, often dominated by heather, on dry or damp but not wet peat.

**Fell** *(4)*   tract of upland moor or hill, often rocky.

**Hillock; Knowe** *(15)*   a small hill or mound.

**Down** *(2)*   a hill, usually a sand dune.

**Ridge; Rig** *(15)*   long narrow raised land formation with sloping sides especially one formed by the meeting of two faces or a mountain. Also a raised strip on ploughed land.

**Crag, Craig; Scar, Cliff; Scaur** *(20)*   steep high exposed rock face.

**Gully or Gulley**   a channel or small valley cut originally by heavy rainwater; deep wide fissure between two buttresses in a mountain face.

steep high exposed rock face.

**Glen** *(45)*   a narrow usually steep sided and deep mountain valley.

**Valley; Vale** *(30)*   a long depression in the land surface, usually through which a river flows and formed by erosion, often steep sided.

**Strath** *(2)*   level land between hills, through which a river flows.

**Howe; Hollow** *(5)* a depression or dip in the land surface.

**Dell/Den** *(11)*   small wooded hollow or valley.

**Heugh** *(2)*   a ravine, or very steep banking.

**Banking** *(53)*   raised earthen bank, often retaining a river or stream, usually grassed over.

**Haugh** *(2)*   low lying flat fields, usually of grass, and beside a river.

**Bawk** *(1)*   strip of untilled land.

**Lallan; Lan'** *(4)*   lowland geographically as opposed to Highlands, also used to describe dialect.

**Plain** *(34)*   a practically level tract of land, especially an extensive treeless area.

**Field; Park** *(33)*   an area of land, cleared of trees and undergrowth, usually enclosed by a hedge or dyke and used for pasture or growing crops.

**Meadow** *(4)*   low lying grassland, often boggy and near a river, cut for hay and grazed.

**Lay; Lea** *(26)*   land under grass.

**Cove** *(3)*   small bay or inlet, or narrow cavern formed by sides of cliffs on mountain.

**Tree** *(59)*   any large woody perennial plant, with a distinct trunk, giving rise to branches and leaves.

**Forest** *(22)*    any large 'wooded' area, with a high density of trees and plants.

**Wood** *(87)*    collection of trees, shrubs, herbs and grasses, usually dominated by one or a few species and smaller than forest.

**Shrub; Bush** *(18)*    any woody perennial plant, smaller than a tree with several major branches arising from near the base of the main stem.

**Herb**    any seed-bearing plant, whose aerial parts do not persist above ground at the end of the growing season (herbaceous).

**Shaw** *(17)*    a wild natural wood, often situated in a hollow.

**Covert** *(5)*    a small wood, shaw or thicket, planted and/or managed, especially to provide shelter for game species.

**Glade** *(4)*    an open area or clearing, in a forest or wood.

**Grove** *(26)*    a very small wooded area.

**Bower** *(30)*    an area of shady, leafy, shelter, usually formed by over hanging branches of either trees, bushes or shrubs.

**Hedge** *(3)*    a continuous row of tree or shrub species, often forming a boundary and providing shelter to a field or garden.

**Soil; Earth; Grun; Yird** *(45)*    the top layer of the land surface of the earth, composed of disintegrated rock particles, humus, water and air.

**Dust; Stour** *(35)*    dry fine powdery material such as particles of earth, sand or pollen.

**Sand** *(8)*    loose material consisting of rock or mineral grains, especially quartz.

**Peat** *(4)*    a compact, brown coloured, deposit of partially decomposed vegetable matter, saturated with water. Used as a fuel and fertilizer when dried.


## NATURAL PHENOMENA

**Sun; Sinn; Pheobus** *(107)*    the star that is the source of heat and light for the planet. *Pheobus* is a poetic personification of the sun via the Latin from Greek *Phoibus* bright; related to *phaos* light

**Moon; Min; Phoebe** *(49)*    the natural satellite of the earth. Moonshine or moonlight is light from the sun received on earth after reflection by the moon.

**Rain** *(16)*    precipitation from clouds in the form of drops of water, formed by the condensation of water vapour in the atmosphere.

**Rainbow** *(2)*    bow shaped display in the sky of the colours of the spectrum, caused by the refraction and reflection of the sun's rays through rain or mist.

**Dew** *(55)*    drops of water condensed on a cool surface especially at night, from vapour in the air.

**Mist** *(7)*    thin fog resulting from condensation in the air near the earth surface.

**Fog** *(5)*    a mass of droplets of condensed water vapour suspended in the air, often greatly reducing visibility, corresponding to a cloud but at a lower level.

**Snow; Snaw** *(38)*    precipitation from clouds in the form of ice crystals, formed in the upper atmosphere. The fall of such precipitation forms a layer of snow flakes on the ground. When driven together by the wind, forms a bank of deep snowflakes or *Drift*.

**Sleet** *(5)*    partly melted, falling snow or hail.

**Frost** *(30)*    white deposit of ice particles, formed by temperatures of either -8°C. or 24°F.

**Hoarfrost; Cranreuch** *(2)* a deposit of needle-like ice crystals, formed on the ground by direct condensation at temperatures below freezing point.

**Thaw; Thowe** *(3)* to melt from a frozen solid state.

**Aurora borealis** *(2)* the aurora seen round the North Pole. Also called 'Borealis' or 'Northern Lights'. Aurora is an atmospheric phenomenon, consisting of bands, curtains or streamers of usually green, red or yellow light, that move across the sky. It is caused by collisions between air molecules and charged particles from the sun, that are trapped in the earth's magnetic field.

**Hail (stanes)** *(3)* small pellets of ice, falling from cumulonimbus clouds, when there are strong air currents.

**Lightning** *(3)* a flash of light in the sky, occurring during a thunderstorm and caused by a discharge of electricity, either between clouds or between a cloud and the earth.

**Thunder** *(7)* a loud cracking or deep rumbling noise, caused by the rapid expansion of atmospheric gases, which are suddenly heated by lightning.

**Tempest** *(20)* a violent wind or storm.

**Storm** *(43)* violent weather condition of strong winds, rain, hail, lightning, thunder, blows of soil, sand, or snow. A violent gale force reaching Force 10 on the Beaufort scale with speed of 55-63 miles per hour.

**Gale** *(9)* a strong wind, specifically one of between Force 7-10 on the Beaufort scale.

**Wind** *(63)* a current of air, sometimes of considerable force, moving generally horizontally from areas of high pressure to areas of low pressure.

**Boreas** *(8)* describes a wind from the North.

**Gust** *(4)* sudden blast of wind.

**Breeze** *(17)* a gentle or light wind of Force 2-6 on the Beaufort scale.

**Zehhyr** *(2)* soft or gentle breeze.

**Calm** *(5)* a registration of zero on the Beaufort scale.

# Bibliography

Adams, L E. *The Harvest Mouse*. Wildlife. 1913

Alexander, W B and Lack, D. 'Changes in Status Among British Breeding Birds'. *British Birds* 1944

Allison, A. *The Scottish Sporting Gazette*. 1991

Bannerman, D A. *The Birds of the British Isles*. 1963

Barke, J and Smith, S G. (Eds). *The Merry Muses of Caledonia* by Robert Burns.

Baxter, E V. and Rintoul, L J. *The Birds of Scotland*. 1953

Bold, A. *A Burns Companion*. 1991

Boyle, A M. *The Ayrshire Book of Burns Lore*. 1986

Corbet and Harris (eds). *The Handbook of British Mammals*.

Corbet, G B. and Southern, H M. (eds). *The Handbook of British Mammals*. 1977

*Collins English Dictionary*. Glasgow 1990

Duncan (Sir) A B. *Report on the Investigation of the Magpie*. 1938.

Elemont, P. *Brithers A'*. Oliphants, Edinburgh (1934)

Fairhurst, A. and Soothill, E. *Trees of the British Countryside* (Blandford). 1981

Gemmill, J F. *Natural History in the Poetry of Robert Burns.* 1928

Gibson, J A. *History of Birds of Ailsa Craig*. 1951

Gladstone, H S. *The Birds of Dumfriesshire*. 1910

——*Notes of the Birds of Dumfriesshire*. 1923

——*Vertebrate Fauna of Dumfriesshire*. 1912

Gray and Anderson. *Birds of Ayrshire and Wigtownshire*. 1869

Gray, R. *Birds of the West of Scotland*. 1871

Gray, W. personal communications. 1991 [Gaelic and Scots names]

Gurney, S H. *The Gannet*. 1913

Hillman, R M. *The Making of the Scottish Landscape*. 1975

Mackay, J A. (Ed). *The Complete Works of Robert Burns* (Bicentenary Souvenir Edition: The Burns Federation). 1986

——*The Complete Letters of Robert Burns* (Bicentenary Souvenir Edition: The Burns Federation). 1987

——(Compiler) *Burns A-Z: The Complete Word Finder*. 1990

——*Burns – Lore of Dumfries and Galloway*. 1988

Madders, M. and Welstead, J. *Where to Watch Birds in Scotland*. 1990

Meikle, H. and Beattie, W. *Poems of Robert Burns*. National Library of Scotland 1946.

Nicholaisen, W F H. 'List of Celtic Bird Names' *in* Bannerman, D A. *The Birds of the British Isles*. 1963

Paton, E R. and Pike, O G. *The Birds of Ayrshire*. 1929

Reid, J B. *A Complete Word and Phrase Concordance to the Poems and Songs of Robert Burns*. 1889

Rennie, F. 'Gaelic Names of Birds' in *Where to Watch Birds in Scotland*: Madders and Welsted. 1990

Sibbald, Sir Robert. *Scotia Illustrata, sive Prodromus histriae naturalis*.

Smith, A. (Ed). *The Works of Robert Burns*: Macmillan

Sprott, G. *Robert Burns, Farmer*. 1990 (National Museums of Scotland)

*Statistical Account of Scotland, The Old*, 1791-1799

*Statistical Account of Scotland, New*, 1832-1845

Symons, A. *Trans. of the Nat. Hist. and Antiquarian Society of Dumfries-Galloway*. 1895-1896

Thom, V M. *Birds in Scotland.* 1986 (Scottish Ornithologists Club)

Watson, Donald. *Birds of Moor and Mountain.* Scottish Academic Press, 1972.

White, G. *The Natural History and Antiquities, in the County of Southamton.* 1789

Witherby, Jourdain, Ticehurst, Tucker. *The Handbook of British Birds.* 1947

Young, J G. 'Distribution, Status and Movement of Feral Greylag Geese in Southern Scotland'. *Scottish Birds* 7.

Young, J G. and Holden T. et al. Unpublished internal reports to N.C.C.

# POEM AND SONG INDEX

# GENERAL INDEX

Adder, 182
Afton, 89
Ague, 184
Ailsa Craig, 141
Allan, 90
Ant, 180
Apple,
    Crab, 64; Domestic, 64
Ash, 56
Aspen, 43
Autumn, 115–16
Ayr, 90

Badger, 81
Barn Owl, 144
Bat, 72
Bay, 57
Beaver, 77
Ben Ledie, 106
Bee, 180–82
Beech, 41, 48
Beetle, 182
Ben Lomond, 106
Bent, 37
Bewick's Swan, 125
Birch, 40, 43–6
Bittern, 123
Blackthorn, 63
Blackbird, 152
Bluebell, 8
Bog Myrtle, 6
Bracken, 10
Bramble, 60
Broad-Leafed Dock, 13
Broom, 61–3
Brown Hare, 73
Brown Rat, 78
Brown Top, 37
Brown Trout, 166
Bruar, 91
Burdock, 24
Butterfly, 176
Buzzard,
    Common, 131; Honey, 131; Rough-
    Legged, 131

Cairn, 91
Canker (worm), 180

Carrion Crow, 155
Cart, 91
Cessnock, 92
Cherry,
    Wild, 50; Bird, 51
Cleg, 179
Clover, 10
Cluden, 92
Clyde, 92
Cockchafer (see beetle), 182
Cockle, 170
Cod, 169
Common,
    Bent, 37; Dog Violet, 7; Hawthorn, 51–
    6; Poppy, 15; Ragwort, 16; Reed, 35;
    Rye, 37; Yew, 66
Coot, 136
Corncrake, 135–6
Corsincon, 106
Cotton Thistle, 9
Cowslip, 15
Coyle, 92
Crab Apple, 64
Craggie, 106
Criffel, 106
Cuckoo, 143
Cumnock, 105
Curlew, 140

Daffodil, 31
Daisy, 20
Daubentons, 72
Dee, 93
Deer,
    Fallow, 83; Red, 83; Roe, 84
Devon, 93
Dog Rose, 24–9
Doon, 93–4
Dove,
    Rock, 142; Stock, 142
Dunnock, 158

Eagle, 128–9
Earn, 95
Earthworm, Common, 171
Eden, 95
Eel, 168
Elder, 63

# PERSONAL POSTSCRIPTS

*I dream'd I lay where flowers were springing*
*Gaily in the sunny beam,*
*List'ning to the wild birds singing,*
*By a falling crystal stream;*
*Straight the sky grew black and daring,*
*Thro the woods the whirlwinds rave,*
*Trees with aged arms were warring*
*O'er the swelling, drumlie wave.*

*Such was my life's deceitful morning,*
*Such the pleasures I enjoy'd!*
*But lang or noon, loud tempests storming,*
*A' my flowery bliss destroy'd.*
*Tho fickle Fortune has deceiv'd me*
*(She promis'd fair, and perform'd but ill),*
*Of monie a Joy and hope bereav'd me,*
*I bear a heart shall support me still."*

------------

*God knows I'm no saint*

------------

*I have a whole host of follies and sins to*
*answer for, but if I could, and I*
*believe I do it as far as I can, I*
*would wipe all tears from all eyes.*

------------

*That I for poor old Scotland's sake*
*Some usefu' plan or book could make*
*Or sing a sang at least...*

------------

*My curse upon your whunstane hearts,*
*Ye E'nbrugh gentry!*

*May Freedom, Harmony, and Love,*
*Unite you in the **Grand Design***
*Beneath th' Omniscient Eye above-*
*The glorious **Architect Divine**.*
*That you may keep th' **Unerring Line**,*
*Still rising by the **Plummet's Law**,*
*Till **Order** bright completely shine,*
*Shall be my pray'r when far awa.*

-----------

Last, white-rob'd Peace, crown'd with a hazel wreath,

-----------

John G. Young, compiler of this book, is currently an Area Officer with Scottish Natural Heritage, Angus and Dundee Districts.

Born and bred in the heart of the Burns' country in an old Burns haunt at Sanquhar, Dumfriesshire (1936), he worked in the building trade throughout Dumfries and Ayrshire. Following a youthful interest in ornithology he joined the Nature Conservancy, the Government nature conservation agency, in 1966. Since then he has served in the Solway area, Fife, Highlands and in Edinburgh before taking up his current post.

Author of some 20 scientific articles on birds, he was a founder member of the North Solway Ringing Group (the first of its type in Scotland) and joint editor of the Region's Bird Report. In demand as a lecturer, he has long sought for greater co-operation between conservationists and people involved in field sports. He retains membership of New Cumnock Burns Club and the Black Joan at Sanquhar.

Now living near Forfar in Angus, he lists his other interests as gardening, music, shooting, Freemasonry and Glasgow Rangers.

*CONSTRUCTIVE COMMENT AND ADDITIONS WELCOMED*

John G Young
11 Restenneth Place
Lunanhead
Forfar
Angus DD8 3NF
Scotland

Golden Plover Chick